W9-AUY-452

POCKET EUROPE

The Economist

═══ POCKET ═══

EUROPE

THE ECONOMIST IN ASSOCIATION WITH
HAMISH HAMILTON LTD

Published by the Penguin Group
Penguin Books Ltd, 27 Wrights Lane, London W8 5TZ, England
Penguin Books USA Inc., 375 Hudson Street, New York,
New York 10014, USA
Penguin Books Australia Ltd, Ringwood, Victoria, Australia
Penguin Books Canada Ltd, 10 Alcorn Avenue, Toronto,
Ontario, Canada M4V 3B2
Penguin Books (NZ) Ltd, 182–190 Wairau Road, Auckland 10,
New Zealand

Penguin Books Ltd, Registered Offices: Harmondsworth,
Middlesex, England

First published by The Economist Books Ltd 1992
This edition published by Hamish Hamilton Ltd in association
with The Economist 1994

1 3 5 7 9 10 8 6 4 2

Contributors
The Economist Intelligence Unit, John Andrews,
Peter Holden, Dick Leonard, David Manasian,
Vlad Sobell, Anna Wolek

Printed in Great Britain by William Clowes Limited,
Beccles and London

A CIP catalogue record for this book is available
from the British Library

ISBN 0-241-00280-X

Contents

INTRODUCTION

Europe has long been used to thinking of itself as the centre of the world. Such self-centredness has not always been justified, but by the early 1990s Europe, as the world's largest economic block and as the stage for communism's collapse, had rightly claimed the world's attention.

The wider Europe

The end of the Cold War and the collapse of the Soviet empire has restored the 19th-century concept of a Europe stretching as far north-east as Russia, and as far south-east as the Balkans. Military arsenals are being reduced, and arms negotiations are being overtaken by unilateral actions on all sides. Western business and industry are investing in Eastern Europe, as they did before, although the German government is giving more aid to the former Soviet Union and Eastern Europe than any other in the West.

Pan-European transport links are getting almost their first serious study since the Romans stopped building their imperial roads. Passport-less travel is becoming a reality within a large part of Western Europe, which no longer imposes visas on visitors from several central European countries. Eastern Europe is beginning to rival North Africa as a source of immigration into Western Europe.

All the countries in the swathe of Eastern Europe that runs from the Baltic to the Balkans are now exhibiting some form of multi-party democracy and the market economy. But even though Europe has expanded in recent years, its economic heart remains the countries which belong, or aspire to belong, to the European Union.

The Union core

The EU, as the Maastricht Treaty has renamed the older, less ambitious, European Community, has become Europe's core institution because no other club offers its members such an array of economic, social, political and (potentially) defence benefits. Turkey applied to join in 1987, Austria in 1989, Malta and Cyprus in 1990, and Sweden in 1991. Finland applied in 1992, and so too did Norway. Poland, Hungary and the Czech and Slovak Republics have negotiated special associations with the EU that clearly state their membership ambitions. Romania and Bulgaria have followed suit. Even Estonia, Latvia and Lithuania formed links with the then EC within days of getting freedom after Soviet communism's collapse in August 1991. In the aftermath of the crisis in former Yugoslavia may come other applications.

Eastern Europe after communism

The collapse of central planning and of the Comecon trading system has pushed Eastern Europe into a sharp recession. It no longer has an easy Soviet outlet for the industrial goods which it could not sell, on quality, in the West, or for farm produce that protectionists in Western Europe shut out. The pain of transition towards market economies has been made worse by very high inflation and large-scale redundancies.

Eastern Europe's collective future is hard to read. Some parts of it could go the successful way of economies in Asia, with which they have in common a high general level of education and skills. Other parts could follow the Latin American trend with hyperinflation and recession fuelling populist nationalism.

The pattern will be mixed. No country has a higher per head debt than Hungary, but neither has any East European country been experimenting with market reform for so long (on and off since 1968). Hungary has also developed its financial and agricultural sectors more than its neighbours. The relative success of their economy has always made Hungarians fret about the less happy fate of fellow Magyars in nearby Romania; this could again become a source of nationalist tension. Czechoslovakia was quite well placed to start off the new era, with a low debt and a broad industrial range that has made it a target for Western venture capitalists. However, after Czechoslovakia's "velvet divorce" in 1993, economic disparities could fuel political tensions between the Czech Republic and less advanced Slovakia.

First to suffer a real industrial crash in the 1980s, Poland has been the first to go for bold economic reform, including currency convertibility. But with old-fashioned industry and a very fragmented and largely private farming sector, it faces a big task in raising average living standards for what is the largest population (38m) in Eastern Europe.

De-communisation has been less rapid in the Balkans. Romania is likely to remain politically unstable for some time to come, in the wake of the Ceausescu dictatorship which had the sole merit of leaving the country virtually debt-free. Bulgaria's non-communist opposition came to power only in autumn 1991 and faces the task of re-directing an economy that used to conduct half its total trade with the Soviet Union. Civil war has since cast a total blight over former Yugoslavia, destroying the economic progress that had been made in 1990.

Towards a bigger European Union

Negotiations to enlarge the European club took second place in 1993 to the EC's desire to implement its single market programme and to ratify the constitutional amendments on monetary and political union that on November 1st brought the European Union into being. The hope then was that Austria, Sweden, Finland and Norway would be ready to join the Union in 1995, with a second wave of central and East European members around the turn of the century. Turkey, with a large, poor, Muslim and semi-European population, seemed unlikely to get in – even though its application was made in 1987.

For the moment, however, the 12 EU states form a relatively small hard core, at the centre of a series of concentric circles formed by other organisations with more limited functions. NATO is not planning any imminent increase in membership beyond 16, but it is trying to extend – through "Partnerships of Peace" – its practical and political consultations to central European countries. The Council of Europe watches over democratic rights in its member countries (now numbering more than 30). Overarching all these bodies is the Conference on Security and Co-operation in Europe (CSCE), whose 37 members (including the USA and Canada) have pledged themselves to the peaceful settlement of disputes.

Single market success

The EU has long been an economic giant because it accounts for more than 40% of total world trade, but it remained a market riddled with internal barriers until a major effort to eliminate them started in the mid-1980s with the single market programme. Capturing the deregulatory mood of many governments, and coinciding happily with a cyclical upswing in the European economy in the late 1980s, this programme has proved astonishingly successful, at least in legislative terms. Most of the 300 measures in the 1992 programme have been passed into law, though many of them have been slow to take effect. The legislation was made possible by the introduction of more majority voting in the Council of Ministers' decision-making.

The impact of the single market will be particularly dramatic for service industries, especially banking, investment and insurance which have up to now been highly regulated on a national basis, and for those sectors like telecommunications which have tended to live off contracts from their own national governments. The opening up of public procurement to competitive cross-border bidding is a key element of the single market. The decision by Brussels to abandon its earlier approach of complete harmonisation of technical standards and marketing rules in favour of setting only a basic regulatory framework and requiring member states to "mutually recognise" all the minor differences in each other's products is having an effect right across the Union. The single market has triggered an increasing number of cross-border takeovers and acquisitions, to which the response of EU governments has been to reinforce the European Commission's anti-trust powers by giving it the right to vet all major mergers.

Most of the difficulties that remain relate to the abolition of frontier checks within the Union. This was supposed to occur by end-1992 but more than a year later governments were still wrangling over how, in the absence of any controls on the Union's internal borders, they were to administer health checks on animals and plants and security controls on people. This last aspect is considered a particular problem by non-continental states like Britain and Ireland, and by Denmark which has a passport union with fellow Nordic countries. However, under the Schengen Agreement, the other nine EU states have agreed to form a free-travel zone, involving a common policy on immigration and a high degree of cross-border co-operation between their police forces.

EMU on the runway

If the ability to travel right across the Union without a passport becomes one of the most striking features of the new Europe, an even more far-reaching ambition is the plan for a single currency by the late 1990s. Economic and monetary union (EMU) has been one of European federalists' older dreams, but it was given new impetus by the success of "1992". A single market needed a single currency, it was argued, to remove the bother and expense of money-changing and to provide complete price transparency throughout the member states. Many of Germany's partners had also grown restive about its de facto dominance of the European Monetary System (EMS), anchored by the D-mark, and felt that a real EMU would give them at least some say in Europe's monetary policy.

By the end of 1991, after a year of negotiations, the shape of the putative EMU had become pretty clear. A single federal central bank would manage the single currency, which would be a variant of the present ecu. The bank's board would be composed of an independent president, and the governors of the 12 national central banks, which themselves – like the Federal Reserve system in America – would act as the European bank's operating arms. The bank's charter would commit it to the overriding goal of price stability. Economic policy decisions on budgets, taxes and borrowing would stay with national governments, but they would have to be co-ordinated and monitored to avoid the risk of a free-spending or over-borrowing country undermining the common currency.

The key remaining questions are which countries will take part and when. Britain is a special case because alone among the Twelve it has from the start stated its clear political reservation about a common currency. As a result it has been allowed to delay the decision on whether to take part in the final stage of EMU. A similar "opt-out" was granted to Denmark. But will any members be ready in time for the planned EMU date of around 1997? No country will be fit for EMU unless it has first brought its economic performance close to that of the best-performing EU states, notably Germany. But in the early 1990s the German economy, too, was underperforming the criteria for EMU. If a majority of states do not qualify by 1997, EMU is to be delayed to 1999. Even then the pattern will be untidy. Austria and Sweden will be able to slip easily into the EMU strait-jacket, but central European countries will not. It may therefore be well into the next century before all citizens are using the same currency.

EPU not far behind ?

Tied to EMU are the Twelve's parallel agreements on European political union (EPU). The link was originally loose. The Twelve reacted to the 1989 collapse of East European communism by deciding that they should assume tighter political order in a Europe which had become more volatile and from which America was partially disengaging. But EMU and EPU became closely intertwined, for the main reason that Germany made it clear that it would not surrender the D-mark unless its partners agreed, in the EPU negotiations, to more powers for the European Parliament and to a common foreign and security policy. Much of Germany's energies and money are going into rescuing the eastern half of the country from 40 years of communism, but its very enlargement makes Germany more pivotal than ever to the rest of Europe.

External events increasingly require the Twelve to act speedily and jointly, but their response to the Gulf crisis and the subsequent war against Iraq in January 1991 was ragged. To some, this proved that the Twelve were simply not ready to face such issues together, and so they should not pretend to do so. But the civil war in the former Yugoslavia produced a crisis on the Union's doorstep with the capacity to tear the Twelve, as well as the Balkans, apart. With the CSCE still in its infancy, with NATO barred from acting outside the alliance territory, and with America tending to take a back seat in Europe, the Union took the lead in seeking a political solution to the crisis – and was seen to fail. By 1994 the Union had managed to commit NATO – and hence America – to help find a solution.

Most EU states now clearly feel that while major issues of EU foreign policy should be decided by unanimity, the measures to implement these decisions should be taken by majority vote. A minority – Britain, Denmark, Portugal and Ireland (which is neutral) – disagree, and argue that foreign policy is too sensitive and volatile to be voted on like some measure to harmonise industrial boiler standards. Even trickier is the debate on defence. France, always NATO's most half-hearted member, has seen in EPU a chance to emancipate Europe from America, and is urging that the EU commit itself to a common defence policy. By contrast, Britain is insisting that a common defence policy should develop only within the overall context of NATO. Meanwhile, France is eagerly developing a "Euro-Corps", with troops from Germany, Belgium and Spain.

Market magnetism

Whatever its occasional setbacks, the Union is unlikely to lose its attraction for the rest of Europe. The magnetic pull stems in large part from the economic fact that it now has a single market of nearly 340m consumers. Negotiations to expand this market resulted in 1993 in the European Economic Area (EEA), a free-trade zone of 380m people linking the Twelve with six members of EFTA (the seventh, Switzerland, voted by referendum not to join). This is acknowledged to be the first step to a wider EU.

The next challenge would then be to extend the EEA concept to Eastern Europe. Poland, the Czech Republic, Slovakia and Hungary are negotiating to achieve free trade with the Union. In the process, they are mounting a heavy attack on the Union's protectionist common agricultural policy (CAP). There is some political sympathy in the Union for the arguments of Eastern Europe. It used to be Europe's granary, and could become so again.

Political clout

The EU has always tended to be viewed by the outside

world in commercial terms, but this changed in 1990–91 when both America and Japan signed declarations with the EC (as it was then called), committing themselves to regular political dialogue with Brussels. This was recognition that it is becoming ever less true to see the organisation as an economic giant and a political pygmy.

═══ Part I ═══
COUNTRY RANKINGS

Area and population

Area *sq km*

1	Russia	17,075,400		25	Georgia	69,700
2	Turkey	779,452		26	Lithuania	65,200
3	Ukraine	603,700		27	Latvia	64,110
4	France	552,000		28	Croatia	56,538
5	Spain	504,782		29	Bosnia-Hercegovina	51,233
6	Sweden	449,964		30	Slovakia	49,035
7	Germany	357,039		31	Estonia	45,100
8	Finland	337,030		32	Denmark	43,069
9	Norway	324,219		33	Switzerland	41,293
10	Poland	312,677		34	Netherlands	37,938
11	Italy	301,225		35	Moldova	33,700
12	United Kingdom	244,046		36	Belgium	30,513
13	Romania	237,500		37	Armenia	29,800
14	Belorussia	207,600		38	Albania	28,750
15	Greece	131,944		39	Macedonia	25,713
16	Bulgaria	110,910		40	Slovenia	20,296
17	Iceland	103,000		41	Cyprus	9,250
18	Serbia	102,350		42	Luxembourg	2,586
19	Hungary	93,030		43	Andorra	450
20	Portugal	92,082		44	Malta	320
21	Azerbaijan	86,600		45	Liechtenstein	160
22	Austria	83,849		46	San Marino	60
23	Czech Republic	78,664		47	Monaco	2
24	Ireland	70,283				

Highest population density *pop. per sq km*

1	Monaco	15,785		25	Romania	96
2	Malta	1,125		26	Austria	94
3	Netherlands	379		27	Ukraine	86
4	San Marino	377		28	Bosnia-Hercegovina	85
5	Belgium	329			Croatia	85
6	United Kingdom	238		30	Azerbaijan	83
7	Germany	226		31	Bulgaria	81
8	Italy	192		32	Turkey	80
9	Liechtenstein	175		33	Macedonia	79
10	Switzerland	168		34	Cyprus	78
11	Luxembourg	151			Georgia	78
12	Andorra	133			Greece	78
13	Moldova	132		37	Spain	78
14	Czech Republic	131		38	Lithuania	57
15	Poland	124		39	Belorussia	49
16	Armenia	123			Ireland	49
17	Denmark	121		41	Latvia	41
18	Albania	117		42	Estonia	34
19	Hungary	113		43	Sweden	19
20	Slovakia	108		44	Finland	15
21	Portugal	107		45	Norway	13
22	France	105		46	Russia	9
23	Serbia	104		47	Iceland	2
24	Slovenia	97				

Largest populations *m*

1	Russia	148.9	23	Switzerland	6.7
2	Germany	80.5	24	Georgia	5.5
3	Turkey	58.5	25	Slovakia	5.3
4	Italy	57.8	26	Denmark	5.1
5	United Kingdom	57.7		Finland	5.1
6	France	57.3	28	Croatia	4.8
7	Ukraine	52.1	29	Moldova	4.5
8	Spain	39.1	30	Bosnia-Hercegovina	4.4
9	Poland	38.4	31	Norway	4.3
10	Romania	22.8	32	Armenia	3.7
11	Netherlands	15.1		Lithuania	3.7
12	Serbia	10.6	34	Ireland	3.5
13	Czech Republic	10.4	35	Albania	3.4
	Greece	10.4	36	Latvia	2.6
15	Belorussia	10.3	37	Slovenia	2.0
16	Hungary	10.2		Macedonia	2.0
17	Belgium	10.0	39	Estonia	1.5
18	Portugal	9.8	40	Cyprus	0.7
19	Bulgaria	9.0	41	Luxembourg	0.4
20	Sweden	8.7		Malta	0.4
21	Austria	7.9	43	Iceland	0.3
22	Azerbaijan	7.2	44	Andorra	0.1

Oldest populations *% aged over 65*

1	Monaco	22.5	21	San Marino	12.8
2	Sweden	17.4	22	Belorussia	12.3
3	Norway	15.9	23	Ex-Czechoslovakia	12.1
4	Belgium	15.7	24	Estonia	11.9
5	Italy	15.6		Lithuania	11.9
	United Kingdom	15.6		Portugal	11.9
6	Austria	15.4	27	Georgia	11.6
	Denmark	15.4		Ireland	11.6
	Greece	15.4	29	Russia	11.2
9	Switzerland	15.1	30	Poland	10.9
10	France	14.9	31	Iceland	10.4
11	Germany	14.8	32	Cyprus	10.3
12	Spain	14.7	33	Malta	10.2
13	Portugal	14.2	34	Romania	10.1
14	Finland	14.1	35	Andorra	9.9
15	Hungary	13.9	36	Liechtenstein	9.8
16	Latvia	13.2	37	Moldova	8.4
	Luxembourg	13.2	38	Armenia	7.6
	Ukraine	13.2	39	Azerbaijan	6.8
19	Bulgaria	13.1	40	Albania	5.3
20	Netherlands	13.0	41	Turkey	4.8

The economy

GDP *$bn*

1	Germany	1,846.1		21	Belorussia	30.1
2	France	1,278.7		22	Hungary	30.0
3	Italy	1,186.6		23	Czech Republic	25.3
4	United Kingdom	1,024.8		24	Romania	24.9
5	Spain	547.9		25	Luxembourg	13.7
6	Russia	397.8		26	Slovenia	12.7
7	Netherlands	312.3		27	Bulgaria	11.9
8	Switzerland	248.7		28	Croatia	10.7
9	Sweden	233.2		29	Slovakia	10.2
10	Belgium	209.6		30	Cyprus	7.1
11	Austria	174.8		31	Azerbaijan	6.3
12	Denmark	133.9		32	Iceland	6.2
13	Finland	116.3		33	Moldova	5.5
14	Turkey	114.2		34	Latvia	5.1
15	Norway	110.4		35	Lithuania	4.9
16	Ukraine	87.0		36	Georgia	4.7
17	Poland	75.3		37	Estonia	4.3
18	Greece	75.1		38	Armenia	2.7
19	Portugal	73.3		39	Malta	2.6
20	Ireland	42.8				

GDP per head *$*

1	Switzerland	36,230		21	Slovenia	6,330
2	Luxembourg	35,260		22	Hungary	3,010
3	Sweden	26,780		23	Belorussia	2,910
4	Denmark	25,930		24	Estonia	2,750
5	Norway	25,800		25	Russia	2,670
6	Iceland	23,670		26	Czech Republic	2,440
7	Finland	22,980		27	Croatia	2,240
8	Germany	22,920		28	Poland	1,960
9	France	22,300		29	Turkey	1,950
10	Austria	22,110		30	Latvia	1,930
11	Belgium	20,880		31	Slovakia	1,920
12	Netherlands	20,590		32	Ukraine	1,670
13	Italy	20,510		33	Bulgaria	1,330
14	United Kingdom	17,760		34	Lithuania	1,310
15	Spain	14,020		35	Moldova	1,260
16	Ireland	12,100		36	Romania	1,090
17	Cyprus	9,820		37	Azerbaijan	870
18	Portugal	7,450		38	Georgia	850
19	Malta	7,300		39	Armenia	780
20	Greece	7,180				

GDP per head in PPP *1991 (USA=100)*

1	Switzerland	98.4	17	Greece	34.7
2	Germany	89.3	18	Latvia	34.1
3	France	83.3	19	Romania	31.2
4	Denmark	80.8	20	Belorussia	31.0
5	Austria	79.9	21	Czech Republic	28.4
6	Belgium	79.1	22	Hungary	27.5
7	Sweden	79.0	23	Lithuania	24.4
8	Norway	77.6	24	Ukraine	23.4
9	Italy	77.0	25	Bulgaria	22.5
10	Netherlands	76.0	26	Turkey	21.9
11	United Kingdom	73.8	27	Moldova	21.0
12	Finland	72.9	28	Armenia	20.8
13	Spain	57.3	29	Poland	20.3
14	Portugal	42.7	30	Azerbaijan	16.6
15	Russia	37.0		Georgia	16.6
16	Estonia	36.6			

GDP growth *% average annual real growth 1985–92*

1	Turkey	5.0	11	Belgium	2.4
2	Ireland	4.8	12	Switzerland	2.3
3	Luxembourg	4.5	13	United Kingdom	2.2
4	Spain	3.5	14	Greece	1.8
5	Austria	2.8	15	Hungary	1.7
	Germany	2.8		Iceland	1.7
7	Netherlands	2.6	17	Denmark	1.4
8	France	2.5	18	Sweden	1.2
	Italy	2.5	19	Finland	1.1
	Norway	2.5			

Industrial output *% average annual real growth 1985–92*

1	Cyprus	5.0		Spain	1.6
2	Portugal	4.8	15	Ireland	1.4
3	Norway	4.4	16	United Kingdom	1.2
4	Luxembourg	3.0	17	Finland	0.8
5	Austria	2.9	18	Greece	-0.1
6	Switzerland	2.6	19	Sweden	-1.0
7	Germany	2.5	20	Hungary	-1.4
8	Belgium	2.0	21	Poland	-4.4
	Italy	2.0	22	Romania	-8.0
10	Denmark	1.8	23	Ex-Czechoslovakia	-10.6
	France	1.8	24	Bulgaria	-16.1
	Netherlands	1.8	25	Russia	-21.0
13	Malta	1.6			

Household spending[a]

Household spending on food and drink % of total

1	Turkey	40		14	Italy	19
2	Ex-Czechoslovakia	34		15	Switzerland	17
	Malta	34		16	Austria	16
	Portugal	34			Finland	16
5	Bulgaria	31			France	16
	Romania	31			Luxembourg	16
7	Greece	30		20	Belgium	15
8	Poland	29			Norway	15
9	Iceland	27		22	Denmark	13
10	Hungary	25			Netherlands	13
11	Spain	24			Sweden	13
12	Cyprus	22		25	Germany	12
	Ireland	22			United Kingdom	12

Household spending on health % of total

1	Switzerland	15		14	Luxembourg	7
2	France	13			Spain	7
	Germany	13		16	Ex-Czechoslovakia	6
4	Netherlands	11			Greece	6
	Norway	11			Poland	6
	Sweden	11			Portugal	6
7	Austria	10		20	Hungary	5
	Belgium	10		21	Bulgaria	4
	Ireland	10			Malta	4
	Italy	10			Romania	4
11	Denmark	9			Turkey	4
	Finland	9		25	Cyprus	2
13	United Kingdom	8				

Household spending on housing and energy % of total

1	Luxembourg	20			Norway	14
2	Denmark	19		15	Turkey	13
	Sweden	19		16	Greece	12
4	Germany	18		17	Iceland	11
	Netherlands	18			Ireland	11
6	Austria	17		19	Cyprus	9
	Belgium	17			Hungary	9
	France	17			Portugal	9
	Switzerland	17		22	Malta	7
	United Kingdom	17		23	Poland	6
11	Spain	16		24	Bulgaria	4
12	Finland	15			Ex-Czechoslovakia	4
13	Italy	14		26	Romania	3

Household spending on clothing and footwear
% of total

1	Cyprus	16		Germany	7
2	Turkey	15		Luxembourg	7
3	Malta	11		Spain	7
4	Bulgaria	10	17	Belgium	6
	Portugal	10		France	6
	Romania	10		Netherlands	6
7	Austria	9		Norway	6
	Hungary	9		United Kingdom	6
	Poland	9	22	Denmark	5
10	Greece	8		Ireland	5
	Iceland	8		Sweden	5
	Italy	8	25	Finland	4
13	Ex Czechoslovakia	7		Switzerland	4

Consumer goods ownership *% of households*

	TV	VCR	Microwave
Denmark	98	39	14
Ireland	98	38	20
Italy	98	25	6
Luxembourg	98	39	16
Netherlands	98	48	19
Spain	98	40	9
United Kingdom	98	58	48
Belgium	97	42	21
Germany	97	42	36
Norway	97	41	34
Sweden	97	48	37
Austria	96	37	31
Ex-Czechoslovakia	95	...	...
Finland	94	46	53
France	94	35	25
Greece	94	37	2
Bulgaria	93	...	...
Switzerland	93	41	15
Portugal	92	22	4
Romania	77	...	...
Poland	70	...	...
Cyprus	56	...	...
Hungary	21	...	...

a All figures are for 1991.

Life and leisure

Human Development Index

1	Norway	98		18	Cyprus	89
	Sweden	98			Ex-Czechoslovakia	89
	Switzerland	98			Hungary	89
4	France	97		21	Lithuania	88
	Netherlands	97		22	Estonia	87
6	Denmark	96			Latvia	87
	Germany	96		24	Belorussia	86
	Iceland	96			Malta	86
	United Kingdom	96			Russia	86
10	Austria	95		27	Bulgaria	85
	Belgium	95			Portugal	85
	Finland	95		29	Ukraine	84
13	Luxembourg	94		30	Armenia	83
14	Ireland	93			Georgia	83
15	Italy	92			Poland	83
	Spain	92		33	Azerbaijan	77
17	Greece	90		34	Moldova	76

Divorce *latest available year, no. per 1,000 pop.*

1	Russia	3.4			Switzerland	1.9
2	Finland	2.9		16	Iceland	1.8
	United Kingdom	2.9		17	Bulgaria	1.7
4	Denmark	2.8		18	Monaco	1.4
5	Ex-Czechoslovakia	2.6			Romania	1.4
6	Hungary	2.4		20	Poland	1.1
7	Norway	2.2		21	Greece	0.9
	Sweden	2.2			Portugal	0.9
9	Germany	2.1		23	Albania	0.8
	Luxembourg	2.1		24	Cyprus	0.5
11	Austria	2.0		25	Italy	0.4
	Belgium	2.0			Turkey	0.4
13	France	1.9		27	Spain	0.2
	Netherlands	1.9				

Tourist arrivals *m*

1	France	51.5		15	Turkey	4.8
2	Spain	34.3		16	Bulgaria	4.5
3	Italy	26.7		17	Ireland	3.7
4	Hungary	20.5		18	Poland	3.4
5	Austria	19.0		19	Belgium	3.2
6	United Kingdom	18.0		20	Norway	2.0
7	Germany	17.0		21	Cyprus	1.6
8	Switzerland	13.2		22	Denmark	1.2
9	Greece	8.9		23	Finland	0.9
10	Ex-Czechoslovakia	8.1			Malta	0.9
11	Portugal	8.0		25	Luxembourg	0.8
12	Russia	7.2			Sweden	0.8
13	Romania	6.5		27	San Marino	0.4
14	Netherlands	5.8		28	Monaco	0.2

=Part II=
COUNTRY PROFILES

ALBANIA

Modern Albania won independence from the Turks in 1912 after four centuries of rule from Istanbul. A major turning point was reached in March 1992 when the country voted, after a period of liberalisation, to shake off the remnants of the communist regime installed in 1946.

Politics: overcoming isolationism

After winning independence from the Turks Albania had to struggle for survival in an unstable region and during the first world war it was occupied by Greek, Italian and Austrian armies. Independence from Italy was re-established in 1920. But the country remained volatile and in 1928 the minister of the interior, Ahmed Zogu, proclaimed himself King Zog I. Italian influence again intensified and Albania was turned into a fully-fledged protectorate by Mussolini in 1939. After the second world war it came under communist rule.

Communist Albania was a creation of Enver Hoxha who ruled it until his death in 1985. The Hoxha regime engaged in a particularly hardline form of communism under which foreign trade was kept to the barest minimum and foreign investment was banned. Even links with other communist countries ended in 1972 when China fell out of favour for improving relations with the United States. After Hoxha's death the regime of Ramiz Alia slowly attempted to overcome the legacy of his misrule. Relations with neighbouring countries were gradually restored. When communism collapsed across Eastern Europe Mr Alia introduced political reforms with the aim of holding on to power. But since the 1992 elections the country has been ruled by a coalition dominated by the Democratic Party and by President Sali Berisha, a cardiologist by profession. Although displaying an authoritarian streak, the new regime has presided over relatively rapid political and economic reforms.

The economy: aid and stabilisation

Albania's economy dived in the last years of communist rule: GDP shrank by 10% in 1990 and by 30% in 1991. But in 1993 growth of 8% was the highest of any former communist country. Much of this was due to foreign aid, especially from Italy, and hard-currency remittances from some 250,000 Albanians working in Greece. Privatisation, particularly of agriculture, is working well and the development of tourism and natural resources such as copper and chromium offers great potential.

| Total area | 28,750 sq km | Capital | Tirana |

Government

System An interim constitution is in force. The People's Assembly has 140 deputies; 100 are elected directly, 40 by proportional representation. The president is elected by the Assembly. The president nominates the prime minister.

Main political parties Democratic Party (DA), Democratic Alliance Party of Albania (DAPA), Socialist Party of Albania (former Communist Party), Social Democratic Party, Union for Human Rights (UHR, Greek minority party)

The economy

GDP $bn	...	GDP per head	...
% av. ann. growth in real GDP	...	GDP per head in purchasing power parity (USA=100)	...

Debt

Foreign debt $m	624.7	Debt service $m	2.0
as % of GDP	...	Debt service ratio	2.4

People

Population m	3.36	% under 15	32.6
Pop. per sq km	117	% over 65	5.3
% urban	35	No. men per 100 women	106
% av. ann. growth 1985–92	1.8	Human Development Index	70

Life expectancy	yrs		per 1,000 pop.
Men	71	Crude birth rate	23
Women	78	Crude death rate	5

Ethnic groups	% of total	Workforce	% of total
Albanian	90	Services[a]	18.5
Greek	8	Industry[a]	23.8
Other	2	Agriculture[a]	50.5
		Construction[a]	7.2
		% unemployed	9.1

Health

Pop. per doctor	719	Pop. per hospital bed	244

a 1989; state sector only.

ANDORRA

This tiny landlocked country in the Pyrenees between France and Spain survives on agriculture and tourism, though low taxes have also helped it to develop as a finance and duty-free centre. From the late 13th century until recently it was a co-principality ruled by French and Spanish feudal overlords. But in 1993 a new constitution was approved by parliament and passed by referendum, establishing Andorra as a sovereign state. Catalan is the official language but Castillian Spanish and French are widely spoken. A large proportion of the population are immigrant workers from Spain.

History: a Franco-Spanish affair

For helping the king of the Franks in his war against the Saracens in Spain, Andorra, it is held, was granted self-government by Charlemagne. Then in 1843 Charles II, Charlemagne's grandson, granted overlordship of the state to the Comte de Foix, but this was later disputed by the Bishop of Urgel in Spain who claimed Andorra as his cathedral's endowment. Eventually a compromise was reached and the count and the bishop became co-princes in 1278. The count's rights later passed to Henry IV of France and his successors until 1793 when the revolutionary government renounced France's title. In 1806, after being petitioned by Andorra, Napoleon restored the title to France.

The economy: servicing skiers

Tourism (mainly skiing) has become the cornerstone of the economy; visitors per year now total some 12m. Agriculture is mostly sheep rearing, and manufacturing is small scale. Andorra's duty-free status, as well as attracting tourists, has made banking and smuggling important to the economy.

Joining the world

In June 1990 Andorra signed a treaty with the European Union, its first international treaty, by which it joined the EU customs union. The treaty was implemented in 1991, thus ending the country's economic isolation. Farm trade is not included but Andorra can now sell other goods within the EU on the same basis as full EU members. Furthermore goods imported from the EU get duty-free transit to encourage the foreign investment which will help modernise the economy. The government also plans to relax the laws that require Andorran participation in every new foreign company.

| Total area | 450 sq km | Capital | Andorra La Vella |

Government

System The one-chamber General Council has 28 members directly elected for four years. It elects the president, who chooses the members of government.

Main political parties No formal political parties

People

Population '000	60	% under 15[a]	18.0
Pop. per sq km	133	% over 65[a]	9.9
% urban	65	No. men per 100 women	...

Life expectancy	yrs		per 1,000 pop.
Men	74	Crude birth rate	12.6
Women	81	Crude death rate	4.2

Ethnic groups	% of total		
Spanish	61	French	6
Andorran	30	Other	3

Health

Pop. per doctor	441	Pop. per hospital bed	437

a 1989.

ARMENIA

During much of its history Armenia has been ruled by foreign powers. It won independence after the collapse of the Soviet Union in 1991, but has suffered severely from the military conflict with Azerbaijan and from the economic consequences of Soviet disintegration.

History: the road to independence

In the early 16th century Armenia became part of the Ottoman empire but in 1639 Turkey lost part of its Armenian territory to Persia. From the early 19th century the country became a source of conflict between Russia and Turkey and the eastern part was annexed by Russia. Armenia's push for independence from Turkey resulted in pogroms and mass deportations in the late 19th century. After the first world war Armenia was too weak to survive as an independent state. In 1922 it became part of the Soviet Union, eventually winning the status of a Union republic in 1936.

Politics: conflict with Azerbaijan

Mikhail Gorbachev's liberalisation programme soon resulted in a resurfacing of old regional tensions. In 1988 the mountainous province of Nagorno-Karabakh, 80% Armenian but under the jurisdiction of Azerbaijan (after Stalin's decree to that effect in 1921), demanded formal unification with Armenia. In early 1992 Nagorno-Karabakh declared independence, and as Soviet troops withdrew from the area full-scale fighting erupted between Armenia and Azerbaijan. The Armenians have proved more adept in the war, despite being ostensibly the weaker side. By the end of 1993 they had expelled Azerbaijani forces from Nagorno-Karabakh and occupied parts of Azerbaijani territory. Their military fortunes, however, suffered some setbacks in early 1994 after a change of regime in Azerbaijan. Several international peace efforts have been attempted but all have failed.

The economy: war damaged

Armenia is dependent on fuel imports, mainly from Russia, but it has significant mineral resources: marble, basalt, granite and numerous non-ferrous metals, including gold and silver. The economy grew at an impressive annual average rate of 7% between 1971 and 1985. But in 1991 national income fell by 12%, and in the following first year of independence it plummeted by 46%, while inflation soared.

Total area	29,800 sq km	Capital	Yerevan

Government

System Armenia has yet to adopt its post-Soviet constitution. Its Soviet-style legislature, the Supreme Soviet, has been renamed Parliament. The highest official is the directly elected president. The president appoints the prime minister.

Main political parties Dashnak Revolutionary Federation, Hentchak Party, Armenian Pan-National Movement, Armenian Democratic Liberal Party, National Democratic Union, Communist Party

The economy

GDP $bn	2.7	GDP per head $	780
% av. ann. growth		GDP per head in purchasing	
in real GDP	...	power parity (USA=100)	20.8

Debt

Foreign debt $m	10.0	Debt service $m	...
as % of GDP, 1985–92	0.4	Debt service ratio	...

People and society

Population m	3.68	% under 15	30.1
Pop. per sq km	123	% over 65	7.6
% urban	54	No. men per 100 women	...
% av. ann. growth 1985–92	1.4	Human Development Index	83

Life expectancy	yrs		per 1,000 pop.
Men	68	Crude birth rate	22
Women	74	Crude death rate	7

Ethnic groups	% of total	Workforce	% of total
Armenian	93	Construction	42
Russian	2	Agriculture	18
Kurd	2	Other	40
Other	3		

Health

Pop. per doctor	250	Pop. per hospital bed	111

AUSTRIA

Total area	83,849 sq km	Population	7.9m
GDP	$175bn	GDP per head	$22,106
Capital	Vienna	Other cities	Graz, Linz, Salzburg

At the geographical heart of Europe, Austria has been subjected to many cultural and political influences through the centuries. After the destruction of the second world war, its economic recovery was almost as remarkable as western Germany's. From the moment it became a founder member of the European Free Trade Association (EFTA) this small export-dependent country has acknowledged that its future lies in a more open and integrated Europe. In 1994, some five years after applying for membership, Austria was invited to join the European Union. It will become a full member in 1995.

History: Habsburg foundation

Although a high level of civilisation can be traced back to the Iron Age, the key event in the country's early development was in 1273 when Ottokar of Bohemia, who controlled much of present-day Austria, refused to swear allegiance to Count Rudolf von Habsburg after he had been appointed emperor of the Germans. Five years later Ottokar was defeated in battle by Rudolf. For the next six and a half centuries the House of Austria was ruled by 19 Habsburg emperors and kings and one empress, although the Austrian empire as such was only founded when in 1804 Franz II renounced his title as emperor of the Germans to become Franz I, emperor of the Austrians.

Politics: post-war tradition of consensus

The degree of co-operation between political parties established in 1945 served Austria well in the reconstruction years and consensus is the natural state of affairs today. Although political debate is active, disputes tend to arise about means rather than ends, with governments tending to follow a line that is close to the centre. The 1991 elections resulted in the continuation of the coalition between the left-of-centre Social Democrats (SPO) and the centre-right People's Party (OVP) that had governed since 1986. But in the late 1980s, largely as a result of fears about large-scale immigration from Eastern Europe, there was increasing support for the right-wing Freedom Party (FPO), under Jorg Haider. It was expected that in the 1994 October elections, it and its off-split, Liberal Forum, would take votes from the OVP.

Foreign policy: neutral tradition

Austria joined the United Nations in 1955, within a month of passing a law on neutrality, and Vienna has become an important city in UN affairs. Already a member of EFTA and the EEA, Austria's application for membership of the European Union was approved in March 1994, and in a referendum in June Austrians voted overwhelmingly in favour of joining the EU.

The economy: from public to private

After the second world war the traditional industries in western Austria that had been taken over by Germany following the invasion of 1938 were nationalised. Those in the rest of the country were managed from Moscow until the State Treaty was signed in 1955 after which they too were nationalised and revived with the help of Marshall Aid. But state control led to complacency; by the mid-1980s Austria's growth rate was among the lowest in Europe and the country had a chronic budget deficit and huge public debt. However, the late 1980s saw a turnaround thanks largely to policies which encouraged privatisation, gave priority to growth sectors such as chemicals and manufacturing, and involved hard cost cutting. Manufacturing has been helped by an emphasis on adding value through high technology, and the country has a vibrant services sector, based initially on its banking tradition and tourism.

Dependent on exports – and Germany

With its relatively small domestic market, Austria depends on exports; the strength of the economy is therefore strongly influenced by Germany, its most important trading partner. It is also affected more than most other countries in Western Europe by the process of change in Eastern Europe. The early 1990s saw the Austrian economy, like that of Germany, in trouble. The recession caused a large number of bankruptcies in the private sector while the public sector was shedding labour. This process is likely to continue due to the need to restructure. However, by early 1994 there were signs that the economy had bottomed out and a revival of GDP growth was forecast for 1994–95.

Total area	83,849 sq km	% agricultural area	41.6
Capital	Vienna	Highest point metres	
Other cities	Graz, Linz, Salzburg	Grossglockner 3,798	
		Main rivers	Danube (Donau), Inn

The economy

GDP $bn	175	GDP per head $	22,106
% av. ann. growth in		GDP per head in purchasing	
real GDP 1985–92	2.8	power parity (USA=100)	79.9

Origins of GDP	% of total	Components of GDP	% of total
Agriculture	3	Private consumption	56
Industry	36	Public consumption	18
of which:		Investment	26
manufacturing	29	Exports	40
Services	61	Imports	-38

Structure of manufacturing

			% of total
Agric. & food processing	15	Other	51
Textiles & clothing	6	Av. ann. increase in industrial	
Machinery & transport	28	output 1985–92	2.9

Inflation and exchange rates

Consumer price 1993	3.6%	Sch per $ av. 1993	11.63
Av. ann. rate 1988–93	3.1%	Sch per ecu av. 1993	13.03

Balance of payments, reserves and aid

			$bn
Visible exports fob	43.4	Capital balance	1.0
Visible imports fob	-52.2	Overall balance	2.6
Trade balance	-8.8	Change in reserves	2.0
Invisible inflows	38.7	Level of reserves	
Invisible outflows	-29.6	end Dec.	15.7
Net transfers	-0.9	Aid given	0.6
Current account balance	-0.7	as % of GDP	0.3
as % of GDP	-0.4		

Principal exports	$bn fob	Principal imports	$bn cif
Machinery & transport equip.	17.3	Machinery & transport equip.	21.4
Manufactures	13.1	Manufactures	10.0
Consumer goods	6.2	Consumer goods	9.6
Chemical products	3.8	Chemical products	5.3
Raw materials excl. fuels	1.8	Fuels & energy	2.8
Food, drink & tobacco	1.2	Food, drink & tobacco	2.3
Total incl. others	44.3	Total incl. others	54.1

Main export destinations	% of total	Main origins of imports	% of total
Germany	39.8	Germany	42.9
Italy	8.8	Italy	8.6
Switzerland	5.9	Japan	4.7
France	4.4	France	4.4
UK	3.6	Switzerland	4.0

Government

System The federal president is ceremonial head of state, directly elected for up to two six-year terms. The federal chancellor heads the council of ministers and is nominally appointed by the president from the strongest party in the National Council. The two-chamber Federal Assembly consists of a 183-member National Council (Nationalrat), elected by a form of proportional representation for four years, and a 63-member Federal Council (Bundesrat), elected by the republic's nine provinces.

Main political parties Socialist Party (SPO), People's Party (OVP), Freedom Party (FPO), Liberal Forum, United Green Party (VGO), Alternative List (ALO)

People

Population m	7.9	% under 15	17.6
Pop. per sq km	94	% over 65	15.4
% urban	59	No. men per 100 women	93
% av. ann. growth 1985–92	0.6	Human Development Index	95

Life expectancy	yrs		per 1,000 pop.
Men	73	Crude birth rate	12
Women	70	Crude death rate	11

Ethnic groups	% of total	Workforce	% of total
Austrian	98	Services	56.4
Yugoslav	1	Industry	35.4
Other	1	Agriculture	8.1
		% unemployed	3.5

Society

		Consumer goods ownership	
No. households m	2.9		% of households
Av. no. per household	2.5	TV	96
Marriages per 1,000 pop.	5.7	Video recorder	37
Divorces per 1,000 pop.	2.0	Microwave oven	31

Household spending	% of total	Education	
Food/drink	16.0	Spending as % of GDP	5.6
Clothing/footwear	9.0	Years of compulsory education	9
Housing/energy	17.0	Enrolment ratios:	
Household goods	7.0	primary school	103
Health	10.0	secondary school	83
Transport/communications	15.0	tertiary education	33
Leisure/other	19.0		

Tourism		Health	
Tourist arrivals m	19.0	Pop. per doctor	230
Tourist receipts $bn	13.0	Pop. per hospital bed	93

AZERBAIJAN

The Azerbaijani culture has been strongly influenced by the neighbouring Turkish, Persian and Arab worlds, and the country was a source of rivalry among the great powers. Russian influence grew in the early 19th century, and the northern part was ceded to Russia in 1828. Since independence from the Soviet Union in 1991, Azerbaijan has suffered from instability.

Politics: conflict with Armenia

The collapse of the Soviet Union plunged Azerbaijan into chaos. The main cause was the conflict with neighbouring Armenia over the mainly Armenian-inhabited enclave of Nagorno-Karabakh, which had been put arbitrarily under Azerbaijani jurisdiction by Stalin in 1921. In the late 1980s relations with Armenia grew increasingly tense as Mikhail Gorbachev's reforms loosened Moscow's control, and in 1992 full-scale fighting began.

The first post-independence leader, Ayaz Mutalibov, was deposed after setbacks in the war. In May 1992 Abulfaz Elchibei, leader of the nationalist Popular Front, was elected president. A month later he was forced to resign after a mutiny by military officers. The parliament then voted to bring back to power Heidar Aliev, Azerbaijan's former communist boss and a member of Brezhnev's Politbureau. In October Mr Aliev was elected president with an overwhelming Soviet-style 98.9% of the vote. One reason why Mr Aliev was able to stage a comeback was disillusionment with flagging support from Azerbaijan's traditional ally, Turkey. The new president brought a more profitable Russian connection. Azerbaijan joined the Commonwealth of Independent States and Russia stepped up its efforts to mediate in the conflict with Armenia.

The economy: oil development

Azerbaijan has substantial deposits of oil; reserves are estimated at about 1bn tons. Large-scale exploration started in 1970, but production fell from nearly 15m tons in 1980 to less than 12m tons in 1991. Oil companies have been negotiating to provide much needed capital investment since 1991, and in early 1994 President Aliev announced his determination to conclude a deal. Azerbaijan's economy has been hit hard by the break-up of the Soviet Union and by the war with Armenia. National income fell by more than 30% in 1992; it declined again the following year.

Total area	86,600 sq km	Capital	Baku

Government

System A new constitution was adopted in 1991. Azerbaijan has a single-chamber legislature, the Mejlis, with 300 members elected for a five-year term. The prime minister is appointed by a directly-elected president, subject to approval by the Mejlis.

Main political parties Azerbaijani Popular Front, National Independence Party, Musavat Party, Grey Wolves (Bozkurt)

The economy

GDP $bn	6.3	GDP per head $	870
% av. ann. growth in real GDP	...	GDP per head in purchasing power parity (USA=100)	16.6

Debt

Foreign debt $m	...	Debt service $m	...
as % of GDP	...	Debt service ratio	...

People

Population m	7.15	% under 15	33.1
Pop. per sq km	83	% over 65	6.8
% urban	54	No. men per 100 women	106
% av. ann. growth 1985–90	1.4	Human Development Index	77

Life expectancy	yrs		per 1,000 pop.
Men	65	Crude birth rate	26
Women	73	Crude death rate	7

Ethnic groups	% of total	Health	
Azeri	83	Pop. per doctor	250
Russian	6	Pop. per hospital bed	98
Armenian	6		
Daghestanis	3		
Other	2		

BELGIUM

Total area	30,510 sq km	Population	10.0m
GDP	$210bn	GDP per head	$20,878
Capital	Brussels	Other cities	Antwerp, Ghent, Charleroi

With its people divided between the French-speaking Walloons and Dutch-speaking Flemish (there is also a small German-speaking community), Belgium has a fragile sense of national identity. It would prefer to see itself as the diplomatic and bureaucratic heart of the European Union.

History: mixing the Low Countries

Belgium's divisions can be traced back 2,000 years to Caesar's Gallic wars. Latin culture swept the south of the "Belgian area" but the tribes of the north resisted Romanisation. Its more recent origins lie in the duchies and counties that emerged some 1,100 years ago in north-west Europe. From the treaty of Verdun in 843 to the break-up of the Napoleonic empire (1814–15) the area between the Meuse river and the North Sea was a battleground for rival principalities. The Dukes of Burgundy, the Spanish, the Habsburgs and Napoleon were all involved, by war and by dynastic marriage, in attempts to unite the Low Countries. The process produced great cities where art and commerce flourished, and an abiding Flemish resentment of the French-speaking elite.

The modern monarchy

Modern Belgium began with the secessionary revolution of 1830 against the 15-year-old "United Kingdom of the Netherlands". The next year an elected National Congress chose a German prince, Leopold of Saxe-Cobourg-Gotha, to be the first "King of the Belgians". However, it was not until the Treaty of London in 1839 that all of Europe recognised the new kingdom.

The dynasty's fortunes have varied. The first king promoted economic development; Leopold II kept Belgium out of the war in 1870 that pitted Bismarck's Germany against the France of Napoleon III, and also founded a Belgian empire with the African colony of the Congo. But the reign of King Albert saw Belgium as a first world war battlefield. Much the same was true for Leopold III, whose policy of neutrality failed to stop the country being overrun by Hitler's troops in 1940. Because the return of the king at the end of the war was unacceptable to public opinion, his brother Charles reigned as regent until 1950, when Leopold abdicated in favour of Baudouin, his eldest son.

The new king was both wise and popular; his death in 1993 was mourned by Flemings and Walloons alike, uncertain as they were at the ability of Baudouin's brother and successor, Albert, to calm intercommunal tensions.

Politics: keeping the balance

Belgium is only superficially a conventional parliamentary democracy and constitutional monarchy. In practice, political life is a constant balancing act across the linguistic divide. One result is that both French- and Dutch-speaking communities have their own parties, even if the ideologies are identical; another is that governments are invariably short-lived coalitions.

In mid-1993 parliament agreed to turn the country into a federal state. The national government would be responsible for foreign affairs, defence, justice, internal security, taxation and social security. All other areas became the responsibility of three regions, Flanders, Wallonia and Brussels, and of the country's three language groups. Meanwhile, the Chamber of Representatives was to be reduced from 212 members to 150 and the Senate from over 180 to 71. As part of the devolutionary process there are directly elected parliaments in Flanders, Wallonia and Brussels (a Francophone island in Dutch-speaking Flanders).

How well federalism works remains to be seen. But at least arguments tend to be confined to domestic issues. On foreign affairs there is agreement: Belgium's place is in the EU, and the more federally-minded that union, the better.

The economy: debt-burdened trader

Belgium has always been a great exporter, from lace in the middle ages to chemicals, pharmaceuticals, steel and diamonds today. From 1960 to the oil shock of 1974 the economy grew by 5% a year. However, inflation-linked pay rises in the aftermath, coupled with generous welfare benefits, have burdened Belgium with Western Europe's highest national debt as a proportion of GDP.

One socially important effect of economic growth is that Wallonia, the centre of coal and steel production, has fallen behind Flanders, which in the 1960s transformed itself from a farming region into one of industry and advanced technology. The challenge for any Belgian government now is to cut debt and public spending.

Total area	30,513 sq km	% agricultural area[a]	45.6
Capital	Brussels	Highest point metres	Botrange 694
Other cities	Antwerp, Ghent ,	Main rivers	Schelde, Meuse,
	Charleroi		Sambre

The economy

GDP $bn	210	GDP per head $	20,878
% av. ann. growth in		GDP per head in purchasing	
real GDP 1985–92	2.4	power parity (USA=100)	79.1

Origins of GDP	% of total	Components of GDP	% of total
Agriculture	2	Private consumption	64
Industry	31	Public consumption	15
of which:		Investment	18
manufacturing	22	Exports	67
Services	62	Imports	-63

Structure of manufacturing

			% of total
Agric. & food processing	17	Other	52
Textiles & clothing	8	Av. ann. increase in industrial	
Machinery & transport	23	output 1985–92	2.0

Inflation and exchange rates

Consumer price 1993	2.8%	BFr per $ av. 1993	34.60
Av. ann. rate 1988–93	2.7%	BFr per ecu av. 1993	40.47

Balance of payments, reserves and aid[a]

			$bn
Visible exports fob	116.6	Capital balance	-6.1
Visible imports fob	-116.4	Overall balance	0.6
Trade balance	0.2	Change in reserves	0.6
Invisible inflows	126.7	Level of reserves	
Invisible outflows	-119.0	end Dec.	22.1
Net transfers	-2.5	Aid given	0.9
Current account balance	5.4	as % of GDP	0.4
as % of GDP	2.6		

Principal exports	$bn fob	Principal imports	$bn cif
Machinery & transport equip.	33.4	Machinery & transport equip.	32.0
Chemicals	18.1	Chemicals	14.9
Metals	13.8	Food & agric. products	10.6
Food and agric. products	10.7	Metals & manufactures	9.5
Textiles & clothing	8.8	Fossil fuels	9.3
Precious stones & jewellery	7.7	Textiles & clothing	7.7
Total incl. others	123.4	Total incl. others	125.2

Main export destinations	% of total	Main origins of imports	% of total
Germany	22.8	Germany	23.9
France	19.3	Netherlands	17.5
Netherlands	13.7	France	16.5
UK	7.8	UK	7.7
Italy	5.9	Italy	4.5

Government

System Belgium agreed to become a federal state (with a constitutional hereditary monarchy) in 1993, with considerable autonomy given to the three regions of Flanders, Wallonia and Brussels, and to the three linguistic communities. Under the reforms the two-house legislature comprises a 150-member Chamber of Representatives and a 71-member Senate. Flanders, Wallonia and Brussels have their own directly-elected parliaments.

Main political parties French: Christian Social Party (PSC), Socialist Party (PS), Liberal Party (PRL), French-speaking Democratic Front (FDF), Ecology Party (Ecolo) National Front (FN); Flemish: Christian People's Party (CVP), Socialist Party (SP), Liberal Party (PVV), People's Union (VU), Ecology Party (Agalev), Flemish Nationalists (VU), Flemish Separatists (VB)

People

Population m	10.0	% under 15	17.9
Pop. per sq km	329	% over 65	15.7
% urban	97	No. men per 100 women	96
% av. ann. growth 1985–92	0.3	Human Development Index	95

Life expectancy	yrs		per 1,000 pop.
Men	73	Crude birth rate	12
Women	79	Crude death rate	10

Ethnic groups	% of total	Workforce	% of total
Fleming	85	Services	69.6
Walloon	33	Industry	21.4
Mixed or other	12	Agriculture	2.7
		Construction	6.3
		% unemployed	11.2

Society

No. households m	3.7	**Consumer goods ownership**	
Av. no. per household	2.6		% of households
Marriages per 1,000 pop.	6.6	TV	97
Divorces per 1,000 pop.	2.0	Video recorder	42
		Microwave oven	21

Household spending	% of total	Education	
Food/drink	15.0	Spending as % of GDP	6.1
Clothing/footwear	6.0	Years of compulsory education	10
Housing/energy	17.0	Enrolment ratios:	
Household goods	7.0	primary school	102
Health	10.0	secondary school	104
Transport/communications	11.0	tertiary education	37
Leisure/other	24.0		

Tourism		Health	
Tourist arrivals m	3.2	Pop. per doctor	310
Tourist receipts $bn	3.6	Pop. per hospital bed	120

a   Including Luxembourg.

BELORUSSIA

After invasion by the Mongols in the 13th and 14th centuries the Slav peoples on Belorussian territory came under the rule of the Grand Duchy of Lithuania, which eventually became part of a Polish-Lithuanian union. After the partition of Poland in the late 18th century the area of today's Belorussia fell under Moscow's rule. A brief period of independence occurred in 1918 before Belorussia was firmly incorporated into Soviet Russia. It became one of the most loyal members of the Soviet Union and after the second world war was developed as a model communist republic. After independence in 1991 links with Moscow were maintained and in early 1994 Belorussia opted for a close union with Russia.

Politics: the conservatives cling on

The nationalist, pro-independence forces started to organise in 1988 under the Popular Front chaired by Zyanon Paznyak. In 1990 members of the Front won 16% of the seats in elections to the Belorussian parliament. After the attempted coup against Mikhail Gorbachev in Moscow in August 1991, the parliament declared independence. Stanislau Shushkevich, the speaker, became the country's leader but he shared power with the prime minister, Vyacheslau Kebich. Mr Shushkevich was removed from office in early 1994 and replaced by a conservative, Miecyslau Hryb. Since independence Belorussia has continued to cling to the remnants of the communist system, with conservatives in parliament refusing to enact political and economic reforms. In mid-1994 the first free presidential elections revealed considerable dissatisfaction with the government but it seemed likely that Belorussia would continue to strengthen its links with Moscow.

The economy: leaning on Russia

During the Soviet period Belorussia was the world's third largest producer of tractors and a major producer of trucks and motorcycles. Industry accounted for over 50% of national income in 1991. About 70% of raw materials continue to be supplied by the former Soviet republics and the country is dependent on fuel imported from Russia. The lack of economic reforms since independence has hindered the chances of recovery. National income fell by 15% in 1992 and by a similar margin in 1993 when, as in neighbouring Ukraine, hyperinflation took hold.

Total area	207,600 sq km	Capital	Minsk

Government
System Belorussia has an amended Soviet-style constitution. There is a unicameral legislature, the Supreme Soviet (eventually to be renamed the Soim), with 360 deputies. The chairman of the Supreme Soviet (sometimes referred to as president) shares power with the prime minister. Belorussia is yet to hold its post-Soviet elections.

Main political parties The Communist Party of Belorussia, Popular Front of Belorussia, Social Democratic Party, National Democratic Party, United Democratic Party, Belorussian Peasant Party

The economy
GDP $bn	30.1	GDP per head $	2,910
% av. ann. growth		GDP per head in purchasing	
in real GDP	...	power parity (USA=100)	31.0

Debt
Foreign debt $m	181.2	Debt service $m	0.6
as % of GDP	0.6	Debt service ratio	...

People
Population m	10.27	% under 15	22.9
Pop. per sq km	49	% over 65	12.3
% urban	66	No. men per 100 women	...
% av. ann. growth 1985–91	0.4	Human Development Index	86

Life expectancy	yrs		per 1,000 pop.
Men	66	Crude birth rate	15
Women	76	Crude death rate	11

Ethnic groups	% of total	Workforce	% of total
Belorussian	78	Services	30.4
Russian	13	Industry	39.1
Polish	4	Agriculture	20.7
Ukrainian	3	Construction	9.8
Other	2	% unemployed	...

Health
Pop. per doctor	250	Pop. per hospital bed	76

BOSNIA

The former Yugoslav republic of Bosnia-Hercegovina is one of the most complex mosaics of nationalities and religions in the Balkans. In 1991 Muslims (ethnic Slavs converted to Islam by the Ottomans) constituted 44% of the population, with Serbs accounting for 31% and Croats 17%.

History: almost constant subjugation

The area of today's Bosnia was settled by southern Slavs in the 6th century and, despite spending most of its history under foreign rule, Bosnia managed to remain a distinct entity. It came under the control of the Austro-Hungarian empire in the late 19th century and the assassination of the heir to the Austro-Hungarian throne in the Bosnian capital, Sarajevo, in June 1914 triggered off the first world war. After the collapse of the empire Bosnia-Hercegovina became part of inter-war Yugoslavia, and then of the Federal Republic created by Josip Broz Tito.

Politics: riven by nationalism

Following the declaration of independence by Slovenia and Croatia in June 1991 Yugoslavia collapsed and a bitter war ensued. The pretext for the war in Bosnia was the reluctance of Bosnian Serbs to live in an independent Bosnian state, proclaimed after a referendum in March 1992. However, the war was fuelled by the desire of Bosnian Serbs to create independent statelets within Bosnia, linked closely with Serbia. This was opposed by the mainly Muslim Bosnian government headed by President Alia Izetbegovic as it was seen as the first step towards the republic's disintegration. In early 1993 fighting also erupted between Bosnian Croats and Muslims, who had been nominal allies. Bosnia became the theatre for the bitterest fighting in former Yugoslavia and of widespread ethnic cleansing. The capital Sarajevo, and other Muslim enclaves, endured a prolonged siege by the Serbs. By 1994 more than 200,000 people had died and a succession of ceasefires and peace plans had made little progress towards a solution.

The economy: bombed out

The country is relatively well endowed with mineral resources, forests and hydroelectric power potential. The economy was rapidly developed during communist rule but was brought to a standstill in the 1990s by the war. Any recovery will depend on large-scale international aid.

Total area	51,233 sq km	Capital	Sarajevo

Government

System The Republic of Bosnia-Hercegovina adopted a new constitution before fighting flared up between Serbs, Muslims and Croats. Elections for the two-chamber parliament, the Chamber of Citizens and the Chamber of Municipalities, were held in December 1990.

Main political parties Normal political life has been suspended in the wake of the fighting.

People

Population m	4.36	% under 15	...
Pop. per sq km	85	% over 65	...
% urban	...	No. men per 100 women	...
% av. ann. growth 1990–91	0.5	Human Development Index	...

Life expectancy*	yrs		per 1,000 pop.
Men	68	Crude birth rate	14.5
Women	73	Crude death rate	6.5

Ethnic groups	% of total	Workforce	% of total
Muslim	44	Services	...
Serb	33	Industry	...
Croat	17	Agriculture	...
Other	6	Construction	...
		% unemployed	...

Health

Pop. per doctor	...	Pop. per hospital bed	...

a Former Yugoslavia.

BULGARIA

Total area	110,910 sq km	Population	8.96m
GDP	$11.9bn	GDP per head	$1,330
Capital	Sofia	Other cities	Plovdiv, Varna, Burgas

Strong historical ties ensured that Bulgaria remained one of the Soviet Union's closest allies until the Todor Zhivkov regime, which had been in power for 35 years, fell in 1989. Newly democratic Bulgaria sees its future closely linked with the market economy of Western Europe.

History: the Russian connection

Modern Bulgarians are the descendants of a Finno-Ugrian people who in the 7th century merged with the Slav population; Bulgarian is a south Slav language closely related to Russian and Serbo-Croat. Orthodox Christianity was introduced in 865 by Boris, khan of the Bulgars. The Bulgarian kingdom prospered under the rule of Simeon, the tsar of the Bulgars, in the late 9th and early 10th centuries, but the eastern part of the country was annexed to the Byzantine empire in 971; Bulgaria was fully absorbed after 1014. In 1396 it was incorporated into the Ottoman empire, but an autonomous Principality of Bulgaria was created at the Congress of Berlin in 1878 after pressure from Russia. Full independence from Turkey was proclaimed in 1908. The intricacies of Balkan politics (a confrontation with Serbia) led Bulgaria to side with Germany in the first world war, and again during the second world war, although Bulgaria did not take part in Germany's attack on the Soviet Union. The authoritarian regime of Tsar Boris III ruled the country in the inter-war period. The presence of the Soviet army on Bulgarian territory after the war eventually ensured the entrenchment of the communist regime headed by Vulko Chervenkov. He was succeeded by Todor Zhivkov in 1954.

Politics: democracy's labour pains

The first free elections held in June 1990 were won – because the opposition was in disarray – by the renamed communists, the Bulgarian Socialist Party. But it failed to win the necessary majority in the Grand National Assembly which resulted in instability and, in late 1991, new elections. The first non-communist government, headed by Filip Dimitrov of the Union of Democratic Forces (UDF), was appointed. The UDF ruled in coalition with the mainly Turkish Movement for Rights and Freedoms. A former dissident philosopher, Zhelyu Zhelev, was elected president by the parliament in 1991. A year later Mr Dimitrov's government was voted out of office by the parliament. Weeks of negotiation followed before a government of "independent experts" was formed, under the leadership of Luyben Berov. Two years later it was still clinging on to power, but elections looked inevitable.

International relations: big changes

Communist Bulgaria had supported the idea of detente between the East and the West but the Zhivkov regime was strongly opposed to the liberalising reforms of Mikhail Gorbachev during the late 1980s. After the collapse of the communist government there was a rapid reorientation to the West. Bulgaria has an association agreement with the European Union and is keen to become a member of NATO. Relations with Turkey, severely damaged in the last years of Zhivkov's rule, have dramatically improved, and relations with Greece have been constructive. At considerable cost, Bulgaria supported UN sanctions against Serbia.

Society: Turkish exodus

An exodus of ethnic Turks due to the repressive policies of the Zhivkov regime in the late 1980s resulted in a drop in population size, but it has grown at an average annual rate of 1.6% in recent years. About 800,000 ethnic Turks remain, concentrated around Shumen and Khaskovo.

The economy: not in the market vanguard

Post-communist Bulgaria embarked on the transition to a market economy but the process generally lagged behind countries run by more aggressive reformists, Poland, the Czech Republic and Hungary. However, the pace of reform has been rapid by the standards of some of the former Soviet republics. In common with other ex-communist countries Bulgaria found the initial impact of market reforms quite shocking; national income fell by about a fifth in both 1990 and 1991. The economy continued to stagnate in 1994 but a modest recovery was expected in 1995. The country has various established strengths: there are considerable deposits of low quality coal and non-ferrous metals, and tourism, concentrated on the Black Sea, has traditionally been a major source of income.

Total area	110,910 sq km	% agricultural area	55.6
Capital	Sofia	Highest point metres	Musala 2,925
Other cities	Plovdiv, Varna, Burgas	Main rivers	Danube (Dunau), Iskur, Maritsa, Tundzha

The economy

GDP $bn	11.9	GDP per head $	1,330
% av. ann. growth in		GDP per head in purchasing	
real GDP 1985–92	...	power parity (USA=100)	22.5

Origins of GDP[ab]	% of total	Components of GDP[ab]	% of total
Agriculture	13	Consumption	75.4
Industry	50	Accumulation	24.6
of which:			
manufacturing	...		
Services	37		

Structure of manufacturing

			% of total
Agric. & food processing	...	Other	...
Textiles & clothing	...	Av. change in industrial	
Machinery & transport	...	output 1992	-16.1

Inflation and exchange rates

Consumer price 1992	85.0%	Lev per $ av. 1993	26.80
Av. ann. rate 1988–93	...	Lev per ecu av. 1993	30.02

Balance of payments and debt

			$bn
Visible exports fob	5.1	Capital balance	...
Visible imports fob	-4.6	Overall balance	...
Trade balance	0.5	Change in reserves	...
Invisible inflows	...	Foreign debt	12.9
Invisible outflows	...	as % of GDP	110.7
Net transfers	0.5	Debt service	0.4
Current account balance	...	Debt service ratio	6.9
as % of GDP	...		

Principal exports[c]	$bn fob	Principal imports[c]	$bn cif
Industrial products	14.0	Industrial products	14.4
Processed agric. products	1.9	Processed agric. products	0.2
Non-processed agricultural		Non-processed agricultural	
products	0.4	products	0.6
Total	16.4	Total	15.2

Main export destinations[c]	% of total	Main origins of imports[c]	% of total
Ex-Soviet Union	65.0	Ex-Soviet Union	53.6
Eastern Germany	5.6	Eastern Germany	5.8
Ex-Czechoslovakia	4.4	Ex-Czechoslovakia	5.0
Poland	3.9	Western Germany	4.9
Romania	2.0	Poland	4.8

Government
System of government Under a new constitution adopted in July 1991, the president, who is head of state, is directly elected and appoints the prime minister. The one-chamber directly elected national assembly has 240 members.
Main political parties Bulgarian Socialist Party (BSP), Bulgarian Agrarian National Union (BANU), Union of Democratic Forces (UDF), Movement for Rights and Freedoms (MRF, ethnic Turkish party)

People

Population m	8.96	% under 15	20.1
Pop. per sq km	81	% over 65	13.1
% urban	68	No. men per 100 women	98
% av. ann. growth 1985–92	nil	Human Development Index	85

Life expectancy	yrs		per 1,000 pop.
Men	69	Crude birth rate	12
Women	76	Crude death rate	12

Ethnic groups	% of total	Workforce[a]	% of total
Bulgarian	85.3	Services	41.9
Turkish	8.5	Industry	33.9
Gypsy	2.6	Agriculture	18.0
Macedonian	2.5	Construction	6.2
Other	1.1	% unemployed	16.4

Society

No. households m	3.0	**Consumer goods ownership**	
Av. no. per household	2.8		% of households
Marriages per 1,000 pop.	7.0	TV	93
Divorces per 1,000 pop.	1.7	Video recorder	...
		Microwave oven	...

Household spending	% of total	Education	
Food/drink	31.0	Spending as % of GDP[ab]	6.9
Clothing/footwear	10.0	Years of compulsory education	8
Housing/energy	4.0	Enrolment ratios:	
Household goods	17.0	primary school	96
Health	4.0	secondary school	74
Transport/communications	9.0	tertiary education	31
Leisure/other	25.0		

Tourism		Health	
Tourist arrivals m	4.5	Pop. per doctor	320
Tourist receipts $bn	0.4	Pop. per hospital bed	102

a   1989.
b   As % of NMP.
c   1990.

CROATIA

The southern Slav nation of Croats settled in the former Roman provinces of Panonia and Dalmatia in the 7th century. The country was later taken by the Ottoman Turks who ceded it to the Austrian Habsburgs at the end of the 17th century.

After the reorganisation of Austria into Austria-Hungary, tensions grew in the late 19th century between Croatia and Hungary, as the Croats called for more autonomy. In 1918 Croatia became part of the kingdom of Serbs, Croats and Slovenes ruled by a Serb dynasty. In 1929 the kingdom was formally renamed Yugoslavia. In the second world war the Nazis installed a puppet government in Croatia, run by the far-right Ustashi, who engaged in genocide against Croatian Serbs and other nationalities. After the war Croatia became part of the Federal Republic of Yugoslavia, run by the League of Communists of Yugoslavia whose leader, Josip Broz Tito, was himself a Croat.

Politics: the forces of nationalism

After Tito's death in 1980 the forces of nationalism gradually began to assert themselves leading to the disintegration of Yugoslavia. In June 1991 Croatia (and neighbouring Slovenia) declared unilateral independence. Franjo Tudjman, a former communist turned nationalist, was elected president. The declaration triggered off a war with Croatian Serbs in Krajina, in eastern Croatia. Croatia lost about one-third of its territory to the Serbs. In 1992–93 Croatia negotiated with Serbia about the partition of Bosnia-Hercegovina and fighting erupted in April 1993 between Bosnian Croats and Muslims. A peace plan in 1994 envisaged a confederation between Croatia and Bosnia.

The economy: the burden of the war

Tito's idiosyncratic version of self-management communism provided considerable devolution to enterprises as well as regions. A range of industries was developed in Croatia, such as electrical engineering, pharmaceuticals and ship-building. Since the 1960s Croatia has also developed its considerable tourist potential. The disintegration of the close-knit Yugoslav economy coupled with the war caused a severe economic decline. The national income fell by 23% in 1991 and 25% in 1992, when inflation reached a giddy 1,250%.

Total area	56,538 sq km	Capital	Zagreb

Government

System A new constitution was passed in 1990. Croatia has a bicameral legislature with a House of Constituencies and House of the Regions. The directly elected president appoints the prime minister.

Main political parties Croatian Democratic Union (HDZ), Croatian Social Liberal Party (HSLS), Croatian Peasants' Party (HSS), Croatian Party of Rights (HSP, far right), Social Democratic Party of Croatia (SDP, former communists), Serbian Democratic Party (SDS), Serbian People's Party

The economy

GDP $bn	10.7	GDP per head $	2,238
% av. ann. growth in real GDP	...	GDP per head in purchasing power parity (USA=100)	...

Debt

Foreign debt $m	...	Debt service $m	...
as % of GDP	...	Debt service ratio	...

People

Population m	4.78	% under 15	...
Pop. per sq km	85	% over 65	...
% urban	...	No. men per 100 women	...
% av. ann. growth 1981–91	0.4	Human Development Index	...

Life expectancy	yrs		per 1,000 pop.
Men	67	Crude birth rate	12.2
Women	74	Crude death rate	11.3

Ethnic groups	% of total	Workforce	% of total
Croat	78	Services	35.3
Serb	12	Industry	52.6
Muslims	1	Agriculture	5.3
Other	9	Construction	6.8
		% unemployed	15.0

Health

Pop. per doctor	...	Pop. per hospital bed	...

CYPRUS

Cyprus has been divided since 1974, with the Turkish Republic of Northern Cyprus recognised only by Turkey. Repeated initiatives to find a solution have failed.

History: from subservience to split

This Mediterranean island was in turn part of the Greek, Roman and Byzantine empires. It was held by Richard the Lionheart at the end of the third crusade after which it was ruled by the French before being annexed by Venice and then, in 1571, conquered by Ottoman Turks. Three centuries of Muslim rule ended when in 1878 the country became a British protectorate. After Turkey entered the first world war Britain annexed Cyprus. Increasing demands by Greek Cypriots for union (*enosis*) with Greece led to riots in 1931 and a campaign of terrorism in the 1950s. In 1959 there was agreement on power sharing; a Greek-Cypriot, Archbishop Makarios, became president, and a Turkish-Cypriot, Fazil Kutchuk, vice-president. In 1960 independence from Britain was granted. But the power-sharing arrangements soon broke down and in 1974, following a right-wing coup by the army in Greece, Turkey invaded the island to protect the Turkish-Cypriot minority. Since then the northern third of the island has been under Turkish-Cypriot control.

The economy: divided progress

Political division has been reflected in economic development. The Greek south has prospered: high levels of state investment in housing and infrastructure not only helped to replace what had been lost in the North, but also to generate growth. However, this was accompanied by a large public sector deficit which remains a problem. Reducing the deficit is top of the economic agenda, coupled with measures to bring the economy in line with the EU. Specialised agriculture and tourism has been developed, as well as off-shore banking and shipping, but with tourism and exports being the economic base.

Because of its relative isolation economic development in the Turkish north has been difficult. It remains heavily dependent on Turkey, which has financed virtually all investment in infrastructure. The economy is reliant on imports for food and other necessities and thus runs a constant balance of payments deficit. Nonetheless, Turkish Cyprus is making progress, albeit slowly, especially in tourism.

Total area	9,250 sq km	Capital	Nicosia

Government

System The Greek-Cypriot administration in the Republic of Cyprus observes the 1960 constitution. The president, who is directly elected for five years, appoints the Council of Ministers, and convenes and presides over their meetings. The one-chamber House of Representatives has nominally 80 members directly elected by proportional representation for five years; however, the 24 seats reserved for Turkish Cypriots remain unfilled. The Turkish-Cypriot administration in the Turkish Republic of Northern Cyprus, which is not recognised internationally, approved its own constitution in 1985.

Main political parties Communist Party (Akel), Adisok (splinter group of Akel), Democratic Party (Diko), Democratic rally (Disy), Socialist Party (Edek)

The economy

GDP $bn	7.1	GDP per head $	9,820
% av. ann. growth in		GDP per head in purchasing	
real GDP 1985–91	5.0	power parity (USA=100)	...

Origins of GDP[a]	% of total	Components of GDP	% of total
Agriculture	7.1	Private consumption	62.9
Industry	27.0	Public consumption	12.8
of which:		Investment	26.7
manufacturing	15.2	Exports	51.3
Services	60.7	Imports	-55.5

Debt

Foreign debt $bn	2.1	Debt service $m	...
as % of GDP	46.7	Debt service ratio	...

People

Population m	720	% under 15	25.6
Pop. per sq km	78	% over 65	10.3
% urban	53	No. men per 100 women	99
% av. ann. growth 1985–92	0.4	Human Development Index	89

Life expectancy	yrs		per 1,000 pop.
Men	74	Crude birth rate	18
Women	78	Crude death rate	8

Ethnic groups	% of total	Health	
Greek	78	Pop. per doctor	516
Turkish	18	Pop. per hospital bed	165
Other	4		

a 1990.

CZECH REPUBLIC

Total area	78,664 sq km	Population	10.4m
GDP	$25.3bn	GDP per head	$2,440
Capital	Prague	Other cities	Brno, Ostrava

The independent Czech Republic came into existence in January 1993 after the split of the Czech and Slovak Federated Republic. Unlike in Slovakia, separation, which was not initially desired by the Czechs, has proved to be a boon to the country. The political scene has stabilised, and economic reforms and the republic's westward reorientation have gathered pace.

History: Germanic influences

The Czechs first shared a common state with the Slovaks in the Great Moravian Empire in the 9th century. After its collapse in the early 10th century, the kingdom of Bohemia, created from its ruins, became part of the Holy Roman Empire built by German emperors. The kingdom prospered culturally and economically in the medieval period and Charles's University was founded in 1348 in Prague, the first in central Europe. King Charles I was crowned Holy Roman Emperor in 1346 (as Charles IV). The kingdom rebelled against Roman Catholicism and German domination during the Hussite wars in 1420–33. The Hussite movement had sprung into existence after the burning at the stake, in 1415, of the reformation martyr Jan Hus. It returned, however, into the Catholic fold after the Battle of the White Mountain near Prague in 1620. Forced Germanisation and conversion to Catholicism followed.

The first stirrings of national revival occurred in the 19th century. These coincided with similar movements in Slovakia, where Slovak intellectuals strove to recreate the common state. The drive for national emancipation culminated during the first world war, and after great efforts by T.G. Masaryk the Czechoslovak Republic was proclaimed in October 1918; Masaryk became president. The inter-war republic, which inherited the bulk of the industrial potential of the Austro-Hungarian empire, prospered economically and enjoyed the reputation of a stable democracy. It was dismembered and occupied by the Nazis between March 1939 and May 1945.

Politics: emancipation from Moscow

After a communist coup in February 1948 the country fell under Soviet domination. A reform movement, headed by the Slovak Communist Party leader, Alexander Dubcek, was suppressed by the Soviet army in August 1968. Mr Dubcek was replaced by the reactionary Gustav Husak whose "normalisation" policies over the following two decades resulted in severe cultural and economic decline. Moscow's shackles were finally thrown off in late 1989 when demonstrations led to the demise of the communist regime in a peaceful "velvet revolution". A playright and former dissident, Vaclav Havel, became president and the first free elections were held in June 1990. A right-of-centre coalition headed by Vaclav Klaus won the second elections in June 1992. Because post-communist Czechoslovakia was riven with Czech-Slovak disputes, Mr Klaus soon became convinced that separation of the federation was the only lasting solution.

Foreign policy: shift to the West

Since its democratisation the country has sought to "return to Europe". An association agreement has been concluded with the European Union, and links have been created with NATO under the Partnership for Peace scheme. Relations with Slovakia are often tense but generally constructive. The Czech Republic is a member of the central European Visegrad group, which also includes Poland, Hungary and Slovakia.

The economy: hopes on the horizon

Like all former Soviet satellites the Czech Republic was forced to develop costly and inefficient heavy industries at the expense of light industry and services. Industry and mining accounted for over 60% of the country's production in recent years. Market-oriented reforms induced a severe recession in 1990, which lasted through to 1993, but by early 1994 recovery looked under way. Machinery and equipment and other industrial products account for about 60% of total exports, and fuels are a major import item. An ambitious mass privatisation programme, engineered by Mr Klaus, has proved successful and large numbers of tourists have flocked to post-communist Prague, thus boosting growth in the service sector.

Total area	78,664 sq km	% agricultural area	54.3
Capital	Prague	Highest point metres	
Other cities	Brno, Ostrava		Snezka 1,603
		Main river	Elbe

The economy

GDP $bn	25.3	GDP per head $	2,440
% av. ann. growth in		GDP per head in purchasing	
real GDP 1985–92[a]	-1.4	power parity (USA=100)	28.4

Origins of GDP[a]	% of total	Components of GDP[a]	% of total
Agriculture	8	Private consumption	67
Industry	56	Public consumption	...
of which:		Investment	31
manufacturing	...	Exports	42
Services	36	Imports	...

Structure of manufacturing

			% of total
Agric. & food processing	10	Other	37
Textiles & clothing	11	Av. change in industrial	
Machinery & transport	35	output 1985–91	-3.8

Inflation and exchange rates

Consumer price 1993[a]	20.8%	Kcs per $ av. 1993	29.15
Av. ann. rate 1988–93[a]	15.9%	Kcs per ecu av. 1993	32.65

Balance of payments and debt[a]

			$bn
Visible exports fob	11.5	Capital balance	-0.2
Visible imports fob	-13.3	Overall balance	-0.4
Trade balance	-1.8	Change in reserves	-2.3
Invisible inflows	4.8	Foreign debt	9.3
Invisible outflows	-3.1	as % of GDP	28.8
Net transfers	0.1	Debt service	2.0
Current account balance	-0.03	Debt service ratio	...
as % of GDP	-0.1		

Principal exports[abc]	$bn fob	Principal imports[abc]	$bn cif
Fuels, minerals & metals	1.34	Machinery & equipment	2.11
Machinery & equipment	1.27	Foodstuffs & livestock	0.89
Consumer goods excl. food	1.02	Fuels, minerals & metals	0.83
Chemicals, fertilisers & rubber	0.68	Chemicals, fertilisers & rubber	0.63
Organic raw materials		Organic raw materials	
excl. food	0.66	excl. food	0.34
Total incl. others	5.66	Total incl. others	5.38

Main export destinations[ac]	% of total	Main origins of imports[ac]	% of total
Ex-Soviet Union	30.5	Ex-Soviet Union	29.7
Poland	8.5	Western Germany	9.3
Western Germany	8.3	Poland	8.6
Eastern Germany	6.6	Eastern Germany	7.8
Austria	4.6	Austria	5.5

Government

System A new constitution was adopted after the break up of Czechoslovakia in January 1993. The lower chamber, Parliament, has 200 deputies and elects the president. An upper house, the Senate, with 81 members is planned. Parliament is elected on the basis of proportional representation. Parties failing to gain 5% of the vote are not represented.

Main political parties Civic Democratic Party (CDP), Civic Democratic Alliance, Christian Democratic Party, Social Democratic Party, Communist Party of Bohemia and Moravia, Republican Party

People

Population m	10.4	% under 15	20.9[a]
Pop. per sq km	131	% over 65	12.1[a]
% urban	78[a]	No. men per 100 women	95[a]
% av. ann. growth 1985–92	0.1[a]	Human Development Index	89[a]

Life expectancy[a]	yrs		per 1,000 pop.
Men	69	Crude birth rate	13
Women	76	Crude death rate	11

Ethnic groups	% of total	Workforce	% of total
Czech	62.9	Services	46.0
Slovak	31.8	Industry	36.1
Hungarian	3.8	Agriculture	9.9
Polish	0.5	Construction	8.0
Other	1.0	% unemployed	5.1

Society[a]

No. households m	5.6	**Consumer goods ownership**	
Av. no. per household	2.7		% of households
Marriages per 1,000 pop.	8.4	TV	95
Divorces per 1,000 pop.	2.6	Video recorder	…
		Microwave oven	…

Household spending[a]	% of total	Education	
Food/drink	34.0	Spending as % of GDP[ac]	5.3
Clothing/footwear	7.0	Years of compulsory education	10
Housing/energy	4.0	Enrolment ratios:	
Household goods	13.0	primary school	93
Health	6.0	secondary school	84
Transport/communications	6.0	tertiary education	18
Leisure/other	24.0		
		Health[a]	
Tourist arrivals[c] m	8.1	Pop. per doctor	310
Tourist receipts $bn	0.5	Pop. per hospital bed	127

a Former Czechoslovakia.
b To/from non-socialist countries.
c 1990.

DENMARK

Total area	43,069 sq km	Population	5.1m
GDP	$134bn	GDP per head	$25,927
Capital	Copenhagen	Other cities	Aarhus, Odense, Alborg

Denmark was the first Scandinavian country to join the European Union but it has maintained close links with the rest of Scandinavia, which will be strengthened by the proposed road and rail link between Denmark and Sweden. In common with the citizens of the other Scandinavian countries, the Danes enjoy one of the highest living standards in the world. The challenge is to maintain that state of affairs.

History: lesser power now

Until 1866 Denmark was a power of importance in northern Europe. It was under the rule of the Danish regent, Margrethe (1375–1412), that Denmark, Norway and Sweden were united for the first and only time. This period was followed by a series of short-lived Scandinavian alliances until the overthrow of Christian II in 1523. Then began a steady shrinking of Denmark's frontiers, culminating in the loss of Schleswig and Holstein after defeat by the Prussians in 1886. This destroyed Denmark's influence in Europe (though North Schleswig rejoined Denmark after a plebiscite in 1920). In the first world war the country was neutral; it tried to preserve its neutrality in 1939 by signing a pact with Hitler but was occupied in 1940.

Politics: constant coalition

With a system of proportional representation and up to 13 parties contesting just 179 legislative seats, it is no surprise that no single party has been able to secure an absolute majority in post-war Denmark. In consequence there has been a succession of minority and coalition governments almost every two years. Most of these have been led by the centre-left Social Democrats (SDP), though centre-right coalitions were in power from 1982 to 1993.

Foreign policy: keenish Europeans

The failure of its policy of neutrality led Denmark to ally itself with mainstream Europe. It was a founder member of NATO and EFTA, which it left when, together with Britain and Ireland, it joined the European Community in 1973. But the Danes have at times shown embarrassing independence from the European line. Conflict with NATO policy came in 1988 when the parliament voted to ban nuclear weapons from Danish territory and led to a new election less than a year after the previous one. Conflict over the EU came when it took two referendums to approve the Maastricht treaty. In June 1992 the people rejected (by a very small margin) the treaty; and it was only approved in May 1993 after various opt-out clauses had been negotiated. However, the issue is likely to re-emerge in the run up to the 1995 elections, with the Liberals pushing for full integration into the EU.

The economy: return to stability

The drift from agriculture to industry became a surge in the 1960s, with agricultural exports falling from some two-thirds of total exports to just over a quarter in little more than a decade. The oil price rises of the early 1970s led to a doubling of foreign debt in six years and exacerbated the imbalance in the economy. During the 1980s governments were in constant battle with the problems of reducing the current-account and budget deficits, controlling inflation and restraining domestic demand. By the early 1990s the current account was in surplus, the inflation rate was one of the lowest in the OECD, and growth was similar to that of other EU countries.

GREENLAND

The world's largest island came under Danish rule in 1380. A nationalist movement developed after the island was taken into the European Union with Denmark in 1973 despite a majority vote by Greenlanders against joining. A 1979 referendum produced a large majority in favour of home rule and in 1985 Greenland withdrew from the EU. Seal-hunting, fishing and sheep-rearing are the main economic activities, and the island still depends on subsidies from Denmark, its largest trading partner.

THE FAROE ISLANDS

Lying between Scotland and Iceland the Faroes have been administered by Denmark since 1380. They have their own government and parliament for internal affairs, and did not join the EU. About a third of the population lives on the main island, Streymoy. Fishing accounts for 90% of exports and the economy is heavily dependent on Danish subsidies.

Total area	43,069 sq km	% agricultural area	64.7
Capital	Copenhagen	Highest point metres	
Other cities	Arhus, Odense, Alborg		Ydıng Skovhoj 173
		Main river	Gudena

The economy

GDP $bn	134	GDP per head $	25,927
% av. ann. growth in		GDP per head in purchasing	
real GDP 1985–92	1.4	power parity (USA=100)	80.8

Origins of GDP	% of total	Components of GDP	% of total
Agriculture	6	Private consumption	52
Industry	29	Public consumption	25
of which:		Investment	15
manufacturing	22	Exports	37
Services	65	Imports	-29

Structure of manufacturing

			% of total
Agric. & food processing	21	Other	51
Textiles & clothing	4	Av. ann. increase in industrial	
Machinery & transport	23	output 1985–92	1.8

Inflation and exchange rates

Consumer price 1993	1.3%	DKr per $ av. 1993	6.48
Av. ann. rate 1988–93	2.9%	DKr per ecu av. 1993	7.59

Balance of payments, reserves and aid

			$bn
Visible exports fob	40.6	Capital balance	-5.0
Visible imports fob	-33.4	Overall balance	-0.2
Trade balance	7.2	Change in reserves	3.7
Invisible inflows	30.2	Level of reserves	
Invisible outflows	-32.2	end Dec.	11.6
Net transfers	-0.5	Aid given	1.4
Current account balance	4.7	as % of GDP	1.0
as % of GDP	3.5		

Principal exports[*]	$bn fob	Principal imports[*]	$bn cif
Food & agric. products	9.0	Machinery, incl. electric	6.9
Machinery, incl. electric	8.3	Transport equipment	2.7
Chemicals	3.4	Chemicals	2.7
Furniture	1.5	Textiles & clothing	2.3
Fuels & energy products	1.5	Fuels & energy products	2.2
Total incl. others	35.9	Total incl. others	32.3

Main export destinations[*]	% of total	Main origins of imports[*]	% of total
Germany	22.4	Germany	22.1
Sweden	11.5	Sweden	10.8
UK	10.3	UK	8.0
France	5.8	USA	6.3
Norway	5.5	Netherlands	5.7

Government

System The monarch is ceremonial head of state. The crown nominally appoints a prime minister, who commands a majority in the Folketing (parliament), who in turn chooses a state council (cabinet). All the ministers are responsible to parliament. The one-chamber Folketing has 179 members, including two each from the Faroe islands and Greenland, elected by a form of proportional representation for four years.

Main political parties Social Democratic Party, Conservative People's Party (KF), Liberal Party (V), Socialist People's Party, Progress Party, Centre Democrats, Social Liberal Party, Christian People's Party

People

Population m	5.1	% under 15	17.1
Pop. per sq km	121	% over 65	15.4
% urban	87	No. men per 100 women	98
% av. ann. growth 1985–92	0.1	Human Development Index	96

Life expectancy	yrs		per 1,000 pop.
Men	73	Crude birth rate	13
Women	79	Crude death rate	12

Ethnic groups	% of total	Workforce	% of total
Danish	98.0	Services	66.2
Other Scandinavian	0.4	Industry	21.9
Turkish	0.3	Agriculture	5.6
British	0.2	Construction	6.3
		% unemployed	11.4

Society

No. households m	2.2	**Consumer goods ownership**	
Av. no. per household	2.2		% of households
Marriages per 1,000 pop.	6.2	TV	98
Divorces per 1,000 pop.	2.8	Video recorder	39
		Microwave oven	14

Household spending	% of total	Education	
Food/drink	13.0	Spending as % of GDP	6.9
Clothing/footwear	5.0	Years of compulsory education	9
Housing/energy	19.0	Enrolment ratios:	
Household goods	7.0	primary school	98
Health	9.0	secondary school	109
Transport/communications	13.0	tertiary education	32
Leisure/other	26.0		

Tourism		Health	
Tourist arrivals m	1.2	Pop. per doctor	390
Tourist receipts $bn	3.3	Pop. per hospital bed	175

a 1991.

ESTONIA

Estonia was incorporated into the Russian empire in 1721 after years of conflict between Russia and Sweden. National revival began in the 19th century and in 1920 Soviet Russia recognised Estonia's independence. A parliamentary republic was proclaimed, but in 1934 the prime minister, Konstantin Pats, reverted to dictatorship. Democracy was restored in 1938 but two years later Soviet control was imposed, following the Molotov-Ribbentrop pact between the Soviet Union and Germany (whose secret protocols ceded control over all Baltic states to Moscow). Large-scale immigration of Russians and other Slavs followed; in 1989 only 61.5% of the population were Estonians.

Politics: breaking away

Mikhail Gorbachev's liberalising reforms in the Soviet Union permitted the revival of pro-independence forces and in 1988 the Popular Front of Estonia was formed. Estonian was recognised as the official language a year later and in 1990 confrontation with Moscow's hardliners intensified. Independence was proclaimed in September 1991, and the country was recognised by the UN. The first free elections were held in September 1992 and brought to power a right-wing coalition. Lennart Meri became the country's president.

Since independence the country has struggled to reduce its dependence on the former Soviet economy and ensure the withdrawal of former Soviet troops. It has clashed with Moscow over the treatment of Russian nationals. The controversial Aliens Law was passed, which considers non-Estonians as foreigners. Moscow has accused Estonia of pursuing policies of ethnic cleansing and apartheid.

The economy: hopeful signs

Under Soviet rule the economy was industrialised, with engineering, metalworking, electronics and consumer goods predominating. Also developed were the timber and paper industries, drawing on Estonia's forestry resources. After independence a programme of rapid privatisation was carried out and a policy of reorienting trade away from the former Soviet Union was set in motion. Industrial output fell by 39% in the first year of independence, but recovery was expected in 1994. Estonia was the first former Soviet republic to introduce its own currency, the kroon. Unlike the currencies of many former Soviet republics, it has been a success.

Total area	45,100 sq km	Capital	Tallinn

Government

System A new constitution was adopted in 1992. The country has a unicameral parliament, the 101-member Riigikogu. Deputies are elected for four years by proportional representation, with a 5% threshold. In 1992 the president was elected by the Riigikogu after direct elections did not produce a clear winner.

Main political parties Fatherland Alliance (Pro Patria), Popular Front, Estonian National Independence Party (ENIP), Moderates, Independent Royalists, Estonian Liberal Democratic Party, Representative Assembly (representing ethnic Russians)

The economy

GDP $bn	4.3	GDP per head $	2,750
% av. ann. growth		GDP per head in purchasing	
in real GDP 1985–92	...	power parity (USA–100)	36.6

Debt

Foreign debt $m	51.2	Debt service $m	11.0
as % of GDP	1.2	Debt service ratio	...

People

Population m	1.54	% under 15	22.3
Pop. per sq km	34	% over 65	11.9
% urban	72	No. men per 100 women	...
% av. ann. growth 1985–92	0.2	Human Development Index	87

Life expectancy	yrs		per 1,000 pop.
Men	65	Crude birth rate	16.0
Women	74	Crude death rate	12.0

Ethnic groups	% of total	Workforce	% of total
Estonian	61.5	Services	34.1
Russian	30.3	Industry	43.3
Ukrainian	3.2	Agriculture	12.7
Belorussian	1.8	Construction	9.9
Other	3.2	% unemployed	...

Health

Pop. per doctor	210	Pop. per hospital bed	...

FINLAND

Total area	337,030 sq km	Population	5.06m
GDP	$116bn	GDP per head	$22,977
Capital	Helsinki	Other cities	Tampere, Turku, Vantaa

Finland is among the top ten countries in the world for income per head. During the cold-war years relations with its neighbour, the Soviet Union, were of prime importance. In recent years Finland has been forging closer links with the rest of Europe.

History: between Scandinavia and the Bear

From the days of the Swedish crusaders in the 12th century to the end of the Swedish-Russian wars in 1809, Finland was part of the kingdom of Sweden. It then became an autonomous Grand Duchy under the Russian tsar until the Russian revolution in 1917. Following Finland's declaration of independence later that year a brief civil war ensued, which was won by the non-socialist "whites". In 1919 a new constitution was proclaimed, establishing the new republic as a democracy, and in 1920 the Soviet Union recognised Finland's independence. However, in 1939 – and despite a treaty of non-aggression – Finland was attacked by Soviet troops and was forced to give up the northern Arctic territories it had gained only in 1920, as well as most of Karelia. When Germany attacked the Soviet Union in 1941, the Finns tried to recover these lands. They failed and were forced to sign a peace treaty under which they had to cede yet more land and make reparations worth $300m. Although there were difficult moments, the pragmatic Finns pursued a policy of peaceful co-existence with their superpower neighbour during the post-war years, which gave them political stability and the economic benefit of access to a huge market.

Politics: consensus rules

In the post-war period Finland has been ruled by minority governments or coalitions because there are too many political parties for any one to win an absolute majority. The result has been the development of consensus policies as the only practical way of getting legislation passed by the necessary majority. Most of the governments have been left-leaning but the 1991 election resulted in Finland's first wholly non-socialist government for a quarter of a century.

Foreign policy: neutrally pragmatic

After the second world war Finland adopted a policy of neutrality, but it signed in 1948 a Treaty of Friendship with its communist neighbour whereby it agreed to resist – with the assistance of the Soviet Union, if necessary, and subject to mutual agreement – any attack over Finnish territory aimed at the USSR. In 1991 the treaty was scrapped, but in 1992 Finland and Russia signed a new agreement about trade and international politics (but not defence). Finland became an associate member of EFTA in 1961 and a full member in 1986. In 1972 it signed a free-trade agreement with the EU and in 1991 it demonstrated its desire for closer links with the European Union by signing up for the EEA. In 1992 Finland went one step further and applied to join the European Union. In March 1994 the EU agreed to admit Finland as a member in 1995. However, accession was to be subject to a referendum. Past opinion polls have shown the Finns to be sharply divided on whether they should become members

The economy: adapting to circumstances

In the post-war years Finland's economy has shifted from agriculture to manufacturing and become increasingly dependent on trade; export earnings now account for a quarter of GDP. In 1950 the forest industry accounted for almost 80% of Finnish exports, and metal and engineering products for only 5%. By 1990 their respective shares were roughly equal, with both sectors accounting for about 40% of total merchandise exports. But such a development has also required imports of raw materials (notably energy) on a large scale, resulting in an almost constant current-account deficit. The country also borrowed heavily to secure its rapid growth in living standards.

During the 1980s stable trade relations with the USSR enabled Finland to secure growth in export markets. This was accompanied by a high level of investment with emphasis on specialised industry. At the same time, however, growing consumer demand soon led the economy into overheating and a subsequent slide into recession in 1990. The collapse of the Soviet Union in 1991 combined with global economic sluggishness exacerbated the situation. Finland experienced a particularly deep recession with unemployment as high as 13.1% in 1992. By 1994, however, there were signs that the economy might be recovering.

Total area	337,030 sq km	% agricultural area	7.8
Capital	Helsinki	Highest point metres	Haltia 1,324
Other cities	Tampere, Turku, Vantaa	Main rivers	Paatsjoki, Kemijoki, Kokemaenjoki

The economy

GDP $bn	116	GDP per head $	22,977
% av. ann. growth in		GDP per head in purchasing	
real GDP 1985–92	1.1	power parity (USA=100)	72.9

Origins of GDP	% of total	Components of GDP	% of total
Agriculture[a]	6	Private consumption	56
Industry	34	Public consumption	23
of which:		Investment	22
manufacturing	25	Exports	31
Services	59	Imports	-32

Structure of manufacturing

			% of total
Agric. & food processing	13	Other	60
Textiles & clothing	4	Av. ann. increase in industrial	
Machinery & transport	23	output 1985–92	0.8

Inflation and exchange rates

Consumer price 1993	2.1%	Fmk per $ av. 1993	5.71
Av. ann. rate 1988–93	4.4%	Fmk per ecu av. 1993	6.39

Balance of payments, reserves and aid

			$bn
Visible exports fob	23.6	Capital balance	3.4
Visible imports fob	-19.7	Overall balance	-2.2
Trade balance	3.9	Change in reserves	-2.4
Invisible inflows	6.4	Level of reserves	
Invisible outflows	-14.5	end Dec.	5.6
Net transfers	-0.9	Aid given[b]	0.6
Current account balance	-5.1	as % of GDP	0.6
as % of GDP	-4.4		

Principal exports	$bn fob	Principal imports	$bn cif
Metals & engineering	8.0	Raw materials excl.	
Paper industry products	7.3	crude oil	11.1
Chemicals	2.7	Consumer goods	4.6
Wood industry products	1.8	Capital goods	3.0
Total incl. others	24.0	Fuels incl. crude oil	2.2
		Total incl. others	22.5

Main export destinations	% of total	Main origins of imports	% of total
Germany	15.6	Germany	16.9
Sweden	12.8	Sweden	11.7
UK	10.7	UK	8.6
France	6.7	Russia	7.1
USA	5.9	USA	6.1

Government

System The executive president is elected for six years by an absolute majority of votes cast in a direct election, or, failing that, by an electoral college of 301 members, who are themselves directly elected. The president appoints the prime minister and Council of State (Valtioneuvosto). The one-chamber Eduskunta (parliament) has 200 members, directly elected by proportional representation for four years.

Main political parties Centre Party, Social Democratic Party (SDP), National Coalition (Conservatives) Party (KOK), Left Alliance, Swedish People's Party, Green Party, Finnish Christian Union, Finnish Rural Party

People

Population m	5.06	% under 15	18.9
Pop. per sq km	15	% over 65	14.1
% urban	60	No. men per 100 women	95
% av. ann. growth 1985–92	0.4	Human Development Index	95

Life expectancy	yrs		per 1,000 pop.
Men	72	Crude birth rate	12
Women	80	Crude death rate	10

Ethnic groups[b]	% of total	**Workforce**	% of total
Finnish	93.6	Services	63.9
Swedish	6.0	Industry	20.8
Other	0.4	Agriculture	8.5
		Construction	6.8
		% unemployed	13.0

Society

No. households m	2.0	**Consumer goods ownership**
Av. no. per household	2.4	% of households
Marriages per 1,000 pop.	4.8	TV	94
Divorces per 1,000 pop.	2.9	Video recorder	46
		Microwave oven	53

Household spending	% of total	**Education**	
Food/drink	16.0	Spending as % of GDP	6.8
Clothing/footwear	4.0	Years of compulsory education	10
Housing/energy	15.0	Enrolment ratios:	
Household goods	6.0	primary school	99
Health	9.0	secondary school	114
Transport/communications	14.0	tertiary education	47
Leisure/other	29.0		

Tourism		**Health**	
Tourist arrivals m	0.9	Pop. per doctor	410
Tourist receipts $bn	1.2	Pop. per hospital bed	93

a Including forestry.
b Classified by ethno-linguistic composition.

FRANCE

Total area	552,000 sq km	Population	57.3m
GDP	$1,279bn	GDP per head	$22,300
Capital	Paris	Other cities	Lyons, Marseilles, Lille

The French Republic, straddling Western Europe from the Atlantic to the Mediterranean, has a sense of pride – especially in its history and culture – that few other nations match. Having survived two world wars and the loss of its empire, France now is determined to remain a central political and economic force in the European Union.

History: from the Gauls to de Gaulle

The French can trace their identity back first to the migration from the Rhine valley, around 1500BC, of a Celtic people known as the Gauls; then to the five centuries of Roman colonisation that began in 123BC; and finally to the empire created towards the end of the 8th century AD by Germanic Franks under Charlemagne (Charles I).

But a sense of national stability took time to achieve. Although France emerged as one of the successor kingdoms in 987 to the collapse of the Carolingian empire, there followed centuries of intermittent conflict – between dynasties, against the English (the Hundred Years' War between 1337 and 1453) and, in the 16th century, between the Protestant Huguenots and the ultimately victorious Roman Catholics.

Royalty and revolution

From this turmoil France emerged in the 17th century as Europe's greatest power, ruled by Bourbon monarchs such as the "Sun King", Louis XIV. However, by 1789 royal extravagance and expensive defeats in foreign wars had led the near-bankrupt country to a bloody revolution, toppling the monarchy and proclaiming the rights of man. This "First Republic" was too weak to survive; the Corsican Napoleon Bonaparte took power as the republic's "consul" in 1799, before proclaiming himself emperor in 1804.

But Napoleon, too, over-reached himself in foreign ventures, first in Egypt and Syria and then, in 1812, with his disastrous march on Moscow. The end came with defeat by Britain in 1815 at Waterloo. The monarchy was then restored, only to be followed by the 1848–52 "Second Republic" and the 1852–70 "Second Empire" under Napoleon III.

Coping with the neighbours

The end for the Second Empire – and the creation of the

Third Republic – came with France's defeat in its 1870–71 war with Germany, which thereby took temporary possession of Alsace-Lorraine. The area was returned to France after Germany's defeat in the first world war, but then all of France was occupied by Hitler's troops in 1940. Liberation came in 1944. General Charles de Gaulle, who had established a government-in-exile in Algiers, returned to head a provisional government. This was followed in 1946 by the Fourth Republic.

But the post-war years were agonising. The republic was overwhelmed by its costly war against nationalism in French Indochina, from which it withdrew in 1954, and against the independence movement in Algeria, its biggest North African colony. In 1958 de Gaulle returned as prime minister, obtained the electorate's approval for a new constitution and became the first president of the Fifth Republic.

Politics: Paris rules, president predominant

The system devised by General de Gaulle gives great executive powers to a president who is directly elected (either by an absolute majority or, failing that, in a second-round run-off) for a term of seven years. The president appoints the prime minister and, on his advice, the council of ministers. These form a government which is answerable to a two-chamber parliament: the 577-member National Assembly (including 22 members from overseas territories), elected from individual constituencies for a five-year term; and the 319-member Senate, elected by local councils for a nine-year term, one-third retiring every three years.

The inherent strength of the Fifth Republic's constitution is the relatively strong executive powers of the president (in times of crisis he can assume emergency powers); the weakness is that the different electoral cycles can mean a president and a government are from opposing political parties. This enforced "cohabitation" occurred, for example, with the conservative administrations of Jacques Chirac and Edouard Balladur during the presidency of the socialist François Mitterrand. In the event, however, the strange bedfellows managed to co-exist quite peacefully.

The main political parties are the Parti Socialiste on the left and on the centre-right the Gaullist Rassemblement Pour la République and the Union de la Démocratie Française. The UDF was a coalition partner in the RPR government of Mr Balladur. A recent phenomenon has been the near-collapse of the once-powerful Communist Party; it now gets fewer votes than the extreme right-wing National

Front of Jean-Marie Le Pen.

One important feature of French politics is its centralisation of power; the government in Paris decrees what will happen, and then waits to see how the country will react. The consequence is a tradition of extra-parliamentary violence, such as the student uprising of 1968 (which came close, some say, to toppling the government) and the perennial demonstrations by aggrieved farmers, fishermen and industrial workers.

Foreign policy: independent and European

Humiliation in the second world war and the loss in the 1950s and early 1960s of its colonies in Indochina and North Africa combined to hurt the pride of France. So, too, did the dominance of the Anglo-Saxon world under America's leadership.

In retaliation, modern France has obsessively stressed its independence, while, perhaps paradoxically, striving for an integrated Europe to counterbalance the Anglo-Saxon world. De Gaulle, for example, maintained an independent French nuclear force and took France out of NATO's military arm in 1966. He also, with France a founding member of the European Economic Community, vetoed Britain's application throughout the 1960s (the British finally joined in 1973). More important was the need to forge an alliance with Germany within an integrating Europe so that Germany should never again flex its muscles at France's expense.

Those political instincts have been shared by de Gaulle's successors. The question is whether they can still be indulged. A united Germany, for example, is increasingly less willing to play the political subordinate to France.

Society: a matter of culture

France is the largest state in Europe after Russia and, not surprisingly, has strong regional differences (including some regional languages). Yet the French think of themselves as a single culture, with successive governments jealously (and unsuccessfully) guarding the purity of the French language and culture.

Part of this culture is a respect for intellectualism. So too is a strong class system and the concentration of political and administrative power among graduates of the elite *grandes écoles*.

The self-confidence of French culture is not, however,

immune to threat. The influence of the English language, be it in rock music or in business, dismays many. Meanwhile, those who value France's tradition of providing refuge to refugees point to the disturbing rise of the far right, and the risk of racism in a country in which nearly a tenth of the population are either immigrants, mainly from Morocco and Algeria, or children of immigrants.

The economy: all change

For all the damage suffered in world wars and lost colonial wars, modern France has emerged as a force to be reckoned with. It is now the world's fourth biggest economy (and so a member of the policy-making G7); second biggest exporter of commercial services; second biggest agricultural exporter; and fourth biggest exporter of manufactured goods.

All this has been achieved not just by the bounty of nature (the climate and soil, for example, are particularly suited to make France the world's leading wine exporter), but also through government policies in the 1960s and 1970s that supported industry, much of it state-owned, in chemicals, iron and steel, automobiles, nuclear power and – in the adventurous 1980s – high-technology areas such as aerospace and computers. Meanwhile, the shrinking farming community (it now represents only 5% or so of the workforce) was cosetted by huge subsidies under the European Union's Common Agricultural Policy.

But the process was hardly painless. As the economic centre of gravity shifted southwards in the 1960s and 1970s from the coal, steel and textiles industries of the north-east, so came frequent bouts of industrial strife.

Meanwhile, a welfare state was created whose costs threatened to become unsustainable – hence the decision in 1986 to begin a programme of privatisation (in contrast to the nationalisations made by President Mitterrand in 1981). In 1993 the government of Edouard Balladur announced a new plan to privatise some 21 companies valued at Fr400 billion. These included state icons such as the Renault car company, Air France and the Elf oil company. At the same time the government pursued a *franc fort* policy, keeping the currency in line with the Deutschemark even if it meant – as it did – high interest rates and record unemployment.

This policy, the government argued, was necessary to avoid inflation and ensure a modern, competitive economy for the future. That may well be so. But it implies an embrace of free-market forces that is at odds with France's traditions.

Total area	552,000 sq km	% agricultural area	56.7
Capital	Paris	Highest point metres	Mont Blanc
Other cities Lyons, Marseilles, Lille			4,810
		Main rivers Loire, Rhône, Seine,	
		Garonne, Rhine (Rhin)	

The economy

GDP $bn	1,279	GDP per head $	22,300
% av. ann. growth in		GDP per head in purchasing	
real GDP 1985–92	2.5	power parity (USA=100)	83.3

Origins of GDP	% of total	Components of GDP	% of total
Agriculture	3	Private consumption	61
Industry	31	Public consumption	19
of which:		Investment	20
manufacturing	22	Exports	23
Services	66	Imports	-22

Structure of manufacturing

			% of total
Agric. & food processing	13	Other	50
Textiles & clothing	6	Av. ann. increase in industrial	
Machinery & transport	31	output 1985–92	1.8

Inflation and exchange rates

Consumer price 1993	2.1%	Fr per $ av. 1993	5.66
Av. ann. rate 1988–93	2.9%	Fr per ecu av. 1993	6.63

Balance of payments, reserves and aid

			$bn
Visible exports fob	225.2	Capital balance	-19.0
Visible imports fob	-223.6	Overall balance	-13.1
Trade balance	1.7	Change in reserves	-5.4
Invisible inflows	181.4	Level of reserves	
Invisible outflows	-170.4	end Dec.	27.0
Net transfers	-2.8	Aid given	8.27
Current account balance	4.1	as % of GDP	0.63
as % of GDP	0.3		

Principal exports	$bn fob	Principal imports	$bn cif
Capital goods	64.2	Capital goods	58.4
Agric. produce & foodstuffs	37.9	Non-durable consumer goods	40.5
Non-durable consumer goods	35.5	Chemicals	37.0
Chemicals	33.8	Agric. produce & foodstuffs	27.8
Motor vehicles & transp. equip.	32.5	Motor vehicles & transp. equip.	26.4
Total incl. others	236.0	Total incl. others	239.6

Main export destinations	% of total	Main origins of imports	% of total
Germany	17.6	Germany	18.7
Italy	10.9	Italy	10.6
Belgium/Luxembourg	9.2	Belgium/Luxembourg	8.7
UK	9.2	USA	8.4
Spain	7.2	UK	7.7

Government

System The executive president is directly elected for seven years by an absolute majority of votes cast, or, failing that, in a second round run-off election. The president appoints the prime minister and council of ministers, who are responsible to parliament. The two-chamber parliament comprises the 577-member National Assembly, directly elected from individual constituencies for five years and a 321-member Senate, elected by local councils for nine years, one-third retiring every three years.

Main political parties Socialist Party (PS), Rally for the Republic (RPR), Union for French Democracy, Social Democrat Centre (CDS), Social Democratic Party (PSD), Communist Party of France (PCF), National Front (FN)

People

Population m	57.3	% under 15	19.8
Pop. per sq km	105	% over 65	14.9
% urban	74	No. men per 100 women	95
% av. ann. growth 1985–92	0.6	Human Development Index	97

Life expectancy	yrs		per 1,000 pop.
Men	73	Crude birth rate	14
Women	81	Crude death rate	10

Ethnic groupsa	% of total	**Workforce**	% of total
French	93.2	Services	66.3
Algerian	1.5	Industry	21.5
Portugese	1.4	Agriculture	5.1
Moroccan	0.8	Construction	7.1
		% unemployed	10.2

Society

No. households m	21.6	**Consumer goods ownership**	
Av. no. per household	2.5		% of households
Marriages per 1,000 pop.	5.1	TV	94
Divorces per 1,000 pop.	1.9	Video recorder	35
		Microwave oven	25

Household spending	% of total	**Education**	
Food/drink	16.0	Spending as % of GDP	5.7
Clothing/footwear	6.0	Years of compulsory education	10
Housing/energy	17.0	Enrolment ratios:	
Household goods	7.0	primary school	111
Health	13.0	secondary school	99
Transport/communications	13.0	tertiary education	40
Leisure/other	23.0		

Tourism		**Health**	
Tourist arrivals m	51.5	Pop. per doctor	350
Tourism receipts $bn	20.2	Pop. per hospital bed	107

a Classified by nationality.

GEORGIA

Georgia's history has been marked by a constant struggle for survival – the adoption of Christianity in the 4th century made it an object of hostility among the Arab, Persian and Turkish powers. In 1921 it was invaded by the Red Army only three years after having won independence from the Russian empire, into which it was gradually incorporated in the 19th century. In 1991 it became independent again, since when it has staggered from crisis to crisis, with little prospect of stabilisation.

Politics: preventing disintegration

The Georgians welcomed the collapse of the Soviet Union and in 1991 elected Zviad Gamsakhurdia, a dissident nationalist, president. After an increasingly divisive and dictatorial rule, he was ousted in a coup in December 1992. His successor was Eduard Shevardnadze, the former minister of foreign affairs of the Soviet Union and a man deeply associated with the indignities of Moscow's rule. Mr Shevardnadze, however, enjoyed considerable international prestige and thus offered a hope of being able to deal with the rigours of post-Soviet transition.

However, the new regime faced strong separatist movements in South Ossetia, which wanted to join Russia, and in the Autonomous Republic of Abkhazia. It also faced challenges from the province of Mingrelia, the home of the deposed former President Gamsakhurdia. Fighting with the Abkhaz rebels intensified in 1992 and the Georgians suffered serious setbacks. Under Russian pressure the conflict ended in July 1993. In the end Russian influence proved to be the only factor preventing the looming disintegration of the country. But Mr Shevardnadze paid a price, not popular among many of his countrymen: Georgia joined the Commonwealth of Independent States and was brought closer to Moscow.

The economy: in crisis

Agriculture is still (just) the largest sector; the product range is diverse thanks to a warm climate and mountainous terrain. Georgia supplied the Soviet Union with citrus fruit and tea, but imported grain. It has substantial mineral resources, such as manganese, but the deposits have remained underdeveloped. The country is dependent on imported fuel from Russia. Since independence, output has fallen precipitously and inflation has risen sharply.

Total area	69,700 sq km	Capital	Tbilisi

Government

System A post-independence constitution has yet to be promulgated. There is a unicameral legislature, the Supreme Council, with 234 members. The directly elected chairman of the Council acts as head of state, with the right to appoint the prime minister.

Main political parties National Democratic Party, Mshvidoba (Peace; former Communist Party), 11 Oktomberi, Green party, Unity Bloc, Union of Democratic Citizens

The economy

GDP $bn	4.7	GDP per head $	850
% av. ann. growth		GDP per head in purchasing	
in real GDP 1985–92	...	power parity (USA=100)	16.6

Debt

Foreign debt $m	84.8	Debt service $m	...
as % of GDP	1.8	Debt service ratio	...

People

Population m	5.46	% under 15	23.9
Pop. per sq km	78	% over 65	11.6
% urban	56	No. men per 100 women	...
% av. ann. growth 1985–90	0.9	Human Development Index	83

Life expectancy	yrs		per 1,000 pop.
Men	67	Crude birth rate	17
Women	75	Crude death rate	9

Ethnic groups	% of total	Health	
Georgian	68.8	Pop. per doctor	170
Armenian	9.0	Pop. per hospital bed	90
Azeri	5.1		
Ossetian	3.2		
Other	13.9		

GERMANY

Total area	357,039 sq km	Population	80.5m
GDP	$1,846bn	GDP per head	$22,917
Capital	Berlin	Other cities	Hamburg, Munich, Cologne

The Federal Republic of Germany is the economic giant of modern Europe – but has yet to develop commensurate political weight and confidence. However, as memories of the Hitler regime fade, this is changing. The challenge for the recently reunited Germany is to make the change acceptable both to Germans themselves and to their neighbours, be they in Western or Eastern Europe.

History: the flexing of muscles

The Germans were not brought into a cohesive political unit until the 19th century, but their influence had been felt long before. More than 2,000 years ago the German tribes such as the Goths and Vandals were pushing the Celts out of central Europe; the same tribes were defeated by Julius Caesar in 55–53BC, but by 9AD had succeeded in halting Rome's colonial expansion north of the Rhine. By the 5th century the pressure of German invasions finally destroyed the western Roman empire.

The first sense of unity came towards the end of the 8th century with the Frankish empire of Charlemagne (Charles the Great) holding sway over Saxon, Bavarian, Rhenish and other lands. After Charlemagne's death in 814 came a series of dynasties, variously laying claim to the Holy Roman Empire (the Habsburgs, for example, occupied the imperial throne almost continuously from 1273 until 1806). But imperial reality was, in fact, usually disunity and turmoil.

The turmoil was both religious and nationalist. The reforming zeal of Martin Luther, for example, led to the Peasants' Revolt of 1524–25 and to subsequent struggles by Protestants against a Catholic establishment. Then came the devastating Thirty Years' War (1618–48), which ended with Germany divided into more than 300 principalities.

From Bismarck to Hitler

The Holy Roman Empire finally ended in 1806 with the Napoleonic Wars, leaving Germany a jigsaw of divisions despite the creation in 1815 of a German Confederation. This was dominated by the Habsburgs of Austria, but gradually the Prussians increased their power, defeating the Danes in 1864 and the Austrians in 1866. The Prussian chancellor, Otto von Bismarck, then manoeuvred France's

Napoleon III in 1870 into declaring war – and losing. Bismarck was then free to form a united German Empire in 1871, with King Wilhelm I of Prussia proclaimed in Versailles as kaiser, or emperor.

But Germany's glory was not to last. In 1914 the first world war broke out, with Germany (now under Wilhelm II and without Bismarck), Austria and Turkey against Britain, France, Russia, Italy, Japan and, in 1917, America. German defeat came in 1918. The humiliating terms of the Versailles Treaty dispossessed Germany of its colonial empire in Africa and Asia; Alsace and Lorraine were returned to France; other areas were given to Belgium, Denmark and Poland; and the Saar valley was put under the League of Nations until 1935. All this reduced Germany's land and population by about 10% and, with the imposition of crippling reparations, caused intense resentment.

The Nazi nightmare

The national humiliation of what was known as the Weimar Republic was worsened by the economic depression of the 1930s. The consequence was the rise of the Austrian-born Adolf Hitler and his intensely pan-German and anti-Semitic National Socialist German Workers' (Nazi) party. After the party tried to overthrow the government of Bavaria in 1923, Hitler spent eight months in prison. Even so, the party grew in strength. By the 1932 elections the combined vote of the Nazis and the Communists was over 50%, and in 1933 – with the Nazis the dominant party – President von Hindenburg named Hitler as chancellor. In August 1934, the day after the president's death, the cabinet amalgamated the offices of president and chancellor and declared Hitler fuehrer (leader). So began the infamous Third Reich.

Hitler's recipe for the economic woes of the Weimar Republic was a mix of defiance and aggression. Freedom of speech and assembly were abolished; the Versailles Treaty was repudiated; and payment of reparations was halted. In 1936 he re-armed the Rhineland and then, in 1938, launched the Anschluss – the annexation of Austria. In Munich he signed an agreement with Britain's prime minister, Neville Chamberlain, which the following year allowed him to annex part of Czechoslovakia. In September 1939, having signed a non-aggression pact with the Soviet Union, Hitler invaded Poland. Two days later, Britain and France declared war.

From triumph to defeat

Initially the Axis powers – Germany, Italy and Japan – seemed unstoppable. By the summer of 1940, for example,

France was occupied and Germany was preparing to invade Britain. However, Britain's Royal Air Force managed to defeat the German Luftwaffe in the first big turning point of the war. Then, in 1941, Hitler abandoned the non-aggression pact and invaded the Soviet Union. For Hitler, just as for Napoleon, it proved to be a military blunder.

But perhaps the biggest turning point was the air attack by Japan in December 1941 on the American naval base at Pearl Harbor, Hawaii. This brought America into the war on the side of Britain and the other "Allies". In November 1942 the Allied counter-attack began with the landing of American and British troops in German-occupied North Africa. Less than a year later the Allies had landed in Italy. Then, in 1943, the Soviet Red Army began to push the Germans back. Next came the "D-Day" landing of Allied troops in Normandy, France, on June 6, 1944. By the spring of 1945 Germany had been invaded by the Allies. On April 30, 1945, Hitler committed suicide, and nine days later Germany unconditionally surrendered.

The Cold War divide

But the victors were themselves divided. The western part of the country was occupied by Britain, America and (subsequently) France; the eastern part by the Soviet Union. By 1949 the west had been formally consolidated into the Federal Republic of Germany; the east was the German Democratic Republic. The old capital of Berlin, though inside East Germany, was itself divided into Western and Soviet zones.

For both victors and vanquished the damage of the war had been colossal. Particularly horrifying was the systematic extermination by the Nazis of the racially "inferior", among whom were some 6m Jews. That stain on German history remains to influence today's politics.

Politics: democracy – and finally unity

While East Germany, the GDR, became a conventional Soviet satellite – the Communist Party did not renounce its constitutional monopoly on power until December 1989 – West Germany, the FRG, developed as a determinedly democratic federation of 11 *länder* (states), including West Berlin, with a capital in Bonn and under a constitution known as the Basic Law.

This emphasises that the state exists for the benefit of the people and that powers should, wherever possible, be devolved from the centre. For some years, however, these powers had to co-exist with those of the occupying countries. Only in 1955 did the republic become a sovereign state (accepted as such by the Soviet Union) and a member of NATO; and only in 1968 did the Western Allies renounce their right to assume government powers in any state of emergency. Meanwhile, the freedom and relative prosperity of West Germany had attracted over 3m refugees from East Germany, leading the GDR in 1961 to erect the Berlin Wall.

As communism collapsed throughout Europe, so too, in November 1989, did the Berlin Wall. This led to a diplomatic drive by West Germany's Chancellor Helmut Kohl to reunite the divided country. A treaty on economic and monetary union came into effect in July 1990, and approval by the occupying powers – the potential problem was the Soviet Union – was gained in September. Finally, in October 1990, the five *länder* of East Germany formally became part of the Federal Republic.

The democratic balance

Germany's president is elected for up to two five-year terms by a college drawn from the federal and *länder* legislatures. But the role is largely ceremonial: real power rests with the chancellor, elected by the Bundestag, a lower house of the federal parliament which is elected for four years. Of the Bundestag's 662 members (the constitutional minimum is 656), 328 are elected from single-member constituencies and 334 by proportional representation. To be represented in parliament, a party must win at least 5% of the total vote. The idea of the system is to represent the people, but without the fragmention of politics that characterised the Weimar Republic.

A further balance comes with the upper house, the Bundesrat. This 68-member body is appointed by the governments of the *länder*, with each *länd* having between three and five votes depending on population. Since *länder* elections can be held at any time during the life of the federal parliament, the composition of the Bundesrat frequently changes. Politically this is important since the consent of the Bundesrat is needed for certain legislation, notably the budget and matters affecting the *länder*.

The system has led to remarkable stability and a succession of long-serving chancellors, such as Konrad Adenauer, Willy Brandt, Helmut Schmidt and Helmut Kohl. Probably the most important political party has been the Christian Democratic Union (with both Catholic and Protestant members), the party of the two fathers of post-war Germany, Adenauer and Ludwig Erhard. Its Bavarian sister party is the Christian Socialist Union. A significant ally is the small, liberal Free Democrat Party. The opposition to the CDU is dominated by the Social Democrat Party, which governed in the 1960s and 1970s under the leadership of Brandt and Schmidt. The small party of the Greens, although internally at odds, has influenced other parties. One disturbing element in recent years has been the growth of the Republicans and the Deutsche Volksunion, extreme right-wingers who play on fears of immigration.

Foreign policy: at Europe's heart

One legacy of the second world war was a desire to avoid any repetition by anchoring Germany within multinational organisations. Thus Germany was a founder member in the 1950s of the European Economic Community and, in close alliance with France, has ever since been a leader (and then paymaster) of the EU. Another legacy has been a close relationship with America, expressed by membership of NATO in 1955 and the stationing of American troops in Germany.

But the second world war also explains Germany's diffidence in foreign policy and a constitutional bar on military action overseas. This is changing. In the early 1990s, for example, Germany led the way in recognising the republics of former Yugoslavia, and in 1993 – the year in which it publicly hoped for a permanent seat in the UN Security Council – German troops joined the UN peacekeepers in Somalia.

The question is whether Germany's growing confidence can be easily accommodated. France, for example, fears its alliance with Germany may be downgraded as Germany focuses more on the ex-communist countries to its east.

Society: the family line

Although relatively young as a modern nation, the Germans have always had a sense of their own identity. The "Teutonic" traits of discipline and thoroughness are sometimes ridiculed (even within Germany) but are nonetheless real.

The sense of being German is such that citizenship is a matter of blood – and so is available to ethnic Germans in central and Eastern Europe – rather than place of birth. This can cause resentment, not least among the 6m *gastarbeiter* (guestworkers) and others of foreign origin, especially Turks. One particular worry in the early 1990s was a spate of racist violence, aggravated by economic malaise, economic migration from the east and an extremely liberal asylum law. This law was amended in early 1993 so that Germany could return political refugees – genuine or not –

who had arrived in transit from a safe country.

The economy: modern miracle

At the end of the second world war the German economy was in ruins, but a combination of Teutonic virtues, a sensible trade union structure and financial aid from the Marshall Plan produced economic growth in the west that averaged 8% a year through the 1950s. This was the *Wirtschaftswunder* – the economic miracle – and it has resulted in Europe's best developed industrial economy (only about 1% of western Germany's GDP now comes from agriculture). For the past three decades Germany has been a major exporter of cars, machinery and chemicals, particularly to the rest of Europe.

But there are signs that more miracles are needed. One reason is that the social benefits which helped maintain an enviably harmonious record of industrial relations are becoming too costly. A related reason is high labour costs, which by the early 1990s had made it difficult for companies such as Volkswagen to remain internationally competitive. Perhaps the most important reason, however, was unification.

Although East Germany was reputedly the best economy in the Soviet bloc, it proved hopelessly incompetent in comparison with West Germany. In theory this could have been rectified by the forces of the free market, but for political reasons Chancellor Kohl chose to give the currencies of west and east equal value upon unification. Not surprisingly this meant huge unemployment in the east, which had to be offset by social transfers from the west.

Meanwhile, because the government chose to meet the cost by borrowing rather than by raising taxes, the result in the early 1990s was high interest rates – which the independent central bank, the Bundesbank, refused to lower for fear of stoking inflation (hyperinflation had helped end the Weimar Republic). This high interest rate policy caused recession within Germany and, because the Deutschemark anchors the European Monetary System, high interest rates and high unemployment throughout the European Union.

Assessing the future

Pessimists may conclude that the German miracle is coming to an end. However, it is the optimists who are likely to be proved right. They argue that as the east is properly integrated into the overall economy, so Germany will gain more skilled workers with which to remain one of the world's economic powers.

Total area	357,039 sq km	% agricultural area	51.8
Capital	Berlin	Highest point metres	Zugspitze
Other cities	Hamburg, Munich,		2,963
	Cologne	Main rivers	Danube (Donau),
			Rhine (Rhein), Elbe, Oder

The economy

GDP $bn	1,846	GDP per head $	22,917
% av. ann. growth in		GDP per head in purchasing	
real GDP 1985–92[a]	2.8	power parity (USA=100)	89.3

Origins of GDP	% of total	Components of GDP	% of total
Agriculture	2	Private consumption	54
Industry	39	Public consumption	18
of which:		Investment	21
manufacturing	23	Exports	34
Services	59	Imports	-31

Structure of manufacturing[a]

			% of total
Agric. & food processing	9	Other	45
Textiles & clothing	4	Av. ann. increase in industrial	
Machinery & transport	42	output 1985–92	2.5

Inflation[a] and exchange rates

Consumer price 1993	4.1%	DM per $ av. 1993	1.65
Av. ann. rate 1988–93	3.1%	DM per ecu av. 1993	1.94

Balance of payments, reserves and aid

			$bn
Visible exports fob	406.9	Capital balance	68.1
Visible imports fob	-374.0	Overall balance	43.0
Trade balance	32.9	Change in reserves	36.3
Invisible inflows	156.0	Level of reserves	
Invisible outflows	-182.5	end Dec.	99.4
Net transfers	-32.0	Aid given[a]	7.6
Current account balance	-25.6	as % of GDP	0.4
as % of GDP	-1.4		

Principal exports	$bn fob	Principal imports	$bn cif
Road vehicles	120.8	Agric. products & foodstuffs	73.7
Mechanical engineering		Road vehicles	69.8
products	100.9	Electrical engineering	
Chemicals	85.3	products	64.8
Total incl. others	430.4	Chemicals	57.6
		Total incl. others	408.5

Main export destinations	% of total	Main origins of imports	% of total
France	13.0	France	12.0
Italy	9.3	Netherlands	9.6
Netherlands	8.3	Italy	9.2
UK	7.7	Belgium/Luxembourg	7.0
Belgium/Luxembourg	7.4	UK	6.8

Government
System The federal president is elected by a college, comprising members of the federal and state legislatures, for up to two five-year terms. The chancellor, elected by the Bundestag on the nomination of the president, heads the federal government. The two-chamber Federal Assembly comprises the 662-member Bundestag, elected for four years (328 by single-member constituencies and 334 by proportional representation), and the 68-member Bundesrat, chosen by the republic's 16 state governments. Each state (*land*) has its own legislature.

Main political parties Christian Democratic Union (CDU), Christian Social Union (CSU), Social Democratic Party (SPD), Free Democratic Party (FDP), The Greens; eastern Germany: Bündnis 90, Party of Democratic Socialism (PDS)

People

Population m	80.5	% under 15	17.1
Pop. per sq km	226	% over 65	14.8
% urban	84	No. men per 100 women	95
% av. ann. growth 1985–92	0.5	Human Development Index[a]	96

Life expectancy	*yrs*		*per 1,000 pop.*
Men	73	Crude birth rate	11
Women	79	Crude death rate	11

Ethnic groups[b]	*% of total*	Workforce	*% of total*
German	93.2	Services	56.5
Turkish	2.3	Industry	33.3
Yugoslav	0.9	Agriculture	3.5
Italian	0.8	Construction	6.7
		% unemployed[a]	6.6

Society[a]

No. households m	28.2	**Consumer goods ownership**	
Av. no. per household	2.1		*% of households*
Marriages per 1,000 pop.	6.6	TV	97
Divorces per 1,000 pop.	2.1	Video recorder	42
		Microwave oven	36

Household spending	*% of total*	Education	
Food/drink	12.0	Spending as % of GDP	6.2
Clothing/footwear	7.0	Years of compulsory education	10
Housing/energy	18.0	Enrolment ratios:	
Household goods	9.0	primary school	105
Health	13.0	secondary school	97
Transport/communications	13.0	tertiary education	32
Leisure/other	22.0		

Tourism		Health	
Tourist arrivals m	17.0	Pop. per doctor	370
Tourist receipts $bn	10.7	Pop. per hosptial bed	115

a   Western Germany only.   b   Classified by nationality.

GREECE

Total area	131,944 sq km	Population	10.4m
GDP	$75bn	GDP per head	$7,184
Capital	Athens	Other cities	Thessaloniki, Patras

Greece is one of the two least developed countries in the European Union; Portugal is the other. But while the Portuguese economy has been converging towards that of its richer partners, Greece's has been diverging.

History: a troubled road

After nearly four centuries of almost continuous rule by the Turks Greece won its independence in 1829. Prince Otto of Bavaria became king of the Hellenes and ruled despotically until he was deposed and replaced by Prince George of Denmark in 1862. George I was assassinated in 1913 and succeeded by the pro-German Constantine I, who was forced to abdicate in 1917 when Greece entered the first world war on the Allies' side. But he returned after King Alexander died from a monkey bite in 1920, only to abdicate again in 1922 after the Turks had forced the Greek population out of Smyrna. Two years later George II stood down and the country became a republic. He was restored to the throne in 1935, only to establish a dictatorship under General Joannis Metaxas the following year.

In the second world war Greece successfully resisted invasion by Italy in 1940 but was overrun by Germany in 1941. The communists tried to seize power and civil war followed liberation from the Germans. The Communist Party was outlawed in 1947 but it was not until 1949 that the central government won a decisive victory. Conservatives dominated parliament between 1952 and 1963, when the electorate rejected Constantine Karamanlis in favour of a loose amalgam of liberals and socialists. More elections and a period of political muddle followed. Then there was a military coup. King Constantine failed in his attempted constitutional counter-coup and fled into exile. In 1968 the colonels resigned their commissions and entered government. After six years of illiberal rule, the regime collapsed. In 1974 Mr Karamanlis was asked to return and form a government of national unity. After a referendum later that year the country was proclaimed a republic.

Politics: return to democracy

The centre-right New Democracy Party was in power until 1981. The Panhellenic Socialist Movement (PASOK) under

Andreas Papandreou ruled for most of the 1980s but details of financial scandals led to its downfall in 1989 – and to the trial of several former ministers including Mr Papandreou. He was acquitted; the others were not. Three elections took place in ten months before the New Democracy Party in April 1990 got an absolute majority by persuading the single member of the Democratic Renewal Party to support it. Such a fragile majority did not make the job of government easy and the 1993 elections saw PASOK restored to power. Mr Papandreou returned to the prime minister's seat and with him many familiar faces reappeared.

Foreign policy: neighbouring problems

Poor relations with Turkey have dominated Greek foreign policy for two decades. The Greeks feel that the Turks have designs on the eastern Aegean islands and point to north Cyprus as evidence. More recently Macedonia has been worrying the Greeks. They have opposed recognition of the former Yugoslav republic under that name arguing that use of the title implies designs on Greek territory. Nationalists calling for a greater Macedonia stretching as far as Thessaloniki have reinforced Greek fears. In February 1994 Greece closed the port of Thessaloniki to trade with the former Yugoslav republic and suspended diplomatic relations.

The economy: must try harder

Agriculture and manufacturing are the mainstays of the economy. Growth areas include mining and quarrying, oil refining, clothing, some agricultural products and tourism (which, along with shipping, is a useful foreign exchange earner). Tobacco, footwear and leather, and the machinery and transport industries are in decline. During the political uncertainties of 1989–90 inflation reached 25%, and the current-account deficit trebled in the space of a year to $3.6 billion. The New Democracy Party attempted, with varying degrees of success, to deal with this legacy. One of the rewards of its austerity measures was substantial support from the EU, which will continue. Since returning to power the PASOK government has reined back on privatisation but the need to reduce the huge debt burden has given it no choice but to carry on with the austerity measures introduced by its predecessor.

Total area	131,944 sq km	% agricultural area	69.6
Capital	Athens	Highest point metres	
Other cities	Thessaloniki, Patras,		Mt Olympus 2,911
	Larisa, Iraklion	Main rivers	Aliakmon, Pinios,

The economy

GDP $bn	75	GDP per head $	7,184
% av. ann. growth in		GDP per head in purchasing	
real GDP 1985–92	1.8	power parity (USA=100)	34.7

Origins of GDP	% of total	Components of GDP	% of total
Agriculture	15	Private consumption	72
Industry	26	Public consumption	20
of which:		Investment	18
manufacturing	17	Exports	23
Services	59	Imports	-33

Structure of manufacturing

			% of total
Agric. & food processing	22	Other	45
Textiles & clothing	21	Av. ann. increase in industrial	
Machinery & transport	12	output 1985–92	-0.1

Inflation and exchange rates

Consumer price 1993	14.4%	Dr per $ av. 1993	229.3
Av. ann. rate 1988–93	16.2%	Dr per ecu av. 1993	268.0

Balance of payments and debt

			$bn
Visible exports fob	6.0	Capital balance	2.6
Visible imports fob	-17.6	Overall balance	-0.4
Trade balance	-11.6	Change in reserves	-0.3
Invisible inflows	9.3	Foreign debt	30.9
Invisible outflows	-6.3	as % of GDP	39.3
Net transfers	6.5	Debt service	5.7
Current account balance	-2.1	Debt service ratio	27.9
as % of GDP	-2.8		

Principal exports	$bn fob	Principal imports	$bn cif
Manufactures	3.1	Manufactured consumer goods	8.0
Food & beverages	1.5	Machinery	3.5
Petroleum products	0.6	Food	2.8
Minerals	0.3	Crude oil	1.2
Total incl. others	9.5	Chemicals & fertilisers	1.0
		Total incl. others	23.1

Main export destinations	% of total	Main origins of imports	% of total
Germany	23.0	Germany	20.2
Italy	18.0	Italy	14.2
France	7.2	France	7.8
UK	6.9	Netherlands	6.8
USA	4.0	Japan	6.4

Government

System The one-chamber Vouli (parliament) has 300 members directly elected by a form of proportional representation for four years. The president, without executive power, is elected by parliament for five years. The council of ministers is responsible to parliament. It is headed by the prime minister, appointed by the president on the ability to gain support in parliament.

Main political parties New Democracy Party, Panhellenic Socialist Movement (Pasok), Synaspismos – a coalition including the Communist Party of Greece (KKE) and the Greek Left Party (EAR)

People

Population m	10.4	% under 15	17.3
Pop. per sq km	78	% over 65	15.4
% urban	63	No. men per 100 women	97
% av. ann. growth 1985–92	0.7	Human Development Index	90

Life expectancy	yrs		per 1,000 pop.
Men	75	Crude birth rate	11
Women	01	Crude death rate	9

Ethnic groups	% of total	Workforce	% of total
Greek	98	Services	50.2
Other	2	Industry	20.2
		Agriculture	22.2
		Construction	6.8
		% unemployed	7.7

Society

No. households m	3.6	**Consumer goods ownership**	
Av. no. per household	2.7		% of households
Marriages per 1,000 pop.	6.0	TV	94
Divorces per 1,000 pop.	0.9	Video recorder	37
		Microwave oven	2

Household spending	% of total	Education	
Food/drink	30.0	Spending as % of GDP	3.1
Clothing/footwear	8.0	Years of compulsory education	9
Housing/energy	12.0	Enrolment ratios:	
Household goods	5.0	primary school	100
Health	6.0	secondary school	99
Transport/communications	13.0	tertiary education	29
Leisure/other	21.0		

Tourism		Health	
Tourist arrivals m	8.9	Pop. per doctor	580
Tourism receipts $bn	2.6	Pop. per hospital bed	194

HUNGARY

Total area	93,030 sq km	Population	10.2m
GDP	$30bn	GDP per head	$3,006
Capital	Budapest	Other cities	Debrecen, Miskolc, Szeged

Democracy replaced communism in Hungary in 1990. But the country had started moving towards a market economy some two decades earlier and until recently it led the field in post-communist transformation and reorientation towards Western Europe.

History: the struggle for independence

The Hungarians (Magyars) trace their origins to Turkic or Finno-Ugrian tribes who settled in the area of today's Hungary in the 7th century. The medieval kingdom of Hungary encompassed a territory three times as large as today's republic but it was dismembered by the Habsburgs and Ottomans. In 1699 Austria won control of all its territories. The Hungarians struggled for emancipation within the Austrian empire, and an uprising in 1848, led by Louis Kossuth, was put down by Vienna. A major milestone in the struggle for independence was the Compromise (Ausgleich) in 1867 when the Austro-Hungarian empire was created.

Hungary won full independence in 1918 after the disintegration of the empire in the wake of the first world war. However, under the terms of the Treaty of Trianon of 1920, Hungary lost two-thirds of the territory it held within the empire and 40% of its population. The country entered the second world war on the side of the Axis powers hoping to recover the lost territories. After their defeat the territorial arrangements of the Trianon Treaty were confirmed. The consequences still have repercussions as the treatment of Hungarian ethnic minorities in neighbouring Slovakia, Romania and Serbia continues to dog regional relations. It also causes political problems for Hungary's new democracy which is having to accommodate those on the far right who hanker for redress of the perceived injustice at Trianon.

Politics: incremental change

Their history of struggle for independence has equipped modern Hungarians with an acute sense of the art of incremental change within severe constraints. It was demonstrated in their achievement of the dual monarchy which followed Austrian rule, and it came truly into its own during the communist period. Discontent with the early communist regime, initially headed by Matyas Rakosi, boiled over into an anti-Moscow uprising in October 1956. This was promptly put down by the Soviet army and Moscow installed Janos Kadar as head of government. In 1961, after three years of repression, Mr Kadar felt confident enough of his position to promulgate a new conciliatory line: "all those who are not against us are with us", he declared, overturning the standard communist maxim that "those who are not with us are against us". More emphasis was placed on consumerism by a regime sometimes described as practising "goulash communism". Kadar succeeded in introducing incremental change which accelerated with a comprehensive market-oriented reform programme launched in 1968. Because political liberalisation was limited, Kadar's economic reforms survived the period of reaction in the Soviet bloc which followed the crushing of the reformist regime in Czechoslovakia. Hungary was therefore well set on the course of market reform when communism collapsed in 1989, and the coalition, headed by the right-of-centre Hungarian Democratic Forum, which took over lasted longer than any of the other initial post-communist governments in Eastern Europe. The 1994 elections were won by the Hungarian Socialist Party (former communists).

Foreign policy: looking West

Like the other central European countries Hungary has drastically shifted its foreign policy orientation towards the West. It has become an associate member of the European Union and has applied for full membership. It has links with NATO through the Partnership for Peace scheme and would like to be a full member of the organisation.

The economy: heavy indebtedness

Before the fall of communism in 1989 private enterprise already accounted for 10% of economic activity and the government had started to divert trade away from the Soviet bloc. But the collapse of Comecon hit the economy hard and helped send Hungary into deep recession in 1991, when GDP fell by 12%. But by 1994, after four years of decline, a modest recovery was expected. After the initial shock of the economic reforms, stability and growth are now in prospect. However, one serious legacy of communism remains: a foreign debt that was estimated at around $25 billion at the end of 1993, the servicing of which is a significant burden on the economy.

Total area	93,030 sq km	% agricultural area	69.8
Capital	Budapest	Highest point metres	Kekes 1,015
Other cities	Debrecen, Miskolc, Szeged	Main rivers	Danube (Duna), Tisza

The economy

GDP $bn	30	GDP per head $	3,006
% av. ann. growth in real GDP 1985–92	1.7	GDP per head in purchasing power parity (USA=100)	27.5

Origins of GDP	% of total	Components of GDP	% of total
Agriculture	10	Private consumption	67
Industry	34	Public consumption	13
of which:		Investment	19
manufacturing	29	Exports	34
Services	55	Imports	...

Structure of manufacturing

			% of total
Agric. & food processing	10	Other	54
Textiles & clothing	9	Av. ann. increase in industrial	
Machinery & transport	27	output 1985–90	-1.4

Inflation and exchange rates

Consumer price 1993	22.5%	Ft per $ av. 1993	91.93
Av. ann. rate 1985–93	23.4%	Ft per ecu av. 1993	102.96

Balance of payments and debt

			$bn
Visible exports fob	10.0	Capital balance	0.4
Visible imports fob	-10.1	Overall balance	0.8
Trade balance	-0.01	Change in reserves	0.8
Invisible inflows	3.8	Level of reserves end Dec.	4.5
Invisible outflows	-4.3	Foreign debt	21.9
Net transfers	0.9	as % of GDP	64.6
Current account balance	0.4	Debt service	5.0
as % of GDP	1.1	Debt service ratio	35.6

Principal exports	$bn fob	Principal imports	$bn cif
Raw materials	3.8	Raw materials	4.1
Consumer goods	2.8	Consumer goods	2.5
Food products	2.6	Capital equipment	2.3
Capital equipment	1.3	Fuels	1.6
Fuels & electricity	0.3	Food products	0.6
Total incl. others	10.7	Total incl. others	11.1

Main export destinations	% of total	Main origins of imports	% of total
Germany	27.7	Germany	23.6
EU	49.8	EU	42.8
Eastern Europe	22.5	Eastern Europe	24.6
EFTA	14.7	EFTA	20.6
CIS	13.1	CIS	16.8

Government

System The current constitution was revised in 1989. The one-chamber National Assembly has 386 members elected for five years (176 by single-member constituencies, 152 by proportional representation from country lists and 58 from a national list). Supreme power is vested in the parliament. It elects the state president and appoints the prime minister.

Main political parties Hungarian Democratic Forum (HDF), Federation of Free Democrats (FDF), Smallholders' Party, Hungarian Socialist Party (HSP), Federation of Young Democrats, Christian Democratic People's Party (HCP), Social Democratic Party (FZDP)

People

Population m	10.2	% under 15	18.5
Pop. per sq km	113	% over 65	13.9
% urban	62	No. men per 100 women	93
% av. ann. growth 1985–92	-0.6	Human Development Index	89

Life expectancy	yrs		per 1,000 pop.
Men	66	Crude birth rate	12
Women	74	Crude death rate	14

Ethnic groups[a]	% of total	Workforce	% of total
Magyar	96.6	Services	47.7
German	1.6	Industry	26.5
Slovak	1.1	Agriculture	19.3
Other	0.7	Construction	6.5
		% unemployed	12.3

Society

No. households m	3.9	**Consumer goods ownership**	
Av. no. per household	2.6		% of households
Marriages per 1,000 pop.	6.4	TV	21
Divorces per 1,000 pop.	2.4	Video recorder	...
		Microwave oven	...

Household spending	% of total	Education	
Food/drink	25.0	Spending as % of GDP	5.4
Clothing/footwear	9.0	Years of compulsory education	10
Housing/energy	9.0	Enrolment ratios:	
Household goods	8.0	primary school	94
Health	5.0	secondary school	79
Transport/communications	9.0	tertiary education	15
Leisure/other	28.0		

Tourism		Health	
Tourist arrivals m	20.5	Pop. per doctor	340
Tourist receipts $bn	1.0	Pop. per hospital bed	99

a Classified by nationality.

ICELAND

The volcanic island of Iceland lies in the North Atlantic some 900km west of Norway just below the Arctic Circle. The isolated Icelanders enjoy one of the highest standards of living in the world and one of the lowest population densities (only two people per square kilometre).

History: Viking territory

Norse Vikings landed in Iceland in the late 9th century. By the mid-10th century they had founded a parliament (Althing) and at the beginning of the 11th century they had adopted Christianity. In 1263 Iceland declared allegiance to the king of Norway and on the union of the Norwegian and Danish crowns in the late 14th century it came under Danish sovereignty. It kept the wholehearted link with Denmark until 1918 when it became independent though still under the Danish crown. During the second world war, while Denmark was occupied by Germany, Iceland itself was occupied by British and American troops. In 1944 the Icelanders voted for complete independence.

Politics: independent-minded coalitions

National politics are fragmented with a variety of parties getting together to form what have often been short-lived coalitions. Iceland is a member of NATO and EFTA and has a trade agreement with the EU. It also – after a long wrangle about fishing rights – signed up for the EEA. Despite the disadvantage of distance, Iceland sees its future as heavily dependent on close links with the rest of Europe, though it has no intention of joining the EU.

The economy: riding on fish

Fishing is the most important industry, accounting for more than two-thirds of export earnings, which is why Iceland was so keen in the EEA negotiations to protect its fishing rights. Other industries include aluminium smelting and ferro-silicon production. Geothermal and hydro power provide most of the country's heating and electricity, and there are plans to exploit this further for export. Tourism offers another opportunity for growth. But the early 1990s saw Iceland in one of its deepest-ever recessions, with recovery not expected before the middle of the decade.

Total area	103,000 sq km	Capital	Reykjavik

Government

System The head of state, with largely ceremonial duties, is the president directly elected for four years. The president appoints the prime minister and cabinet, who have executive power. The unicameral Althingi (parliament) has 63 members, elected by a form of proportional representation for four years.

Main political parties Independence Party, Progressive Party (PP), Social Democratic Party (SDP), People's Alliance (PA), Women's List

The economy

GDP $bn	6.2	GDP per head $	23,670
% av. ann. growth in real GDP 1985–92	1.7	GDP per head in purchasing power parity (USA=100)	...

Origins of GDP[a]	% of total	Components of GDP	% of total
Agriculture	4	Private consumption	60
Industry	44	Public consumption	19
of which:		Investment	19
manufacturing	...	Exports	37
Services	52	Imports	-36

People

Population '000	260	% under 15	25.0
Pop. per sq km	2	% over 65	10.4
% urban	91	No. men per 100 women	101
% av. ann. growth 1985–92	1.2	Human Development Index	96

Life expectancy	yrs		per 1,000 pop.
Men	76	Crude birth rate	18
Women	81	Crude death rate	7

Ethnic groups[b]	% of total	Health	
Icelandic	96.3	Pop. per doctor	370
Danish	0.9	Pop. per hospital bed	86
American	0.5		
Swedish	0.4		

a 1990.
b Classified by nationality.

IRELAND

Total area	70,283 sq km	Population	3.5m
GDP	$43bn	GDP per head	$12,104
Capital	Dublin	Other cities	Cork, Limerick, Galway

Ireland is the third poorest country in the European Union and its demographic structure is similar to that of many developing nations; more than two-fifths of the population is aged 25 or under, while a quarter is under 15. There are not enough jobs to go round, with the result that many skilled and unskilled workers go to other countries to work.

History: living with Britain

In 1921, after a war of independence and some eight centuries of British influence and rule – which saw Oliver Cromwell's ruthless suppression of rebellion at Drogheda in 1649, the defeat of Irish Catholics at the Battle of the Boyne in 1690, and a million deaths and mass immigration during the potato famine of the mid-18th century – the Anglo-Irish treaty was signed. This conceded dominion status within the British Commonwealth to the 26 counties of the Irish Free State; the six northern counties had been given their own parliament within the United Kingdom the year before. Opposition to partition continued and two years of civil war ensued. In 1949 the last remaining ties with Britain were cut and the Free State became a republic.

Politics: coalition tendency

Ireland's system of proportional representation has increasingly resulted in elections where neither of the two main parties, Fianna Fail and Fine Gael, has obtained an absolute majority and so the largest party has had to govern with the support of the Irish Labour Party or the Progressive Democrats. The 1992 election brought the first ever Fianna Fail-Labour coalition. Although the president has little power, the election in 1990 of a woman, Mary Robinson, to the post was a landmark for Irish politics. It also demonstrated how substantially society's attitudes had changed.

Foreign policy: united aims

Irish unity remains high on the political agenda. It was in 1969 after escalating violence that the British Labour government sent troops into Northern Ireland to keep the peace. More than two decades later they are still there; several thousands of civilians and members of the security forces have been killed in the "troubles" and, for most of the time since 1972, Northern Ireland has been under direct rule from London and has had no separate assembly of its own. Several joint initiatives between the British and Irish governments have been announced and since 1985, under the Anglo-Irish Agreement, the Irish government has had an official consultative role in the affairs of Northern Ireland. But nothing so far has yet succeeded in bringing more than a temporary burst of optimism that a solution to the problem will be found.

Neutral tradition

Ireland has been neutral since independence and neutrality having saved the country from the ravages of war, the Irish government then saw no reason to join NATO. But Ireland has been an enthusiastic member of the European Union, which it joined in 1973 at the same time as Britain, and it participates in the EU's Common Foreign and Security Policy. EU structural funds have helped transform the Irish economy and membership of the European Union has allowed it to move more and more out of Britain's shadow.

The economy: lagging behind

Ireland's economy has always lagged behind that of most others in Western Europe. The 1960s was a period of growth but EU membership coincided with the oil price shocks and the country was soon facing recession, rising inflation and a mounting balance-of-payments deficit. In the late 1970s the Fianna Fail government borrowed heavily to finance an ambitious programme of public spending. The habit continued in the early 1980s when governments came and went in quick succession. Governments since have been dealing with the results of this profligacy.

But picking up

However, by 1994 the outlook for the economy was favourable: the budget deficit was under reasonable control, the currency had performed well in the aftermath of the European exchange rate mechanism crisis of summer 1993, inflation was low and, thanks to EU transfers, there was a healthy current-account surplus. The country remains more reliant than most EU countries on agriculture, which still accounts for roughly one-tenth of GDP, but government incentive schemes and the existence of a well-educated workforce have encouraged growth in high-tech industries and increased Dublin's importance as a services and financial centre.

Total area	70, 283 sq km	% agricultural area	80.4
Capital	Dublin	Highest point metres	Carantuohil
Other cities	Cork, Limerick, Galway		1,041
		Main rivers	Shannon, Barrow,
			Suir, Erne, Boyne

The economy

GDP $bn	43	GDP per head $	12,104
% av. ann. growth in		GDP per head in purchasing	
real GDP 1985–92	4.8	power parity (USA=100)	51.6

Origins of GDP	% of total	Components of GDP	% of total
Agriculture	10	Private consumption	56
Industry	38	Public consumption	16
of which:		Investment	19
manufacturing	…	Exports	62
Services	52	Imports	-53

Structure of manufacturing

			% of total
Agric. & food processing	26	Other	38
Textiles & clothing	4	Av. ann. increase in industrial	
Machinery & transport	32	output 1985–92	1.4

Inflation and exchange rates

Consumer price 1993	1.4%	IR£ per $ av. 1993	0.68
Av. ann. rate 1988–93	2.9%	IR£ per ecu av. 1993	0.76

Balance of payments, reserves and aid

			$bn
Visible exports fob	27.9	Capital balance	-6.2
Visible imports fob	-21.1	Overall balance	-3.5
Trade balance	6.8	Change in reserves	-2.3
Invisible inflows	6.6	Level of reserves	
Invisible outflows	-13.7	end Dec.	3.5
Net transfers	3.0	Aid given	0.07
Current account balance	2.6	as % of GDP	0.16
as % of GDP	6.1		

Principal exports	$bn fob	Principal imports	$bn cif
Machinery, transport		Machinery, transport	
equipment	7.7	equipment	8.0
Food, live animals	6.3	Manufactured goods	6.7
Chemicals	5.5	Chemicals	2.9
Misc. manufactures	4.3		
Total incl. others	28.4	Total incl. others	22.5

Main export destinations	% of total	Main origins of imports	% of total
UK	31.5	UK	42.4
Germany	12.8	USA	14.2
France	9.6	Germany	8.3
USA	8.2	Japan	5.0
Netherlands	7.0	France	4.5

Government

System The president is directly elected for seven years. The *taoiseach* (prime minister) heads the government. The lower house, the Dail, is elected by a form of proportional representation. The upper house is the 60-member Seanad.

Main political parties Fianna Fail, Fine Gael, Labour Party, Progressive Democrats, Democratic Left Party

People

Population m	3.5	% under 15	24.7
Pop. per sq km	49	% over 65	11.6
% urban	57	No. men per 100 women	100
% av. ann. growth 1985–92	0.1	Human Development Index	93

Life expectancy	yrs		per 1,000 pop.
Men	73	Crude birth rate	14
Women	78	Crude death rate	9

Ethnic groups	% of total	Workforce	% of total
Irish	94.0	Services	57.8
		Industry	21.5
		Agriculture	13.7
		Construction	7.0
		% unemployed	15.6

Society

		Consumer goods ownership	
No. households m	0.9		% of households
Av. no. per household	3.8		
Marriages per 1,000 pop.	5.0	TV	98
Divorces per 1,000 pop.	…	Video recorder	38
		Microwave oven	20

Household spending	% of total	Education	
Food/drink	22.0	Spending as % of GDP	6.2
Clothing/footwear	5.0	Years of compulsory education	9
Housing/energy	11.0	Enrolment ratios:	
Household goods	5.0	primary school	100
Health	10.0	secondary school	98
Transport/communications	11.0	tertiary education	26
Leisure/other	29.0		

Tourism		Health	
Tourist arrivals m	3.7	Pop. per doctor	630
Tourist receipts $bn	1.4	Pop. per hospital bed	256

a City borough.

ITALY

Total area	301,225 sq km	Population	57.8m
GDP	$1,187bn	GDP per head	$20,513
Capital	Rome	Other cities	Milan, Naples, Turin

The republic of Italy is undergoing an unparalleled transformation: from the corrupt politics of patronage to the accountability of a proper democracy. This painful process will be eased by Italy's vibrant economy.

History: on Rome's foundations

Italy's birth as a single state is relatively recent, but its origins lie in the Etruscan civilisation of 3,000 years ago and then in the Roman republic established in the 6th century BC. That, in turn, became an empire which by the 2nd century AD stretched as far as Britain, North Africa and what is now Iraq. But the Romans fell victim to barbarian invasions in the 4th and 5th centuries, and Italy was occupied by Byzantines, Lombards, Franks, Saracens and Germans. While the pope kept power in Rome, the south was invaded in the 11th century by the Normans and the north disintegrated into rival city-states.

There followed a long period of political fragmentation which, nonetheless, produced in the 13th to 16th centuries the cultural brilliance of the renaissance. Between the 15th and 18th centuries control of most of Italy was gained first by the French, then the Spanish Habsburgs and then – in the north – the Austrians. When the Napoleonic invasion of 1796 ended in 1815, Italy fragmented again into rival states.

Risorgimento

Modern Italy is the product of the Risorgimento – the "resurrection" – in the 19th century carried out under the House of Savoy (the kingdom of Sardinia) and through the nationalist zeal of Giuseppe Mazzini and the guerrilla exploits of Giuseppe Garibaldi. By 1861 they had succeeded well enough in wars against the Austrians and the French to proclaim the kingdom of Italy. Five years later Venice was annexed and then, in 1870, Rome.

Difficult childhood

The new nation had a troubled infancy. Few outside Rome and Tuscany spoke Italian (using regional dialects instead); crime was ubiquitous; the country's troops were humiliated in Ethiopia. True, Italy benefited from the first world war by siding with Britain and France rather than its traditional German and Austrian allies and so gaining from the war-spoils

Trieste and Trentino Alto-Adige. But the reality was rising unemployment and inflation coupled with increasing civil unrest, hence the rise of Benito Mussolini and his National Fascist Party. In 1922 a general strike gave the fascists an excuse to march on Rome, where King Vittorio Emanuele III invited Mussolini to form a government.

Mussolini may have made the trains run on time but his era was otherwise disastrous. The attempt to expand the colonies of Eritrea and Somaliland by invading Abyssinia in 1935 was opposed by Britain and brought sanctions from the League of Nations. Then Mussolini's support for Spain's General Franco soured relations with France and pushed Italy into the embrace of Hitler's Germany. In 1940 Italy entered the second world war on Germany's side.

As the economy worsened, there was little support for the war. In July 1943, just after the Allied landing in Sicily, the king dismissed Mussolini. But the armistice signed with the Allies in September was badly handled; the Germans invaded the north and installed Mussolini as head of a puppet regime. This lasted until April 1945, when the Germans fled and partisans shot Mussolini and hung him upside down in Milan's Piazza Loreto. In May 1946 King Vittorio Emanuele III stepped down in favour of his son, Umberto, only for a referendum to decide the following month that Italy should become a republic.

Politics: dishonest democracy

As the Cold War divided Europe, Britain and America were determined that Italy should not fall into the Soviet sphere. America, therefore, ensured Italy's economic survival, providing some $1.4 billion in Marshall Plan aid in 1948–52.

The political part of the equation was entrusted to the Christian Democrats, who were expected to keep their erstwhile partners in government, the Communists, out of government.

Because of proportional representation, the Christian Democrats could rarely on their own rebuff the Communists. Instead, they had to make coalitions – with Socialists, Social Democrats, Republicans and Liberals – and ensure that the Socialists, the third largest party, did not make common cause with the Communists.

Sharing the spoils

The way to do this was through the allocation of office, from the cabinet down even to schools and offices. This was *lottizzazione*, sharing out the spoils according to the strengths of the parties, and the power of patronage was helped by the enormous state sector.

One quirk of the system was that the Communist Party connived in it, at first because it did not want to risk confrontation with America but later because it, too, benefited from the patronage. Indeed, in the 1970s the Communists (having seen the overthrow of the Marxist Allende government in Chile) decided that a left-wing government in Italy would be too dangerous for the country. The party therefore announced that in return for being consulted it would not vote against the Christian Democrats. Although post-war Italy had over 50 governments in 45 years, including Socialist-led ones, there was never any real weakening of the Christian Democrats' hold on power.

Basta, basta

The longer the system lasted, the more corrupt it became. While the Cold War existed Italians were prepared to keep the system going, but not once Soviet and European communism collapsed at the end of the 1980s.

In early 1993 a Milan businessman complained about a bribe he was being asked to pay. So began an investigation which quickly implicated hundreds of politicians of all parties, often drawing links with the Mafia. Indeed, Giulio Andreotti, seven times a Christian Democrat prime minister, was alleged to be linked with both the Mafia and the killing by the extreme-left Red Brigades in 1978 of Aldo Moro, also once a Christian Democrat prime minister.

All this produced popular revulsion, hence the growing power of the Northern League, a coalition in the industrial north which flirted with the idea of seceding from Rome. In April 1993 the electorate, inspired by Mario Segni, a disaffected Christian Democrat, voted in a clutch of eight referendums for wholesale political change.

Sweet revolution

The change was to limit the scope of proportional representation. In time for elections in March 1994, three-quarters of both senators and deputies were to be elected in first-past-the-post contests. The idea was to eliminate the weaknesses of the old system: too many parties and too big a gap between voters and the politicians on a party list. The political scene is changing. The Socialist and Christian Democrat parties have been discredited (the Christian Democrats have renamed themselves the Popular Party); the Northern League has prospered, as has the anti-Mafia and "progressive" La Rete. A big winner has been the Democratic Party of the Left (PDS), a moderate offspring of the defunct Communist Party. But the biggest winner in the March 1994 elections was the new Forza Italia (Let's go Italy), founded by the tycoon Silvio Berlusconi. His "Freedom Alliance" with the Northern League and the neo-fascist National Alliance took more than half the seats in the lower house and almost half in the senate.

Society: regions first

All Italians share a reputation for *joie de vivre*, but the industrious northerners tend to deride those in the south – the Mezzogiorno – as lazy and corrupt. Whatever the truth, regional identification is strong everywhere, often at the expense of the national identity. Although the country is almost entirely Roman Catholic, the pope's strictures are very often ignored – which is why Italy now has one of the world's lowest birth rates. A looming problem, harped on by the Northern League, is immigration. There are about 1.4m immigrants in Italy, and in 1991 the government ruthlessly turned back immigrants from Albania. Meanwhile, some 5m Italians are themselves living abroad.

The economy: a miracle of black and white

From a small industrial base at the end of the second world war, Italy has grown to become a member of the G7 industrial powers. In 1987, when the government decided to assess the black economy as 18% of GDP, the economy overtook Britain's in size. The makers of the miracle are the small family firms of the north, helped in the 1950s and 1960s by immigrant labour from the south. The number of world-scale companies, such as Fiat, Pirelli and Olivetti, is small and they are usually under family control.

But the miracle has flaws. One is the relative poverty of the Mezzogiorno, traditionally dependent on aid from Rome doled out to companies controlled by the Mafia. The other is a public debt that is greater than annual GDP and keeps the public sector borrowing requirement uncomfortably high. One remedy is a programme to privatise state-owned companies, especially those of the state holding company IRI (Istituto per la Riconstruzione Industriale).

For all its economic vigour, the challenge for Italy remains immense. A whole political class is being dispossessed of power and a generation of businessmen is being undermined. But their sins were representative of Italy's culture, not its aberrations. The transformation of Italy involves Italians transforming themselves, too.

Total area	301,225 sq km	% agricultural area	56.6
Capital	Rome	Highest point metres	Mont Blanc
Other cities	Milan, Naples, Turin		4,810
		Main rivers	Po, Tiber (Tevere), Arno, Adige

The economy

GDP $bn	1,187	GDP per head $	20,513
% av. ann. growth in		GDP per head in purchasing	
real GDP 1985–92	2.5	power parity (USA=100)	77.0

Origins of GDP*	% of total	Components of GDP*	% of total
Agriculture	3	Private consumption	63
Industry	32	Public consumption	18
of which:		Investment	19
manufacturing	26	Exports	18
Services	65	Imports	-18

Structure of manufacturing

			% of total
Agric. & food processing	8	Other	46
Textiles & clothing	13	Av. ann. increase in industrial	
Machinery & transport	33	output 1985–92	2.0

Inflation and exchange rates

Consumer price 1993	4.3%	Lira per $ av. 1993	1,574
Av. ann. rate 1988–93	5.6%	Lira per ecu av. 1993	1,842

Balance of payments, reserves and aid

			$bn
Visible exports fob	177.7	Capital balance	5.0
Visible imports fob	-175.2	Overall balance	-31.7
Trade balance	2.4	Change in reserves	-21.0
Invisible inflows	90.0	Level of reserves	
Invisible outflows	-112.1	end Dec.	50.8
Net transfers	-5.7	Aid given	4.1
Current account balance	-25.4	as % of GDP	0.3
as % of GDP	-2.1		

Principal exports*	$bn fob	Principal imports*	$bn cif
Engineering products	28.2	Chemicals	22.0
Textiles, leather products		Transport equipment	17.0
& clothing	20.2	Metals & minerals	16.6
Transport equipment	12.4	Energy	16.4
Chemicals	12.4	Electrical equipment	12.6
Total incl. others	178.1	Total incl. others	193.6

Main export destinations*	% of total	Main origins of imports*	% of total
Germany	21.0	Germany	20.9
France	15.2	France	14.2
USA	6.9	UK	5.7
UK	6.7	USA	5.6
Spain	5.1	Switzerland	4.4

Government

System The president is ceremonial head of state, elected for seven years by members of parliament and regional representatives. The president nominates the prime minister. The two-chamber parliament is elected for five years; the Chamber of Deputies has 630 members and the Senate 315 members plus five life members nominated by the president and two former presidents of the republic.

Main political parties Italian Popular Party, Democratic Party of the Left (PDS), Socialist Unity (US-PSI), Republican Party (PRI), Union of the Democratic Centre, Radical Party (PR), Social Democratic Party (PSDI), Forza Italia, National Alliance, Lombard League, the Network, Communist Refoundation

People

Population m	57.8	% under 15	15.4
Pop. per sq km	192	% over 65	15.6
% urban	69	No. men per 100 women	95
% av. ann. growth 1985–92	0.2	Human Development Index	92

Life expectancy	yrs		per 1,000 pop.
Men	74	Crude birth rate	10
Women	81	Crude death rate	10

Ethnic groups[b]	% of total	Workforce	% of total
Italian	98.8	Services	59.5
Austrian	0.4	Industry	23.0
French	0.2	Agriculture	8.4
Slovene	0.2	Construction	9.1
		% unemployed	11.5

Society

No. households m	18.2	**Consumer goods ownership**	
Av. no. per household	3.0		% of households
Marriages per 1,000 pop.	5.4	TV	98
Divorces per 1,000 pop.	0.4	Video recorder	25
		Microwave oven	6

Household spending	% of total	Education	
Food/drink	19.0	Spending as % of GDP	4.8
Clothing/footwear	8.0	Years of compulsory education	8
Housing/energy	14.0	Enrolment ratios:	
Household goods	7.0	primary school	97
Health	10.0	secondary school	79
Transport/communications	11.0	tertiary education	31
Leisure/other	23.0		

Tourism		Health	
Tourist arrivals m	26.7	Pop. per doctor	210
Tourist receipts $bn	19.7	Pop. per hospital bed	133

a 1991.
b Classified by ethno-linguistic composition.

LATVIA

Latvia's history, like that of the other Baltic republics, is one of foreign domination. In the 17th century it was conquered by Sweden and in 1772 it was annexed by Russia. The stirrings of independence commenced in the 19th century and an independent republic was promulgated in November 1918. However, the parliamentary democracy proved unstable and the prime minister, Karlis Ulmanis, assumed dictatorial powers in 1934. Independence came to an end when Latvia was subsumed into the Soviet Union as a result of the Molotov-Ribbentrop pact of 1939. Moscow briefly lost Latvia to the Germans but resumed its stranglehold in 1944. Ruthless Sovietisation and an influx of Russian and nationals from other Soviet republics followed. In 1989 only 51.8% of the population were ethnic Latvians.

Politics: problems with Russia

The promotion of independence by the Latvian Popular Front gathered pace in the late 1980s as Mikhail Gorbachev introduced reforms in the Soviet Union. The objective became reality in September 1991, after the abortive coup against Mr Gorbachev in Moscow. Instability followed independence, largely due to the rigours of adjusting to the economic shock caused by the collapse of the Soviet Union and Comecon.

Confrontation with Moscow over the status of ethnic Russians and the slow withdrawal of Russian troops have been another source of tension. The majority of Russians were prevented from voting in the June 1993 elections, which saw the increasingly unpopular government of the Popular Front replaced by a coalition dominated by a less nationalistic movement, Latvian Way.

The economy: return to prosperity?

After the annexation by the Soviet Union a massive industrialisation programme took place and Latvia became an important Eastern bloc producer of such diverse items as railway carriages, buses, freezers, fertilisers and consumer goods. A severe economic crisis followed independence. In 1992 national income fell by 33% and inflation reached 950%. But a year later inflation was down to 100% and the fall in national income was 10%. Radical economic reforms and privatisation have proceeded at a reasonable pace and, like the other Baltic republics, Latvia can look forward to a relatively speedy adjustment to life after the Soviet Union.

Total area	64,100 sq km	Capital	Riga

Government

System The parliament (Saiema) has 100 deputies who are elected on the basis of proportional representation, with a 4% threshold. The Saiema elects the president.

Main political parties Latvian Way (Latvijas Cels), Latvian National Independence Movement (LNNK), Peasants' Union, Harmony Movement, For Fatherland and Freedom, Christian Democratic Union, Ravnopravie (Russian citizens' association)

The economy

GDP $bn	5.1	GDP per head $	1,930
% av. ann. growth		GDP per head in purchasing	
in real GDP 1985–92	...	power parity (USA=100)	34.1

Structure of GDP	% of total		% of total
Agriculture	20	Manufacturing	41
Industry	48	Services	32

Debt			
Foreign debt $m	60.6	Debt service $m	0.2
as % of GDP	1.2	Debt service ratio	...

People

Population m	2.63	% under 15	21.7
Pop. per sq km	41	% over 65	13.2
% urban	71	No. men per 100 women	...
% av. ann. growth 1985–92	0.3	Human Development Index	87

Life expectancy	yrs		per 1,000 pop.
Men	65	Crude birth rate	15
Women	75	Crude death rate	12

Ethnic groups	% of total	Health	
Latvian	51.8	Pop. per doctor	200
Russian	33.8	Pop. per hospital bed	...
Belorussian	4.5		
Ukrainian	3.4		
Other	9.5		

LIECHTENSTEIN

This tiny principality lies landlocked on the foothills of the Alps in the flood plain of the Rhine between Switzerland and Austria. It is a tax haven and has a postal and customs union with Switzerland.

History: saved by neutrality

Although created in the 14th century, it was not until 1719, when it became an independent principality within the Holy Roman Empire, that the country became known by its present name. During the Napoleonic era it came under French control but it regained independence in 1815 as part of the newly created German Confederation. In 1868, two years after the Confederation was dissolved, Liechtenstein declared itself neutral, an act that saved it from the ravages of the two world wars.

Politics: conservative tradition

Conservative forces have dominated politics in the principality. It is only since 1984 that women were granted national voting rights and the proposal of including a provision in the constitution of equality of sex has been rejected. However, the 1993 election saw the Greens win representation in parliament, depriving the Vaterlandische Union of two of their seats. They continue in government, however, although now in a coalition with the Fortschrittliche Burgerpartei.

The economy: not too taxing

In the 1980s Liechtenstein established itself as a prosperous country. The country's tax-haven status and its easy incorporation laws are probably its most important strengths; foreign holding companies established in Liechtenstein for tax reasons provide the government with roughly one-third of its revenues. The banking sector is also of great importance. The industrial sector, for example, manufacturing of precision instruments and construction have flourished. Postage stamps bring in as much as a tenth of government revenues. All this has brought the people of the principality one of the highest standards of living in the world in terms of GDP per head, which is at a level comparable with Switzerland's. The economy is closely linked with its neighbour's and therefore the possibility that Switzerland may join the European Union has large implications.

Total area	160 sq km	Capital	Vaduz

Government
System The prince is head of state. The government, including the prime minister, is formally appointed by the prince, on the proposal of the Landtag (parliament). The one-chamber Landtag has 25 members elected by a form of proportional representation for four years.

Main political parties Patriotic Union (VU), Progressive Citizens' Party (FBP)

People

Population '000	28	% under 15[a]	19.8
Pop. per sq km	175	% over 65[a]	9.8

Life expectancy	yrs		per 1,000 pop.
Men	74	Crude birth rate[a]	13
Women	81	Crude death rate[a]	7

Ethnic groups[b]	% of total		
Liechtensteiner	63.6	Austrian	7.7
Swiss	15.7	German	3.7

Society

No. households m	0.01	Marriages per 1,000 pop.	11.3
Av. no. per household	2.6	Divorces per 1,000 pop.	1.0

Household spending	% of total		
Food/drink	19.0	Health	12.0
Clothing/footwear	7.0	Transport/communications	12.0
Housing, energy	22.0	Leisure/other	21.0
Household goods	6.0		

Health

Pop. per doctor	932	Pop. per hospital bed	269

a 1987.
b Classified by nationality.

LITHUANIA

The medieval Grand Duchy of Lithuania grew increasingly powerful and reached its zenith in the 16th century when its union with Poland meant it dominated Ukraine, Belorussia and parts of Western Russia. It was annexed to the Russian empire in 1795 after the third partition of Poland. After German occupation during the first world war independence from Russia was won in 1919. The republic's democratic system was suspended in 1926 by Antanas Smetona. and Lithuania lost its independence again after the infamous Nazi-Soviet pact of 1939. The Soviet Union temporarily lost possession of Lithuania during the war with Germany, but returned with a vengeance in 1944. Lithuania spearheaded the push for independence within the Soviet Union, but a more conciliatory pro-Moscow course was adopted in late 1992.

Politics: spearheading independence

The pro-independence Lithuanian Movement for Reconstruction (Sajudis) was formed in 1988 and in March 1990 the Lithuanian parliament, headed by Vytautas Landsbergis, unilaterally declared independence. Moscow reacted by applying intense economic and political pressure, fearing that to make concessions to Lithuania would be the beginning of the end of the Soviet Union. Independence came in September 1991 when the Soviet Union did in fact collapse, but not before 13 demonstrators had been killed in anti-Moscow protests in January that year.

The post-independence Sajudis government faced a deep economic crisis and in the October 1992 elections lost power to the Democratic Labour Party, made up of former communists and headed by Algirdas Brazauskas. He set about improving relations with Russia, a task made easier by the fact that, unlike Estonia and Latvia, Lithuania does not have a large Russian population. By August 1993 all Russian troops had been withdrawn from Lithuania.

The economy: on the turn

Rapid industrialisation took place in the post-war years, together with the collectivisation of agriculture. In 1991 industry accounted for 43% of national income and agriculture for 30%. GDP fell by 35% in the first year of independence, but by late 1993 there were signs of recovery.

Total area	65,200 sq km	Capital	Vilnius

Government

System Under a constitution adopted after independence in 1992 Lithuania has a unicameral legislature, the Seimas. It has 141 deputies, of whom 71 are elected directly and 70 on the basis of proportional representation, subject to a 4% threshold. The president is elected directly for a five-year term.

Main political parties Lithuanian Democratic Labour Party (LDLP, former communists), Social Democratic Party, Sajudis (nationalist movement), Union of Poles, Christian Democratic Party, Lithuanian Democratic Party

The economy

GDP $bn	4.9	GDP per head $	1,310
% av. ann. growth		GDP per head in purchasing	
in real GDP 1985–92	...	power parity (USA=100)	24.4

Structure of GDP	% of total		% of total
Agriculture	20	Services	35
Industry	45		

Debt

Foreign debt $m	37.7	Debt service $m	...
as % of GDP	0.8	Debt service ratio	...

People

Population m	3.74	% under 15	22.5
Pop. per sq km	57	% over 65	11.9
% urban	68	No. men per 100 women	...
% av. ann. growth 1985–92	0.8	Human Development Index	88

Life expectancy	yrs		per 1,000 pop.
Men	66	Crude birth rate	15
Women	76	Crude death rate	11

Ethnic groups	% of total	Health	
Lithuanian	80.1	Pop. per doctor	220
Russian	8.6	Pop. per hospital bed	...
Polish	7.7		
Other	3.6		

LUXEMBOURG

The Grand Duchy of Luxembourg is bordered by Belgium, France and Germany. The official language is Letzeburgish but French and German are widely used. Although only a small country, it has played an important role in the evolution of post-war Europe, having been a founder member of NATO and the WEU, and of the organisations which were the forebears of what is now the European Union.

History: a Low Country story

Nearly a century after it was created a duchy in 1354, Luxembourg came under Burgundian control. Four decades later it was absorbed into the Habsburg empire. In the mid-15th century it became part of the Spanish-ruled Low Countries. Then, at the end of the War of the Spanish Succession, it was the Austrian Habsburgs' turn to rule, which they did until the late 18th century when Luxembourg was ceded to France. The 1815 Congress of Vienna resulted in it becoming a grand duchy within the new kingdom of the Netherlands, but 15 years later Belgium seceded taking a large part of Luxembourg with it. The link with the Netherlands lasted until the accession of a Dutch queen in 1890. Under Luxembourg's salic law monarchs had to be male. During both world wars Luxembourg was occupied by Germany, an experience that explains its enthusiasm for the EU.

The economy: small but strong

Luxembourg formed an economic union with Belgium in 1922 and joined the Benelux Union with Belgium and the Netherlands in 1948. It has an even closer economic union with Belgium (BLEU), involving parity of currencies, integrated foreign trade and balance-of-payments accounts and a joint central bank. The economy is stable and in 1993 the unemployment rate was the lowest in Western Europe. Being a small country, trade is very important. In recent years the main impetus to economic growth has come from construction and wholesale and retail trade, as well as a growing number of financial institutions and holding companies, attracted by low taxes. Government efforts to diversify the economy and reduce dependence on the steel sector since the 1970s has resulted in an increase in foreign investment in industry (rubber and plastics in particular) and financial services. Although to a much less extent than its neighbours, Luxembourg has been affected by recession. GDP growth has slowed and concern has been expressed about the deteriorating state of public finances.

Total area	2,586 sq km	Capital	Luxembourg-Ville

Government

System The grand duke (or duchess) is head of state and, constitutionally, has executive power. These powers are exercised, however, through a council of ministers, headed by a prime minister and appointed by the grand duke. The legislature is the 60-member Chamber of Deputies directly elected by a form of proportional representation for five years. However, the 21-member Council of State, appointed by the grand duke, has some legislative power.

Main political parties Christian Social Party (CSV/PCS), Socialist Party (LSAP/POSL), Democratic Party, Communist Party, Ecology Party, Green Party

The economy

GDP $bn	13.7	GDP per head $	35,260
% av. ann. growth in real GDP 1985–92	4.5	GDP per head in purchasing power parity (USA=100)	...

Origins of GDP	% of total	Components of GDP	% of total
Agriculture	2	Private consumption	48
Industry	30	Public consumption	13
of which:		Investment	23
manufacturing	22	Exports	112
Services	68	Imports	-96

Inflation and exchange rates

Consumer price 1993	4.5%	LuxFr per $ av. 1993	34.60
Av. ann. rate 1988–93	3.6%	LuxFr per ecu av. 1993	40.47

Balance of payments, reserves and aid
See Belgium.

People

Population '000	390	% under 15	17.2
Pop. per sq km	151	% over 65	13.2
% urban	84	No. men per 100 women	95
% av. ann. growth 1985–92	0.8	Human Development Index	94

Life expectancy	yrs		per 1,000 pop.
Men	73	Crude birth rate	12
Women	80	Crude death rate	10

Health

Pop. per doctor	527	Pop. per hospital bed	80

MACEDONIA

At many times during its history Macedonia has been the target of attempts by foreign powers to destabilise it, and its recent independence from the debris of former Yugoslavia has been marked by a dispute with Greece.

History: the shifting Balkan sands

The empire of Alexander the Great disintegrated after his death in 323BC and Macedonia became a Roman province in 148BC. Slavic tribes migrated into the area in the 6th century and merged with the indigenous population. In the 9th century Christianity was introduced by Byzantine missionaries, who used a Macedonian dialect as the basis for the first written Slavonic language, Old Church Slavonic. Byzantine influence was contested by Bulgaria, which dominated Macedonia at the time (and which continues to regard Macedonians as ethnic Bulgarians), but Serbia also made claims on the territory. In 1371 Macedonia was conquered by the Ottomans. Some five centuries later, after the disintegration of the Ottoman empire, it became the object of rivalry among neighbouring Balkan powers. Conflict flared in particular between Greece and Bulgaria. The push for autonomy began in 1893 but simultaneously others were pushing for incorporation into Bulgaria. After the Balkan wars of 1912–13, Macedonia was partitioned between Serbia and Greece, and in 1918 the Serbian part was incorporated into the Yugoslav kingdom .

After the second world war Macedonia became part of the Federal Republic of Yugoslavia led by Tito, who promoted the notion of Macedonian statehood in order to resist Bulgaria's claims to the region. In 1991, as Yugoslavia collapsed, Macedonia declared independence, which was recognised by the UN in April 1993. The former communist, Kiro Gligorov, became president. However, the republic ran into a conflict with Greece, which objected to the use of the name of Macedonia, fearing that this would fuel Macedonia's claims on the Greek province of the same name. As a result and as a temporary measure, the country adopted the official name of the Former Yugoslav Republic of Macedonia.

Economy: fragile

Macedonia was the poorest part of Yugoslavia and has been severely affected by the federation's collapse. Chronic unemployment has led to substantial emigration, and sanctions against Serbia have dealt further blows to the fragile Macedonian economy.

Total area	25,713 sq km	Capital	Skopje

Government

System A new constitution was passed in January 1991. It provides for a unicameral parliament (Sobranie) which elects the president. The president appoints the prime minister subject to approval by Sobranie.

Main political parties Internal Macedonian Revolutionary Organisation-Democratic Party for Macedonian National Unity (VMRO-DPMNE), Social Democratic Alliance of Macedonia, Alliance of the Party of Democratic Prosperity (PDP, Albanian party), Reform Forces of Macedonia-Liberal Party

People

Population m	2.03	% under 15	...
Pop. per sq km	79	% over 65	...
% urban	...	No. men per 100 women	...
% av. ann. growth 1981–91	0.6	Human Development Index	...

Life expectancy[a]	yrs		per 1,000 pop.
Men	68	Crude birth rate	14.5
Women	73	Crude death rate	6.5

Ethnic groups	% of total	Workforce	% of total
Macedonians	65	Services	43
Albanians	21	Industry	40
Turks	5	Agriculture	8
Gypsies	3	Construction	9
Others	6	% unemployed	24.8

Health

Pop. per doctor	...	Pop. per hospital bed	...

a Former Yugoslavia.

MALTA

For much of its recent history this central Mediterranean archipelago has been supported by the contribution made by those who valued its strategic position as a naval base. After the last British forces left in 1979, the country had to adapt to the removal of this economic prop. However, by 1990 the Maltese government was sufficiently confident about the condition of the economy to apply for membership of the European Union.

History: Knights, Napoleon and the navy

Before the Habsburg emperor Charles V granted Malta to the Knights of St John of Jerusalem in 1530, it had been under Phoenician, Carthaginian, Greek, Roman, Arab, Sicilian and Spanish rule. In 1798 the Knights surrendered to Napoleon but the island was taken two years later by the British who later backtracked on a commitment to return it to the Knights. Under the British, Malta became an important naval base and it withstood extremely heavy bombing in the second world war. The island became self-governing in 1947 and, after seriously considering full integration with Britain in the 1950s, fully independent in 1964.

Politics: swinging back and forth

The Nationalist Party regained power in 1987. Their previous term, which lasted from 1962 to 1971, was notable for the achievement of independence and the negotiation of a ten-year defence and economic aid treaty. The Labour government under Dom Mintoff which followed tore up that treaty but negotiated another with NATO; it also pursued much closer links with communist and Arab countries, notably Libya. Malta became a republic within the Commonwealth in 1974. In 1979, when the last British/NATO forces left, it declared itself neutral and non-aligned – though this did not deter Dom Mintoff from arranging for Libyan forces to train Malta's army shortly before he retired in 1984. Since the Nationalists returned to government Maltese politics have shifted to the right and towards Europe.

The economy: doing better, but...

The Nationalists have focused on improving the infrastructure, boosting tourism and promoting Malta as an offshore business centre. In 1992 a stockmarket opened. In 1993 the European Commission, in a formal opinion, stated that radical structural reforms of the economy were still needed.

Total area	320 sq km	Capital	Valletta

Government

System The president is the constitutional head of state, elected by the House of Representatives for five years. The president appoints the prime minister, usually the leader of the majority party, and on the the latter's advice the other government ministers. The one-chamber House of Representatives has 69 members directly elected by a form of proportional representation for five years.

Main political parties Nationalist Party, Malta Labour Party, Democratic Alternative

The economy

GDP $bn	2.6	GDP per head $	7,300
% av. ann. growth in real GDP 1985–90	6.1	GDP per head in purchasing power parity (USA=100)	...

Origins of GDP[a]	% of total	Components of GDP[b]	% of total
Agriculture	4	Private consumption	66
Industry	11	Public consumption	18
of which:		Investment	20
manufacturing	27	Exports	79
Services	56	Imports	-91

People

Population '000	360	% under 15	23.1
Pop. per sq km	1,125	% over 65	10.2
% urban	87	No. men per 100 women	97
% av. ann. growth 1985–92	0.8	Human Development Index	86

Life expectancy	yrs		per 1,000 pop.
Men	74	Crude birth rate	14
Women	79	Crude death rate	8

Ethnic groups	% of total	Health	
Maltese	95.7	Pop. per doctor	489
British	2.1	Pop. per hospital bed	108
Other	2.2		

MOLDOVA

Moldova was the smallest republic of the Soviet Union. Its independence has been marred by tensions with mainly Russian separatists in the Transdniestr region, a source of instability that affects Russia, Ukraine and Romania.

History: much fought over

The ethnic Romanian medieval principality of Moldavia spent much of its history under Hungarian rule. In the 16th century its eastern part, Bessarabia, fell under Turkish suzerainty but was annexed by Russia in 1812. Russia lost control over Southern Bessarabia to Romania after its defeat in the Crimean war, but regained it in 1878. In 1918 Russia lost the whole of Bessarabia again to Romania. In 1940 the Soviet Union retook Bessarabia and a new Moldavian Autonomous Republic was formed in 1947. This was followed by severance of all links with Romania and an influx of ethnic Russians and Ukrainians, mainly to the industrial centres. In 1989 Moldovans (ethnic Romanians) accounted for about 65% of the total population.

Politics: separatist threat

In the late 1980s pressure from the Popular Front resulted in the removal of Moldova's pro-Moscow communist leaders, and nationalists gained a majority in the 1990 parliamentary elections. However, as the country moved towards independence (which came in 1991) ethnic Russians on the east bank of the Dniestr became fearful of the possibility incorporation into Romania. Similar separatist movements sprang up among the 150,000-strong community of ethnic Gagauz (Christian ethnic Turks). The conflict with Transdniestr separatists, who were supported by extreme nationalists in Russia, became more tense. Fighting broke out in late 1991 and it was not until mid-1992 that a ceasefire, brokered by Russia, was agreed, establishing an uneasy peace.

Economy: agricultural potential

Unlike most former Soviet republics Moldova's economy remained based mainly on agriculture, which accounted for 42% of national income in 1991. Tiraspol, in the Transdniestr is the chief industrial centre – hence the alarm at its possible secession. The economy has been severely hit by the collapse of the Soviet Union. National income fell by 30% in 1992 and by 10% in 1993. But there has been foreign interest in the country's agribusiness potential.

Total area	33,700 sq km	Capital	Chisinan

Government

System A new post-Soviet constitution is yet to be adopted, but a new parliament, with 104 members, was elected in February 1994. The president, elected directly, is the highest executive official and has the right to appoint the prime minister.

Main political parties Agrarian Democratic Party, Socialist Party (former communists), Popular Front for Moldova (PFM), Christian Democratic Party, Reform Party

The economy

GDP $bn	5.5	GDP per head $	1,260
% av. ann. growth		GDP per head in purchasing	
in real GDP 1985–92	...	power parity (USA=100)	21.0

Debt

Foreign debt $m	37.5	Debt service $m	5.0
as % of GDP	0.7	Debt service ratio	...

People

Population m	4.46	% under 15	31.6
Pop. per sq km	132	% over 65	8.4
% urban	47	No. men per 100 women	...
% av. ann. growth 1991–92	0.7	Human Development Index	76

Life expectancy	yrs		per 1,000 pop.
Men	64	Crude birth rate	19
Women	71	Crude death rate	10

Ethnic groups	% of total	Workforce	
Moldovan	64.5	Services	31.4
Ukrainian	13.8	Industry	22.8
Russian	13.0	Agriculture	40.0
Bulgarian	2.0	Construction	5.8
Other	6.7	% unemployed	...

Health

Pop. per doctor	250	Pop. per hospital bed	128

MONACO

This tiny principality on the border of south-east France is ruled by the Grimaldi family and a national council. Agreements with France established in 1918 and 1919 mean that Monaco will be incorporated into France if the reigning prince should die without leaving a male heir.

History: long time in the family

The Grimaldi family first ruled Monaco in 1297. It became a Spanish protectorate in 1542 and a French one a century later. It was annexed by France during the revolution but by 1815 was independent again, this time under Sardinian protection. In 1861 it reverted to French protection. During the second world war it was occupied first by the Italians (in 1940) and then by the Germans (in 1943).

The economy: linked to France

The principality has close economic links with France and figures for Monaco's national income and external trade are included in the French statistics and not available separately. Furthermore, after a row over Monaco's role as a tax haven in the early 1960s certain Monaco-based companies were made subject to French tax laws.

Offshore ambitions

The economy is dependent on services, particularly tourism, banking and finance. However, Monaco is subject to French foreign-exchange controls, which has prevented it from becoming a major offshore banking centre despite low tax rates. But with the relaxation of these controls as part of the European Union's single market there are hopes that the principality will develop as an offshore centre.

Total area	1.9 sq km	Capital	Monaco-Ville

Government

System The prince, as head of state, appoints and exercises executive authority with a four-member council of government, headed by a minister of state (a French national). Legislative power is held jointly by the prince and the 18-member National Council directly elected for five years.

Main political parties National and Democratic Union

People

Population '000	30	% under 15[a]	11.9
Pop. per sq km	15,785	% over 65[a]	22.5

Life expectancy	yrs		per 1,000 pop.
Men	72	Crude birth rate[b]	7
Women	80	Crude death rate[b]	7

Ethnic groups[c]	% of total		
French	46.8	Italian	16.5
Monégasque	16.6	Other	20.1

Society

No. households m	0.01	Marriages per 1,000 pop.	7.3
Av. no. per household	2.1	Divorces per 1,000 pop.	1.4

Household spending	% of total		
Food/drink	21.0	Health	15.0
Clothing/footwear	9.0	Transport/communications	11.0
Housing/energy	19.0	Leisure/other	11.0
Household goods	14.0		

Tourism		Health	
Tourist arrivals m	0.2	Pop. per doctor	360
Tourist receipts $bn	0.6	Pop. per hospital bed	54

a 1982.
b 1983.
c Classified by nationality.

NETHERLANDS

Total area	37,938 sq km	Population	15.1m
GDP	$312bn	GDP per head	$20,593
Capital	Amsterdam	Other cities	Rotterdam, The Hague, Utrecht

The Dutch are a prosperous nation. Income per head is higher than in Britain, though lower than in its northern European neighbours. They have always been traders and have one of the most international outlooks of any European nation. In building up their post-war prosperity, the Dutch have also treated themselves to one of the most extensive welfare systems in the whole of Europe. Reform of that into a system that the country can afford has proved hard and controversial.

History: the provinces unite

The Dutch emerged as a distinct people in the 13th and 14th centuries. During the late 16th and early 17th centuries they fought an 80-year war of independence against their Spanish rulers, leading to the establishment of their independence in 1648 under the Treaty of Westphalia. But the United Provinces had been an effective political entity for many years before then.

The 17th century was the golden age in Dutch history, a period of great artistic and intellectual achievement, and colonisation by what had become the world's leading maritime nation. During the 18th century the United Provinces saw its power eclipsed by Britain and France, and by the end of the century the region was under French rule. But the defeat of Napoleon saw the House of Orange restored to the throne in 1815, with William I as king of the United Kingdom of the Netherlands. In 1830 Belgium seceded from the kingdom and its independence was recognised by the Netherlands in 1839. The House of Orange has remained on the throne ever since, except for a period of exile during the second world war when the country was occupied by the Germans. (In the first world war the Netherlands succeeded in remaining neutral.)

Politics: leaning left together

Since the second world war the Netherlands has enjoyed a high degree of political stability despite frequently shifting coalition governments. In theory there is a big ideological gap between the various political parties. In practice there has usually been a considerable degree of political consensus around a centre of gravity that is to the left of that in neighbouring countries. Compromise always has to prevail in the end, not least because no single party gets enough votes to rule alone. From November 1982 to May 1994 Ruud Lubbers, the leader of the Christian Democratic Appeal, headed a series of coalition governments. Coalition partners were either the Liberals or the Labour Party. However, the vote for Democratic Appeal fell dramatically in the May 1994 election. Labour also lost electoral support. The Liberal Party and the social democratic Democrats '66 were the main winners, although there was also a rise in support for the extreme right.

Society: agreeing on differences

The Dutch obsession with consensus could only be found in a country fearful of the internal diversity that has at times threatened to pull it apart. By 1919 universal suffrage had been established, as had the principle of "pillarisation" whereby schools, political parties, unions, business groupings and sports clubs were organised along Catholic, Protestant or Socialist lines. It was only in the 1960s that these divisions began to break down. However, even today Protestants, Catholics, Socialists and Liberals have their own TV networks.

North-south divide

Geographically, there is a strong divide between those who live in the traditional Protestant areas north of the Rhine delta and those in the Catholic south, who are by reputation more gregarious.

The economy: a difficult restructuring

The Netherlands' prosperity is based on its industry, natural gas, intensive agriculture and trade; over half of GDP consists of exports and imports. Chemicals, rubber, paper and food and drink have led economic growth but service industries have also grown. However, in the 1980s economic policies that were both equivocal in conception and implementation led to growth that was below the EU average. At the beginning of the 1990s, with the costs of the welfare state amounting to some 7% of GDP (in 1990) and with recession spreading across the world, the economic outlook was gloomy. By 1994 it still did not look too bright, but unpopular austerity measures and reforms of the welfare system had at least put the economy in structurally better shape.

Total area[a]	37,938 sq km	% agricultural area	53.9
Capital	Amsterdam	Highest point metres	Vaalserberg
Other cities	Rotterdam, The Hague,		321
	Utrecht	Main rivers	Rhine (Rhein),
			Maas (Meuse), Sheldt

The economy

GDP $bn	312	GDP per head $	20,593
% av. ann. growth in		GDP per head in purchasing	
real GDP 1985–92	2.6	power parity (USA=100)	76.0

Origins of GDP	% of total	Components of GDP	% of total
Agriculture	4	Private consumption	60
Industry	30	Public consumption	14
of which:		Investment	21
manufacturing	24	Exports	52
Services	66	Imports	-47

Structure of manufacturing

			% of total
Agric. & food processing	16	Other	57
Textiles & clothing	3	Av. ann. increase in industrial	
Machinery & transport	25	output 1985–92	1.8

Inflation and exchange rates

Consumer price 1993	2.1%	G per $ av. 1993	1.86
Av. ann. rate 1988–93	2.3%	G per ecu av. 1993	2.17

Balance of payments, reserves and aid

			$bn
Visible exports fob	128.5	Capital balance	-0.1
Visible imports fob	-117.8	Overall balance	6.4
Trade balance	10.7	Change in reserves	4.1
Invisible inflows	63.6	Level of reserves	
Invisible outflows	-62.8	end Dec.	35.6
Net transfers	-4.8	Aid given	2.75
Current account balance	6.8	as % of GDP	0.9
as % of GDP	2.2		

Principal exports	$bn fob	Principal imports	$bn cif
Machinery & transport equip.	33.3	Machinery & transport equip.	42.4
Chemicals, plastics, etc	31.1	Chemicals, plastics, etc	24.7
Food, drink & tobacco	28.7	Food, drink & tobacco	16.6
Fuels	12.0	Fuels	11.5
Raw materials, oils & fats	9.0	Raw materials, oils & fats	7.1
Total incl. others	139.8	Total incl. others	134.3

Main export destinations	% of total	Main origins of imports	% of total
Germany	28.8	Germany	25.2
Belgium/Luxembourg	14.3	Belgium/Luxembourg	14.2
France	10.6	UK	8.7
UK	9.2	France	7.9
Italy	6.4	USA	7.8

Government

System The monarch has mainly formal powers. Executive power lies with the Council of Ministers, headed by a prime minister who is appointed by the monarch and responsible to the legislature. The two-chamber Staten Generaal (parliament) comprises the 75-member First Chamber, elected by the 12 provincial councils, and the 150-member Second Chamber, directly elected by a form of proportional representation for four years.

Main political parties Christian Democrat Appeal (CDA), Labour Party (PvdA), People's Party for Freedom & Democracy (VVD), Democrats 1966 (D66), Green Left, Political Reformed Party (SGP), Reformed Political Association (GPV), Reformed Political Federation (RPF), Centre Democrats (CD), Socialist Party (SP)

People

Population m	15.1	% under 15	18.7
Pop. per sq km	379	% over 65	13.0
% urban	89	No. men per 100 women	98
% av. ann. growth 1985–92	0.7	Human Development Index	97

Life expectancy	yrs		per 1,000 pop.
Men	74	Crude birth rate	14
Women	81	Crude death rate	9

Ethnic groups	% of total	Workforce	% of total
Dutch	96	Services	70.4
Turkish	1	Industry	18.8
Moroccan	1	Agriculture	4.4
Other	2	Construction	6.4
		% unemployed	6.8

Society

No. households m	6.2	**Consumer goods ownership**	
Av. no. per household	2.3		% of households
Marriages per 1,000 pop.	6.3	TV	98
Divorces per 1,000 pop.	1.9	Video recorder	48
		Microwave oven	19

Household spending	% of total	Education	
Food/drink	13.0	Spending as % of GDP	6.6
Clothing/footwear	6.0	Years of compulsory education	11
Housing/energy	18.0	Enrolment ratios:	
Household goods	8.0	primary school	117
Health	11.0	secondary school	103
Transport/communications	10.0	tertiary education	34
Leisure/other	24.0		
		Health	
Tourist arrivals m	5.8	Pop. per doctor	410
Tourist receipts $bn	3.6	Pop. per hospital bed	169

a Land only.

NORWAY

Total area	324,219 sq km	Population	4.3m
GDP	$110bn	GDP per head	$25,804
Capital	Oslo	Other cities	Bergen, Trondheim, Stavanger

The development of oil and gas reserves in the 1970s transformed the Norwegian economy from its traditional dependence on forestry and fishing and made Norway, in terms of income per head, one of the richest countries in the world.

History: Scandinavian ties

Norway's history has been closely linked with that of Denmark and Sweden. In 1380 Denmark and Norway were united by royal marriage and in 1397 Sweden joined them under the Union of Kalmar, secured by Queen Margrethe of Denmark. Sweden became independent again in 1523, but Norway remained under Danish rule until 1814 when it was ceded to Sweden. The Norwegians rebelled. Sweden invaded. Under the subsequent compromise Norway was allowed to keep its own parliament, which in 1905 after a plebiscite declared Norway completely independent. Sweden agreed to the separation and Prince Carl of Denmark ascended the Norwegian throne as Haakon VII. During the first world war Norway successfully pursued a policy of neutrality. In the second world war it was occupied by German forces.

Politics: Labour dominant

The Labour Party has dominated Norwegian politics since the 1930s and was the majority party in government for almost two decades following the second world war. However, the past three decades have seen a steady stream of minority or coalition governments. The Conservative Party has traditionally been the main opposition party, but in the 1993 election it was beaten into third place by the Centre Party.

Foreign policy: joining in more

As a result of being occupied in the second world war and because it had acquired a northern frontier with the Soviet Union, Norway gave up its policy of neutrality and joined NATO when it was founded in 1949. Norway is a member of the Nordic Council and of EFTA, but it has blown hot and cold over membership of the European Union. It applied for membership first in 1962 and then again in 1967. Terms were agreed and a treaty of accession was signed in January 1972 for membership to take effect in 1973. But in a referendum in September 1972 a majority, fearful of the effects of membership on Norwegian sovereignty and on farming and fishing, voted against the treaty. Two decades later Norway signed up for membership of the European Economic Area and in 1992 it applied yet again to join the EU. In 1994 it was agreed that Norway would become a member as from January 1995. However, accession was to be subject to a referendum.

The economy: running on oil

Oil and gas were first discovered on the Norwegian continental shelf in 1968 and production started in 1971. Norway became a net exporter of oil in the mid-1970s and by 1980 total production of oil and gas stood at 49.5m tons of oil equivalent (toe) compared with 9.3m toe five years before. Norway is now the largest European oil and gas producer (overtaking Britain in 1991). In 1992 it produced 106.6m tons of oil and 27.7m toe of gas. From 1980 the value of oil and gas exports grew rapidly and soon exceeded the value of all other merchandise exports. In 1992 they amounted to almost half of all merchandise exports.

Vulnerability

Because of its dependence on oil and gas, the economy is vulnerable to sharp shifts in oil prices. The collapse in oil prices in the mid-1980s plunged Norway into economic crisis and led to the adoption of an austerity programme. In 1987 wage restraints were imposed, followed by a tough incomes policy which lasted until spring 1990. Industrial subsidies were also cut back, though the Norwegian business sector (particularly agriculture) remains one of the most heavily subsidised in the OECD. The concentration on oil led to a degree of stagnation in other productive sectors, though there has been some growth in sectors such as engineering and chemicals. The global economic downturn has also been felt in Norway. Low GDP growth and higher unemployment, though still low by OECD comparison, has been accompanied by a growing budget deficit.

Total area	324,219 sq km	% agricultural area	3.0
Capital	Oslo	Highest point metres	
Other cities	Bergen, Trondheim,		Galdhopiggen 2,469
	Stavanger	Main rivers	Glåma, Lågen

The economy

GDP $bn	110	GDP per head $	25,804
% av. ann. growth in		GDP per head in purchasing	
real GDP 1985–92	2.5	power parity (USA=100)	77.6

Origins of GDP	% of total	Components of GDP	% of total
Agriculture	3	Private consumption	52
Industry	33	Public consumption	22
of which:		Investment	19
manufacturing	14	Exports	43
Services	65	Imports	-36

Structure of manufacturing
%\ of total

Agric. & food processing	21	Other	53
Textiles & clothing	2	Av. ann. increase in industrial	
Machinery & transport	24	output 1985–92	4.4

Inflation and exchange rates

Consumer price 1993	2.2%	NKr per $ av. 1993	7.09
Av. ann. rate 1988–93	3.9%	NKr per ecu av. 1993	8.35

Balance of payments, reserves and aid
$bn

Visible exports fob	35.2	Capital balance	-0.2
Visible imports fob	-25.9	Overall balance	-0.5
Trade balance	9.3	Change in reserves	-1.3
Invisible inflows	17.1	Level of reserves	
Invisible outflows	-21.6	end Dec.	11.9
Net transfers	-1.8	Aid given	1.3
Current account balance	2.9	as % of GDP	1.2
as % of GDP	2.6		

Principal exports	$bn fob	Principal imports	$bn cif
Oil, gas & products	17.6	Machinery incl. electric	6.3
Non-ferrous metals	2.4	Transport equipment excl. ships	2.4
Machinery incl. electric	2.4	Food, drink & tobacco	1.6
Fish & fish products	2.3	Clothing	1.4
Iron & steel	2.2	Iron & steel	1.2
Total incl. others	35.2	Total incl. others	25.9

Main export destinations	% of total	Main origins of imports	% of total
UK	24.2	Sweden	15.5
Germany	13.5	Germany	14.7
Sweden	9.4	UK	9.4
France	7.9	USA	8.4
Netherlands	7.2	Denmark	7.5

Government

System The monarch is largely a ceremonial head of state. Executive power is exercised by a prime minister and a council of state. The Storting (parliament) has 165 members directly elected by a form of proportional representation for four years. When dealing with legislative matters members elect one-quarter of their number to constitute the Lagting, the other three-quarters forming the Odelsting. There is no right of dissolution between elections.

Main political parties Labour Party, Conservative Party, Progress Party, Socialist Left Party, Christian People's Party, Centre Party

People

Population m	4.3	% under 15	19.7
Pop. per sq km	13	% over 65	15.9
% urban	75	No. men per 100 women	98
% av. ann. growth 1985–92	0.4	Human Development Index	98

Life expectancy	yrs		per 1,000 pop.
Men	74	Crude birth rate	15
Women	81	Crude death rate	11

Ethnic groups*	% of total	Workforce	% of total
Norwegian	95.8	Services	71.4
Danish	0.5	Industry	17.0
Swedish	0.5	Agriculture	5.5
British	0.4	Construction	6.1
		% unemployed	5.9

Society

No. households m	1.7	**Consumer goods ownership**	
Av. no. per household	2.4		% of households
Marriages per 1,000 pop.	4.9	TV	97
Divorces per 1,000 pop.	2.2	Video recorder	41
		Microwave oven	34

Household spending	% of total	Education	
Food/drink	15.0	Spending as % of GDP	6.6
Clothing/footwear	6.0	Years of compulsory education	9
Housing/energy	14.0	Enrolment ratios:	
Household goods	7.0	primary school	99
Health	11.0	secondary school	100
Transport/communications	14.0	tertiary education	43
Leisure/other	25.0		

Tourism		Health	
Tourist arrivals m	2.0	Pop. per doctor	440
Tourist receipt $bn	1.5	Pop. per hospital bed	208

a Classified by nationality.

POLAND

Total area	312,677 sq km	Population	38.4m
GDP	$75bn	GDP per head	$1,962
Capital	Warsaw	Other cities	Lodz, Krakow, Wroclaw

This predominantly lowland central European country has frequently been the victim of the rivalry of major powers. In 1989 it finally freed itself from its most recent period of foreign domination.

History: between East and West

The Polish state owes its origins to the unification of Slavic tribes settled around the Warta river but its centre gradually moved southwards. Christianity was introduced in 966 by King Mieszko. The kingdom grew stronger and in 1569 entered a full union with Lithuania, which stretched from the Baltic to the Black Sea. After the last of the Jagellon dynasty died in 1572 Poland entered a period of decline, caused by numerous wars and economic weakness. In 1772 the kingdom's territory was partitioned between Russia, Prussia and Austria. Further partitions followed in 1793 and 1795, the latter resulting in complete obliteration of the Polish state. A Duchy of Warsaw was created by Napoleon in 1807 and the kingdom of Poland was recreated under Russian patronage at the Congress of Vienna in 1815. Two abortive insurrections against Russian rule took place, in 1830 and 1861. Poland regained its independence in 1916 as the three empires which had partitioned it collapsed. A republic was promulgated in November 1918 by Jozef Pilsudski and its independence was underwritten by the Treaty of Versailles. But the country lacked stability; its borders were unclear, the presence of large ethnic minorities gave rise to tensions and the economy was in poor shape. In 1926 Marshal Pilsudski took over and ruled as a dictator until his death 1935, when he was replaced by a military council.

On September 1st 1939 Poland was invaded by the Nazis, causing Britain and France to declare war on Germany. Two weeks later the Soviet Union invaded and annexed eastern Poland. But in June 1941 Hitler attacked the Soviet Union and Germany occupied the whole of Poland. Nazi occupation proved extremely costly both in human as well as economic terms; about one-sixth of the population lost their lives. A government in exile was formed in London in 1940 under General Wladyslaw Sikorski. Poland's liberation in July 1944 by the Soviet army ensured that the country fell again under Moscow's rule. Once again the great powers played with

Poland's fate: it was agreed in Yalta that Poland would give nearly half of its territory in the east to the Soviet Union but would be compensated by the surrender of parts of Germany's territory to Poland; some 3.5m Germans were forcibly moved to the West.

Politics: rejecting communism

"Imposing communism on Poland is like trying to put a saddle on a cow" – so went a celebrated remark by Josef Stalin. Poland's history under communism has amply confirmed his foresight. First attempts to reject the system came in 1948, a mere year after the declaration of a People's Republic of Poland, when its communist leader, Wladyslaw Gomulka, rebelled against slavish copying of Moscow's model; he was promptly removed. Another crisis followed in 1956. Gomulka returned to preside over "reforms". He was again replaced, after bloody riots in December 1970, by Edward Gierek. His "modernisation programme" ended in an economic crisis by the end of the decade, which eventually spawned the grave-digger of Polish communism, the Solidarity trade union movement. An attempt to put down Solidarity was made in the declaration of martial law in December 1981, but the communist regime eventually collapsed in August 1989. Solidarity's leader, Lech Walesa, was elected president in December 1990.

In 1990 Poland's first post-communist government pioneered radical market-oriented reforms. But the political scene remained unstable, with frequent changes of government. The elections in September 1993 saw a victory by a left-wing coalition with roots in the old Communist Party. However, the reforms have remained firmly on course.

The economy: shock therapy

Poland's liberalising "big bang" of 1990 was linked to tight monetary and fiscal measures. The result was that inflation fell dramatically from its 1989 peak of 1,000%. But so too did industrial production and living standards, while unemployment soared; hence the political instability. However, exports to the West have expanded and the private sector is growing rapidly, augmented by the sell-off of state enterprises. Foreign investors, after initial hesitance, are now showing more interest. The debt burden remains a problem, despite concessions from lenders, but by 1993 Poland was the first of the former Eastern bloc countries to show clear signs of economic recovery.

Total area	312,677 sq km	% agricultural area	61.2
Capital	Warsaw	Highest point metres	Rysy 2,499
Other cities	Lodz, Krakow, Wroclaw	Main rivers	Vistula (Wilsa), Narew, Odra (Oder)

The economy

GDP $bn	75	GDP per head $	1,962
% av. ann. growth in real GDP 1985–92	-0.5	GDP per head in purchasing power parity (USA=100)	20.3

Origins of GDP	% of total	Components of GDP	% of total
Agriculture	7	Private consumption	57
Industry	51	Public consumption	21
of which:		Investment	22
manufacturing	...	Exports	20
Services	42	Imports	-21

Structure of manufacturing

			% of total
Agric. & food processing	21	Other	44
Textiles & clothing	9	Av. ann. increase in industrial	
Machinery & transport	26	output 1985–92	-4.4

Inflation and exchange rates

Consumer price 1993	35.3%	Zl per $ av. 1993	18,115
Av. ann. rate 1988–93	124.2%	Zl per ecu av. 1993	20,288

Balance of payments and debt

			$bn
Visible exports fob	13.9	Capital balance	-1.0
Visible imports fob	-14.1	Overall balance	-4.3
Trade balance	-0.2	Change in reserves	0.5
Invisible inflows	5.5	Level of reserves end Dec.	4.3
Invisible outflows	-8.9	Foreign debt	48.5
Net transfers	0.5	as % of GDP	54.4
Current account balance	-3.1	Debt service	1.5
as % of GDP	-4.1	Debt service ratio	9.5

Principal exports	$bn fob	Principal imports	$bn cif
Machinery	3.2	Machinery	5.7
Chemicals	1.6	Chemicals	2.8
Food & agricultural products	1.3	Energy	2.7
Coal	0.9	Food & agricultural products	1.4
Steel	0.7	Metallurgy	0.7
Total incl. others	13.2	Total incl. others	14.1

Main export destinations	% of total	Main origins of imports	% of total
Germany	31.4	Germany	23.9
Netherlands	6.0	Russia	8.5
Italy	5.6	Italy	6.9
Russia	5.5	UK	6.6
UK	4.4	Netherlands	4.8

Government

System The so-called 'small constitution' is in force pending the passage of post-communist basic law. Poland has a bicameral legislature: Sejm, the lower house, has 460 members; the Senate has 100. The president is elected by direct universal suffrage for a five-year term. The president appoints the prime minister and the latter selects the cabinet.

Main political parties Union of Democratic Left (SLD, former communists), United Peasants' Party (PSL), Democratic Movement (UD), Congress of Liberal Democrats, Christian Democratic Movement, Non-Party Bloc for Reform (BBWR, set up by President Walesa), Congress of Liberal Democrats (KLD)

People

Population m	38.4	% under 15	23.5
Pop. per sq km	124	% over 65	10.9
% urban	62	No. men per 100 women	95
% av. ann. growth 1985–92	0.4	Human Development Index	83

Life expectancy	yrs		per 1,000 pop.
Men	67	Crude birth rate	14
Women	76	Crude death rate	10

Ethnic groups	% of total	Workforce	% of total
Polish	97.6	Services	37.9
German	1.3	Industry	28.1
Ukrainian	0.6	Agriculture	26.7
Other	0.5	Construction	7.3
		% unemployed	13.3

Society

No. households m	12.1	**Consumer goods ownership**	
Av. no. per household	3.0		% of households
Marriages per 1,000 pop.	6.7	TV	70
Divorces per 1,000 pop.	1.1	Video recorder	...
		Microwave oven	...

Household spending	% of total	Education	
Food/drink	29.0	Spending as % of GDP	3.6
Clothing	9.0	Years of compulsory education	8
Housing/energy	6.0	Enrolment ratios:	
Household goods	9.0	primary school	98
Health	6.0	secondary school	82
Transport/communications	8.0	tertiary education	22
Leisure/other	26.0		

Tourism		Health	
Tourist arrivals m	3.4	Pop. per doctor	490
Tourist receipts $bn	0.3	Pop. per hospital bed	152

PORTUGAL

Total area	92,082 sq km	Population	9.8m
GDP	$73bn	GDP per head	$7,451
Capital	Lisbon	Other cities	Loures, Porto

In common with neighbouring Spain, it is only two decades since Portugal ceased being a dictatorship and became a democracy. It remains one of the poorest countries in Western Europe, but since joining the European Union in 1986 its economy has been transformed.

History: once a great power

Portugal became an independent kingdom in the 12th century. Wars with Castile led it to establish an alliance with England in the 14th century and in the following two centuries it developed into one of the world's most important maritime and colonial powers, with an empire that stretched to Africa, India, the Far East and South America. But in 1580 the country was seized by Philip II of Spain and decline set in. After rebellion against Spanish rule the country became independent again in the mid-17th century. The French invaded in 1807 but were expelled by British forces four years later.

Almost a century later republican tensions led to the assassination of King Carlos and his son. His successor, Manuel II, was forced to flee the country during an ensuing republican uprising in 1920 and subsequently a republic was declared. After the first world war the country went through a period of political turmoil until power was handed to Antonio de Oliveira Salazar in 1928. Some 40 years of dictatorship followed. In following isolationist policies Salazar sought to preserve Portugal as a rural and religious society. As a result development was well behind its European neighbours. Mr Salazar stood down after suffering a stroke in 1968. An authoritarian style of government was continued by his successor, Marcello Caetano, until 1974 when there was a bloodless coup organised by military officers who were dissatisfied with endless colonial wars. In 1976 elections were held under a new constitution.

Politics: power to the centre

Portugal's first two governments after the 1976 elections were led by the Socialist leader, Mario Soares. He moved the country back towards the political centre, confirmed Portugal's European outlook by applying to join the European Community and instituted social reforms, but he failed to tackle the structural problems of the economy. The centre-right Democratic Alliance coalition took over in 1980 but was replaced by a coalition between the Socialists (PS) and the Social Democrats (PSD) in 1983. In the 1985 election the PSD – which is pro-market, pro-business and pragmatic – became the largest party and went on to win an absolute majority in the 1987 and 1991 elections. In the 1991 presidential election Mario Soares won a second term as president; the PSD did not put a candidate forward.

Foreign policy: colonists still care

Portugal was a founder member of NATO and joined the European Community in 1986, at the same time as Spain. It has close cultural links with Brazil and, to a much lesser extent, with its former colonies in Africa. It has taken an active part in negotiations for peace in Angola and Mozambique and has protested against Indonesia's annexation of the former Portuguese colony of East Timor. Macao, which has been a Chinese territory under Portuguese administration since 1975, will be handed over to China in 1999.

The economy: the pace slows

In 1975, a year after the coup which brought four decades of dictatorship to an end, large parts of Portugal's economy were nationalised, bringing just over half of industrial fixed investment under state control. Huge amounts of public money were poured into industries that were uncompetitive and had shrinking markets. Similarly, agricultural subsidies heightened the inefficiencies of Portugal's farms. The economy performed poorly for the first decade of democracy. It was only after the country joined the European Union that there was an upswing and, since 1989 when constitutional changes gave the government the power to introduce wideranging privatisation policies, market forces have been the order of the day.

During the latter half of the 1980s GDP growth was, at 4.6% a year, above the OECD average, but in 1992 growth slowed right down and the economy slid into recession in the following year. This was mainly due to falling exports. Restructuring of the economy is essential. Industry needs to move away from low value-added goods and to reduce its dependence on tourism. However, high levels of foreign direct investment are helping the economy move in the right direction, and EU structural funds have made possible a massive infrastructural renewal programme.

Total area	92,082 sq km	% agricultural area	35.5
Capital	Lisbon	Highest point metres	Estrela 1,991
Other cities	Oporto, Setúbal	Main rivers	Tagus (Tejo),
			Douro, Guadiana

The economy

GDP $bn	73	GDP per head $	7,451
% av. ann. growth in		GDP per head in purchasing	
real GDP 1985–90	4.6	power parity (USA=100)	42.7

Origins of GDP	% of total	Components of GDP	% of total
Agriculture	5	Private consumption	66
Industry	36	Public consumption	19
of which:		Investment	28
manufacturing	29	Exports	25
Services	59	Imports	-37

Structure of manufacturing

			% of total
Agric. & food processing	18	Other	49
Textiles & clothing	20	Av. ann. increase in industrial	
Machinery & transport	14	output 1985–92	4.8

Inflation and exchange rates

Consumer price 1993	6.5%	Esc per $ av. 1993	160.8
Av. ann. rate 1988–93	10.5%	Esc per ecu av. 1993	187.8

Balance of payments and debt

			$bn
Visible exports fob	18.2	Capital balance	-1.0
Visible imports fob	-27.7	Overall balance	-0.2
Trade balance	-9.5	Change in reserves	-1.4
Invisible inflows	7.7	Level of reserves end Dec.	24.3
Invisible outflows	-6.2	Foreign debt	32.0
Net transfers	7.8	as % of GDP	40.1
Current account balance	-0.2	Debt service	5.6
as % of GDP	-0.3	Debt service ratio	22.4

Principal exports	$bn fob	Principal imports	$bn cif
Textiles, clothing & footwear	7.0	Machinery & transport equip.	11.5
Machinery & transport equip.	3.9	Foodstuffs	3.8
Forest products	1.9	Chemicals & plastics	3.4
Foodstuffs	1.4	Textiles, clothing & footwear	3.3
Chemicals & plastics	1.0	Combustible fuels	2.4
Total incl. others	18.2	Total incl. others	24.82

Main export destinations	% of total	Main origins of imports	% of total
Germany	19.2	Spain	16.6
Spain	14.7	Germany	15.0
France	14.2	France	12.8
UK	11.2	Italy	10.2
Netherlands	5.4	UK	7.2

Government

System The president is head of state, directly elected for up to two consecutive five-year terms. The Council of Ministers is led by a prime minister, appointed by the president, as leader of the majority party in the assembly, but responsible to the legislature. The one-chamber Assembly of the Republic has 230 members directly elected by a form of proportional representation for four years.

Main political parties Social Democratic Party (PSD), Socialist Party (PS), Communist Party (PCP), Centre Democratic Party (CDS), Popular Democratic Union (UDP)

People

Population m	9.8	% under 15	18.5
Pop. per sq km	107	% over 65	14.2
% urban	34	No. men per 100 women	93
% av. ann. growth 1985–92	-0.7	Human Development Index	85

Life expectancy	yrs		per 1,000 pop.
Men	71	Crude birth rate	12
Women	78	Crude death rate	10

Ethnic groups^a	% of total	Workforce	% of total
Portuguese	98.8	Services	55.4
Angolan	0.2	Industry	24.9
Cape Verdian	0.2	Agriculture	11.5
French	0.1	Construction	8.2
		% unemployed	4.1

Society

No. households m	3.4	**Consumer goods ownership**	
Av. no. per household	2.9		% of households
Marriages per 1,000 pop.	7.0	TV	92
Divorces per 1,000 pop.	0.9	Video recorder	22
		Microwave oven	4

Household spending	% of total	Education	
Food/drink	34.0	Spending as % of GDP	4.9
Clothing/footwear	10.0	Years of compulsory education	8
Housing/energy	9.0	Enrolment ratios:	
Household goods	7.0	primary school	119
Health	6.0	secondary school	59
Transport/communications	13.0	tertiary education	18
Leisure/other	17.0		

Tourism		Health	
Tourist arrivals m	8.0	Pop. per doctor	490
Tourist receipts $bn	3.6	Pop. per hospital bed	238

a Classified by nationality.

ROMANIA

Total area	237,500 sq km	Population	22.8m
GDP	$24.9bn	GDP per head	$1,090
Capital	Bucharest	Other cities	Brasov, Constanta

Post-war Romania had one of the most repressive communist regimes in Eastern Europe. Its collapse in late 1989 was followed by a steady consolidation of democracy and market-oriented reforms.

History: struggle for unification

Moldavia (today making up the bulk of the former Soviet republic of Moldova) and Wallachia fell under Ottoman suzerainty in the 15th century but were united (under Turkish suzerainty) in 1856 by the Treaty of Paris. The state gained independence from Turkey in 1878 at the Congress of Berlin, although it lost to Russia the province of Bessarabia. The kingdom of Romania was created in 1881, since when its overriding objective was the unification of all territories inhabited by Romanians into Greater Romania (Romania Mare). That was attained after the first world war when Romania was awarded Bessarabia, Bukovina, Transylvania and Banat. The new enlarged state, however, proved unviable as it failed to reconcile the interests of its various regions and ethnic minorities. King Carol II instituted a dictatorship in 1938. The regime joined the Nazis' attack on the Soviet Union in June 1941. In August 1944 Ion Antonescu, who as prime minister had ruled the country since 1940, was overthown by King Michael whose coalition government switched sides in the war. But Romania was denied co-belligerent status by Stalin and in 1947 the Soviet Union annexed Bessarabia and northern Bukovina as reparations. Soviet influence strengthened and King Michael was forced to abdicate in 1947. By 1948 a Soviet-style regime, headed by Gheorghe Gheorghui-Dej, was in firm control.

Politics: from dictatorship to democracy

In the early 1960s Romania clashed with Moscow over proposals to turn it largely into a supplier of agricultural products within the Comecon trading bloc. Gheorghiu-Dej was succeeded by a collective leadership in 1965, soon dominated by Nicolae Ceaucescu, who remained in power until he was deposed in December 1989 and executed. He argued that Romania had a right to pursue its own communist model with which nationalism was compatible. This won him popularity, and Romania under Ceaucescu had the distinction of being the only member of the Soviet bloc with a significant degree of external independence. The regime largely ignored Soviet economic and military initiatives and opposed the 1968 Soviet invasion of Czechoslovakia. During the 1970s Romania borrowed heavily from the West to fund Ceaucescu's grandiose economic plans but from 1981 the emphasis shifted to ruthless repayment of the resulting huge foreign debt. Over the years Ceaucescu consolidated the rule of the Ceaucescu clan. The people suffered worsening privations. The regime increasingly relied on the ubiquitous secret police (Securitate). In 1988 Ceaucescu announced a policy of systematisation whereby some 7,000 villages were to be demolished and their inhabitants resettled in ugly agro-industrial centres. At the end of the following year, after fierce fighting in the streets of Bucharest, the regime became the last in Eastern Europe to fall.

The early post-Ceaucescu years were marked by instability and suspicions that neo-communists were taking hold. The government was dominated by the National Salvation Front headed by Ion Iliescu, who had been a close associate of Ceaucescu in the late 1960s. The Salvation Front won the September 1992 elections, but the government has had to rely on the support of nationalists and former communists.

Foreign policy: ethnic tensions

Since 1990 Romania has sought closer links with the West and has signed an association agreement with the EU. Tensions have resurfaced with Hungary over the treatment of ethnic Hungarians in Transylvania, and some Romanians are pushing for reunification with Moldova.

The economy: Soviet-style development

Romania pursued classic Soviet-style development, emphasising heavy industry at the expense of consumer goods and services. Unlike other former Eastern bloc countries Romania is rich in hydrocarbons, which is one reason why it was able to take an independent line from Moscow. Ceaucescu's plans to develop a strong oil and refining sector failed, but the sector has been important; some 294,000 barrels a day (b/d) of crude oil were produced in 1976, though this had fallen to 183,000 b/d by 1989. After the shock of market reforms, the economy was showing signs of recovery in 1994.

Total area	237,500 sq km	% agricultural area	63.6
Capital	Bucharest	Highest point metres	Neglou 2,548
Other cities	Brasov, Constanta	Main rivers	Danube (Dunarea), Mures, Prut

The economy

GDP $bn	24.9	GDP per head $	1,090
% av. ann. growth in		GDP per head in purchasing	
real GDP 1985–92	...	power parity (USA=100)	31.2

Origins of GDP	% of total	Components of GDP	% of total
Agriculture	19	Private consumption	57
Industry	49	Public consumption	14
of which:		Investment	34
manufacturing	...	Exports	17
Services	33	Imports	...

Structure of manufacturing

			% of total
Agric. & food processing	13	Other	43
Textiles & clothing	19	Av. ann. increase in industrial	
Machinery & transport	25	output 1985–92	-8.0

Inflation and exchange rates

Consumer price 1993	255%	Lei per $ av. 1993	760.0
Av. ann. rate 1990–93	135%	Lei per ecu av. 1993	851.2

Balance of payments and debt

			$bn
Visible exports fob	4.0	Capital balance	...
Visible imports fob	6.0	Overall balance	...
Trade balance	-2.0	Change in reserves	...
Invisible inflows	...	Foreign debt	3.5
Invisible outflows	...	as % of GDP	15.9
Net transfers	...	Debt service	0.4
Current account balance	-1.1	Debt service ratio	11.1
as % of GDP	-6.1		

Principal exports*	$bn fob	Principal imports*	$bn cif
Manufactures	2.4	Fuels, minerals & metals	1.7
Machinery & equipment	0.9	Manufactures	1.6
Fuels, minerals & metals	0.5	Machinery & equipment	1.0
Foodstuffs	0.3	Total incl. others	5.5
Total incl. others	4.3		

Main export destinations	% of total	Main origins of imports	% of total
Germany	11.8	Germany	14.0
Russia	9.4	Russia	9.8
Italy	6.2	Italy	8.3
Turkey	5.1	Iran	7.9
Iran	2.8	France	6.1

Government

System Under a new constitution adopted in 1991 there is a bicameral legislature, with a Senate with 143 seats and a Chamber of Deputies with 341 seats. Deputies are elected for four years. The president is elected by direct universal suffrage for four years. He appoints the prime minister.

Main political parties Party of Social Democracy of Romania (PSDR), National Liberal Party, National Peasant-Christian Democratic Party, Hungarian Democratic Union of Romania, Romanian National Unity Party, Socialist Party of Labour

People

Population m	22.8	% under 15	23.1
Pop. per sq km	96	% over 65	10.1
% urban	53	No. men per 100 women	98
% av. ann. growth 1985–92	0.02	Human Development Index	71

Life expectancy	yrs		per 1,000 pop.
Men	68	Crude birth rate	14
Women	74	Crude death rate	10

Ethnic groups	% of total	Workforce	% of total
Romanian	89.1	Services	30.3
Hungarian	8.9	Industry	35.3
German	0.4	Agriculture	29.8
Other	1.6	Construction	4.6
		% unemployed	8.4

Society

No. households m	7.6	**Consumer goods ownership**	
Av. no. per household	2.9		% of households
Marriages per 1,000 pop.	8.3	TV	77
Divorces per 1,000 pop.	1.4	Video recorder	...
		Microwave oven	...

Household spending	% of total	Education	
Food/drink	31.0	Spending as % of GDP	2.1
Clothing	10.0	Years of compulsory education	10
Housing/energy	3.0	Enrolment ratios:	
Household goods	6.0	primary school	91
Health	4.0	secondary school	44
Transport/communications	4.0	tertiary education	9
Leisure/other	43.0		

Tourism		Health	
Tourist arrivals m	6.5	Pop. per doctor	560
Tourist receipts $bn	0.1	Pop. per hospital bed	112

a Convertible currency transactions only.

RUSSIA

Total area	17,075,400 sq km	Population	148.9m
GDP	$397.8bn	GDP per head	$2,670
Capital	Moscow	Other cities	St Petersburg, Nizhni-Novgorod

Russia and its capital, Moscow, were the super power-house of the Soviet Union. Today it remains the most powerful country in the region but since the collapse of the Union in 1991, Russia has stumbled from crisis to crisis. The instability is in many ways inevitable for such a great power reduced to admitting that it had been on the wrong track for more than eight decades. But an unstable Russia poses dangers for the whole region.

History: from imperial expansion to Marxism

The first Slav state on the territory of the former Soviet Union was the principality of Kievan Rus created in 862 in today's Ukraine. Other principalities were subsequently founded with Novgorod and eventually Muscovy (Moscow) becoming the dominant power. Eastern orthodox Christianity was adopted in 988. The Russian principalities were attacked by the Mongols in the 11th century and fully subjugated by 1240. Full liberation was not achieved until 1480 when Muscovy, ruled by Ivan III, managed to unite them against the common enemy. That provided the base for subsequent expansion of the Moscow state; when the first tsar (Caesar) Ivan IV (also known as Ivan the Terrible) died in 1582 it possessed territories stretching from the Caspian Sea to the Ural mountains. Ukraine was subjugated during the rule of Tsar Alexis in 1654. The moderniser Peter the Great conquered the Baltic territories after a protracted war with Sweden in the early 18th century, and during the reign of Catherine the Great there was major expansion, especially in the east. The 19th century saw an intensified interaction and rivalry with the Western powers.

While being part of the European culture Russia always pursued an independent path, partly because of its imperial interests in the East. It also lagged behind the West in its political and economic development. Serfdom was abolished only in 1861 and the tsars continued to rule in an autocratic fashion. Despite this some industrialisation and a rudimentary form of capitalism were established in the second half of the 19th century, and a (restricted) parliament was elected in 1905.

1917 and all that

The privations suffered by the Russian people during the

first world war led to the overthrow of the Romanov dynasty in March 1917. In November the Bolsheviks, a relatively small splinter of the Social Democratic Party, headed by Vladimir Iliych Lenin, staged a coup which eventually resulted in the restoration of the empire and its conversion into the Union of Soviet Socialist Republics (USSR) run along communist lines. In the 1930s Lenin's successor, Joseph Stalin, shifted the emphasis and created a highly centralised and repressive communist state. It involved rapid industrialisation and the collectivisation of agriculture. The new class of prosperous peasants which evolved after the Stolypin reforms of 1905–11 was completely destroyed. Serfdom was in effect reinstated; much of the industrial development was achieved by using slave labour from the prison camps set up by Stalin.

The burden of the Cold War

Buoyed by the spoils of the second world war, Stalin became even more repressive and extended Soviet influence deep into central Europe. Convinced of the natural superiority of the communist system he also pursued a policy of confrontation with the West, particularly the United States. An intense arms race developed with the accumulation of ridiculous numbers of nuclear weapons. The high point in the confrontation was reached during Leonid Brezhnev's period in office in the 1970s and early 1980s when Soviet influence stretched well into Africa and Latin America. Yet this was also a period of increasing co-operation with the West. The arms race was becoming too costly for both East and West, though it was the Soviet economy that was beginning to show signs of severe strain.

From the USSR to the CIS

Brezhnev died in 1982 after nearly two decades in power. He was succeeded by Yuri Andropov who died two years later. Konstantin Chernenko's period in power was even shorter. He died in 1985 and was replaced by Mikhail Gorbachev. He was convinced that the Soviet system had reached the end of the road and so sought to introduce political and economic reforms which, he believed, would bring new dynamism into the economy. It was a risky policy but Mr Gorbachev believed that it could be pursued without the Soviet Union plunging into chaos or disintegrating. He was proved wrong. Abroad his popularity rating soared. At home his policy of *glasnost* (openness) reforms unleashed a separatist surge and by 1990 it was clear that his policy of *perestroika* (restructuring) had failed. Crisis followed crisis. Mr Gorbachev responded by increasing the power of the presidency at the expense of parliament and the Communist Party. In August 1991 reactionary elements in Moscow attempted a coup. It failed but the result was a weaker Gorbachev, the end of Communist Party supremacy and the beginning of the break-up of the Union. Some had predicted that a looser federation would emerge. In fact the result was that all the republics became fully independent but most soon joined a Commonwealth of Independent States (CIS).

Russia alone

The dissolution of the Soviet Union in 1991 is often portrayed as the collapse of the Russian empire. This is misleading since Russia itself, under the charismatic Boris Yeltsin, desired independence from the Soviet regime imposed on it by the communist rulers. Indeed, the biggest nail in the USSR's coffin was the growing desire of the Russian government – a Moscow-based administration separate from the Kremlin – to divest itself of the economic and political burden of the Union. Boris Yeltsin was elected president of the newly independent Russia and started off with high hopes. But the economic and social aftershock of market reforms strengthened the hand of the conservatives who in 1993 occupied the parliament building. With the help of the army, Mr Yeltsin removed them by force and succeeded in getting a new constitution passed. But elections to the parliament resulted in defeat for the reformist parties, as extreme nationalists and communists did unexpectedly well. Liberal ministers such as Yegor Gaidar, architect of the economic reforms, resigned from the government.

Foreign policy: adjusting to new realities

As the largest successor state to the Soviet Union, Russia took over its role in world affairs, although with large rather than superpower status. Relations with the West remained on an even keel, continuing the accommodating course started by Mikhail Gorbachev. Russia undertook to comply with the nuclear disarmament treaties signed by the Soviet government. Then, in 1994, it signed a cooperation agreement with the EU and a partnership agreement with NATO. But Russia also had to strike a new relationship with the former Soviet republics. This was tricky because of the large Russian communities in these newly independent countries and their suspicion that Russia might revert to its old imperialist way. Relations were particularly tense with the Baltic republics where the sizeable Russian communities were discriminated against, and with Ukraine which also had a big nationalist Russian population. Several republics have found themselves drifting back into the Russian embrace since independence.

Society: mixed and divided

Russians account for about four-fifths of the population but there are over 100 different nationalities and ethnic groups in the country, the biggest of which live in the 21 autonomous regions. Cities grew rapidly in the wake of Soviet industrialisation. The Soviet system promoted a reasonable standard of education, especially in scientific and technical areas. Nominally, Russia compares well with some of the Western countries. The system also promoted social welfare with a minimum provision available to virtually every citizen. Since the move to a market economy, the safety net has been removed, racketeering and crime have taken off, and some Russians have become very rich indeed while ever increasing numbers find themselves in desperate poverty.

The economy: the times they are a changing

Russia is rich in mineral resources and in human potential. Its handicap is that its Soviet leaders left it with an economy dependent on worn-out, low-tech, energy-consumptive heavy industry manned by people who produced shoddy goods that no-one, given a free choice, wanted. Agriculture was just as inefficient; even when there were bumper harvests, huge imports were still required because much of the home-grown crop was wasted due to the failure to transport it to where it was needed.

One sector in which the Soviet Union was advanced was defence, and many of the high-tech skills of the defence industry have been redirected towards the development of non-defence industry.

The collapse of the Soviet Union plunged Russia into economic crisis and considerable disagreement about the shape and pace of economic reform needed to tackle it. Output slumped, inflation soared and the value of the currency dived. But by 1994, after a programme of privatisation and the liberalisation of prices in 1992, inflation was gradually coming down from a peak of 1,350% that year and there was at least some hope of recovery.

Total area	17,075,400 sq km	% agricultural area	...
Capital	Moscow	Highest point metres	Elbrus 5,642
Other cities	St Petersburg,	Main rivers	Yenisey, Lena, Ob,
	Nizhni-Novgorod		Amur, Volga

The economy

GDP $bn	397.8	GDP per head $	2,670
% av. ann. growth in		GDP per head in purchasing	
real GDP 1985–92	-4.1	power parity (USA=100)	37

Origins of GDP	% of total	Components of GDP	% of total
Agriculture	13	Private consumption	41
Industry	60	Public consumption	20
of which:		Investment	39
manufacturing	...	Exports	...
Services	39	Imports	...

Structure of manufacturing

			% of total
Agric. & food processing	...	Other	...
Textiles & clothing	...	Av. change in industrial	
Machinery & transport	...	output 1991–92	-21.0

Inflation and exchange rates

Consumer price 1993	940%	Rbl per $ end 1993	1,244
Av. ann. rate 1988–93	162.3%	Rbl per ecu end 1993	1,394

Balance of payments, reserves and aid

			$bn
Visible exports fob[a]	40.0	Capital balance	...
Visible imports fob[a]	35.0	Overall balance	...
Trade balance	5.0	Change in reserves	...
Invisible inflows	...	Debt	78.7
Invisible outflows	...	% GNP	...
Net transfers	...	Debt service ratio	1.6
Current account balance	-0.1		
as % of GDP	-0.7		

Principal exports[b]	$bn fob	Principal imports[b]	$bn cif
Fuels & raw materials	26.8	Machinery & equipment	13.7
Machinery & equipment	3.6	Food products	9.5
Chemicals & rubber	2.4	Chemicals & rubber	3.9
Consumer goods	1.6	Fuels & raw materials	2.1
Total incl. others	40.0	Total incl. others	35.0

Main export destinations	% of total	Main origins of imports	% of total
Germany	14.7	Germany	19.2
OECD countries	59.5	OECD countries	64.3
CMEA	20.0	CMEA	15.2

Government
System Under the constitution adopted in December 1993 Russia has a bicameral legislature which comprises the State Duma (lower house) with 450 deputies, and the Federation Council (upper house) with 178 deputies. The Council represents Russia's regions. The constitution gives strong powers to the president, who is elected directly for a five-year term. He appoints the prime minister, who also acts as president's deputy.

Main political parties Russia's Choice (RC), Democratic Party of Russia, the Communist Party of the Russian Federation, Agrarian Party, Liberal Democratic Party, Party of Russian Unity and Accord, Civic Union, the Yablokobloc

People

Population m	148.9	% under 15	23.2
Pop. per sq km	9	% over 65	11.2
% urban	74	No. men per 100 women	88[c]
% av. ann. growth 1985–91	0.5	Human Development Index	86

Life expectancy	yrs		per 1,000 pop.
Men	63	Crude birth rate	15
Women	74	Crude death rate	11

Ethnic groups	% of total	Workforce	% of total
Russian	81.5	Services	...
Tatars	3.0	Industry	...
Ukrainians	1.2	Agriculture	...
Others	14.3	% unemployed	...

Society

No. households m	68.7	**Consumer goods ownership**	
Av. no. per household	3.9		% of households
Marriages per 1,000 pop.	9.7	TV	45
Divorces per 1,000 pop.	3.4	Video recorder	...
		Microwave oven	...

Household spending	% of total	Education	
Food/drink	...	Spending as % of GNP	...
Clothing/footwear	...	Years of compulsory education	...
Housing/energy	...	Enrolment ratios:	
Household goods	...	primary school	...
Health	...	secondary school	...
Transport/communications	...	tertiary education	...
Leisure/other	...		

Tourism		Health	
Tourist arrivals m	7.2	Pop. per doctor	210
Tourist receipts $bn	0.3[b]	Pop. per hospital bed	72

a   Hard currency only.
b   To and from countries outside former Soviet Union.
c   Ex-Soviet Union.

SAN MARINO

This independent city state lies landlocked in central-east Italy. It was reputedly established in the 4th century by St Marinus and it secured papal recognition in 1631. After the Risorgimento in the mid-19th century, San Marino was the only one of the papal states not to join the new unified Italian state. However, it has had a friendship treaty with Italy since 1862.

Politics: left-wing coalitions

San Marino's political scene has been dominated by left-wing coalitions. In recent years the balance has shifted from Communists to Social Democrats, reflecting the collapse of communism in the Eastern bloc.

The economy: the Italian connection

San Marino maintains a customs union with Italy and uses the Italian lira next to its own currency. The economy is very closely linked with Italy's and the government receives an annual subsidy in return for accepting Italy's rules on foreign exchange and forgoing any income from customs duties. The country is mainly dependent on tourism but is trying to reduce this dependence by developing more light industry. Agriculture has become less important over recent decades but stone-quarrying remains an important activity.

Total area	60 sq km	Capital	San Marino

Government

System Two *capitani reggenti* (co-regents) act as joint heads of state and government. They are elected every six months by parliament from its own members. They exercise executive power through the Congress of State, which they head. The one-chamber Great and General Council has 60 members directly elected by a form of proportional representation for five years.

Main political parties Christian Democratic Party, Socialist Party, Communist Party, Progressive Democratic Party

People

Population '000	23	% under 15[a]	17.7
Pop. per sq km	377	% over 65[a]	12.8
% urban	90	No. men per 100 women	...

Life expectancy	yrs		per 1,000 pop.
Men	74	Crude birth rate[a]	8
Women	79	Crude death rate[a]	7

Ethnic groups	% of total		
Sammarinesi	84.9	Other	0.5
Italian	14.6		

Society

No. households m	...	Marriages per 1,000 pop.	8.7
Av. no. per household	...	Divorces per 1,000 pop.	1.0

Tourism		Health	
Tourist arrivals m	0.4	Pop. per doctor	375
Tourist receipts $bn	...	Pop. per hospital bed	150

a 1987.

SERBIA

The Serbs settled in the Balkans in the 6th century. They were converted to Christianity and fell under Byzantine suzerainty. Independence from Constantinople was established in 1187. After the death of King Dusan in 1355 Serbia gradually succumbed to Ottoman power. A major turning point – and one of the grievances of modern Serb nationalism – occurred in 1389 when the Serbs suffered a crushing defeat in the battle of Kosovo. Serbia was fully incorporated into the Ottoman empire by 1459. Full independence was not achieved until 1878. The kingdom of Serbia was attacked by Austro-Hungarian forces, which led to the outbreak of the first world war. After the collapse of the Austro-Hungarian empire in 1918 Serbia became the pillar of the kingdom renamed Yugoslavia in 1929. In 1941 Serbia was invaded by the Nazis despite an undertaking that it would support the Axis powers. After the war Serbia became the most powerful of the republics in the federation of Yugoslavia.

Politics: all-powerful Milosevic

The stability of post-war Yugoslavia rested on a delicate balance between the republics, in particular between Serbia and Croatia. Yet long-standing enmity soon resurfaced after Tito's death in 1980. Serbia began to assert itself and by 1985 the process of Yugoslavia's disintegration was well under way. It accelerated after Slobodan Milosevic became Communist Party leader in 1986. After taking an increasingly nationalist line, he was re-elected president in December 1992. His Socialist Party won the December 1993 parliamentary elections by a large margin, due to his hold over the media and intimidation of the opposition. His position was strengthened by the siege mentality that took hold after the imposition of the trade embargo in response to Serbia's role in the Bosnian war.

The economy: blown apart

Serbia's economy grew rapidly in the 1950s and 1960s under the impact of Tito's industrialisation policies. But in the 1970s it became clear that the wrong kind of industries had been built and that a major structural adjustment was needed. A large foreign debt was accumulated. The disintegration of Yugoslavia, the burden of the war in Croatia and Bosnia together with the international embargo resulted in a collapse of the Serbian economy. In 1993 the economy shrank by 35% and hyperinflation took hold.

| Total area | 102,350 sq km | Capital | Belgrade |

Government

System A new constitution was adopted in 1989. The single-chamber parliament, the Skupstina, has 250 members. The directly elected president appoints the prime minister.

Main political parties Socialist Party of Serbia (SPS, former communists), Serbian Radical Party (SRS), Party of Serbian Solidarity (SSJ), Democratic Party of Serbia (DSS), Serbian Renewal Movement (SPO)

People

Population m	10.64	% under 15	...
Pop. per sq km	104	% over 65	...
% urban	...	No. men per 100 women	...
% av. ann. growth 1985–92	...	Human Development Index	...

Life expectancy	yrs		per 1,000 pop.
Men	70	Crude birth rate	...
Women	75	Crude death rate	...

Ethnic groups	% of total	Workforce	% of total
Serbs	63	Services	...
Albanian	14	Industry	...
Montenegrin	6	Agriculture	...
Hungarian	4	Construction	...
		% unemployed	...

Health

| Pop. per doctor | ... | Pop. per hospital bed | ... |

Montenegro

Montenegro is a separate republic in what remains of the Federal Republic of Yugoslavia. A large minority in Montenegro want it to become fully independent but Serbia is keen to prevent this and may even seek to make Montenegro formally a province of Serbia.

SLOVAKIA

The area of today's Slovakia was part of a common Czech and Slovak state in the 9th century, but subsequently fell under Hungarian rule. Independence from Austria-Hungary was won with the foundation of Czechoslovakia in 1918, but Slovak aspirations for a fully independent state did not materialise until January 1993.

History: fact and fiction

Its incorporation into the kingdom of Hungary in the 11th century placed Slovakia on a separate path of development from that of the Czech lands. Paradoxically, Hungarian influence in Slovakia intensified after the establishment of dual Austro-Hungarian monarchy in 1867. Thus the history and political culture of the Czech and Slovak nations has diverged, and, although very close, Czech and Slovak are distinct languages. Yet the Czechoslovak republic established in 1918 was based on the fiction of "Czechoslovakism", according to which Slovaks were not considered a separate nation. The post-war communist Czechoslovakia maintained the unitary state until 1969 when Czech and Slovak republics were created under a federal structure.

Politics: starting anew

The first free elections were held in June 1990 and the constitution for the new parliamentary republic was passed in September 1992. The widely respected Michal Kovac was elected as the republic's first president. Yet independence has proved difficult and disillusionment with it has grown. Economic reforms have foundered and there has been a lack of stability, largely due to the confrontational style of the prime minister, Vladimir Meciar, who was forced to resign in March 1994 after a no-confidence vote in parliament. The presence of a 600,000-strong Hungarian minority has generated further tensions.

The economy: the rigours of transition

Communism has left Slovakia with an economy dependent on inefficient heavy industry. Output has collapsed in recent years and unemployment has risen sharply. Machinery and equipment, fuels, chemicals and raw materials are the main exports and about half of exports go to the EU, with which Slovakia has an association agreement. There is considerable tourist potential in the Tatras mountains but the general outlook for the economy is bleak.

Total area	49,035 sq km	Capital	Bratislava

Government

System A new constitution was adopted after the dissolution of Czechoslovakia. The legislature is the Slovak National Council. Its 150 deputies are elected on a proportional representation basis, with a 5% threshold. The president is elected by the Council.

Main political parties Movement for a Democratic Slovakia (MDS), Slovak National Party, Party of the Democratic Left (PSL, former communists), Christian Democratic Movement, Hungarian Christian Democrats (representing the Hungarian minority)

The economy

GDP $bn	10.2	GDP per head $	1,920
% av. ann. growth in real GDP 1985–92	...	GDP per head in purchasing power parity (USA=100)	...

Debt

Foreign debt	...	Debt service	...
as % of GDP	...	Debt service ratio	...

People

Population m	5.29	% under 15	20.9ª
Pop. per sq km	108	% over 65	12.1ª
% urban	78ª	No. men per 100 women	95ª
% av. ann. growth 1985–92	0.1ª	Human Development Index	89ª

Life expectancyª	yrs		per 1,000 pop.
Men	69	Crude birth rate	13
Women	76	Crude death rate	11

Ethnic groups	% of total	Workforce	% of total
...		Services	44
		Industry	33
		Agriculture	13
		Construction	10
		% unemployed	9.6

Health ª

Pop. per doctor	310	Pop. per hospital bed	127

a Former Czechoslovakia.

SLOVENIA

The Slavic tribe of Slovenes is known to have settled in the area of today's Slovenia in the 5th century. They were converted to Christianity and eventually integrated within the Habsburg empire. This left a deep Germanic imprint on Slovenia, though the Slovenes have preserved their Slavic identity and language. Since the early 19th century the Slovenes strove to unite the Slovene-populated provinces under one administrative unit within the Austrian empire. Realising this was unobtainable, they turned to strengthening links with other Slav nations in the Balkans, which led to Slovenian participation in the kingdom of Serbs, Croats and Slovenes created in 1918. However, the kingdom, renamed Yugoslavia in 1929, frustrated the aspirations of the Slovenes as it was dominated by the Serbs. It disintegrated in April 1941 when Slovenia was divided between Germany and Italy. Slovene communists played a leading part in wartime resistance and after the war the country became part of the Federal Republic of Yugoslavia, created by the Croatian communist leader, Josip Broz Tito.

Politics: escaping the federation

The fragile harmony among the Yugoslav republics began to crack soon after the death of Tito in 1980. The Slovenes became especially alarmed when Serbia terminated the autonomous status of the provinces of Vojvodina and Kosovo. Slovene nationalism grew and in September 1989 the Slovenian parliament proclaimed sovereignty. Full independence was declared two years later. A former communist, Milan Kucan, was elected president. Bitter, but brief, fighting with the federal army followed, but independence was sustained. Slovenia did not take part in the war which followed elsewhere. The political scene remained relatively stable.

The economy: comparatively advanced

Slovenia was the most advanced republic of the former Yugoslavia, with well-established manufacturing and tourism sectors. In 1990 it accounted for 20% of Yugoslavia's gross social product, while having only 8% of the federation's total population. On average productivity was twice as high as in Yugoslavia as a whole. After independence a rapid programme of market-oriented reforms was introduced, with the result that Slovenia has already started to recover from the disintegration of the federation.

Total area	20,296 sq km	Capital	Ljubljana

Government

System A new constitution was promulgated in 1991. Slovenia has a two-chamber legislature: the State Assembly, the lower house, has 90 members elected directly for a four-year term; the upper house is the 40-member State Council. The president is elected directly for a five-year term. He appoints the prime minister subject to consultations with parliament.

Main political parties Liberal Democrat Party (LDS), Slovene Christian Democratic Party (SKD), United List of Social Democrats, Slovene National Party, Slovene Christian Democratic Party, Greens of Slovenia

The economy

GDP $bn	12.7	GDP per head $	6,330
% av. ann. growth in real GDP 1985–92	...	GDP per head in purchasing power parity (USA=100)	...

Debt

Foreign debt	...	Debt service	...
as % of GDP	...	Debt service ratio	...

People and society

Population m	1.96	% under 15	...
Pop. per sq km	97	% over 65	...
% urban	...	No. men per 100 women	...
% av. ann. growth 1991–92	0.2	Human Development Index	...

Life expectancy	yrs		per 1,000 pop.
Men	70	Crude birth rate	...
Women	78	Crude death rate	...

Ethnic groups	% of total	Workforce	% of total
Slovene	91	Services	42.5
Croat	3	Industry	43.5
Serb	2	Agriculture	9.2
Muslim	1	Construction	4.8
Other	2	% unemployed	11.6

Health

Pop. per doctor	...	Pop. per hospital bed	...

SPAIN

Total area	504,782 sq km	Population	39.1m
GDP	$548bn	GDP per head	$14,022
Capital	Madrid	Other cities	Barcelona, Valencia, Seville

By casting away its fascist past and adopting the democratic norms of Western Europe, Spain has begun to exploit its human and economic potential. It may still be poorer than most countries in the European Union, but it has the energy and enthusiasm to catch up – and to overtake.

History: Romans, Muslims, kings and Franco

The Iberian peninsula was for centuries swept by migrations and invasions: the Celtic tribes of central Europe crossed the Pyrennean mountains in the 9th and 8th centuries BC; at the end of the 3rd century BC the Romans began a gradual process of colonisation; in the 5th century AD the German tribes arrived, with the Visigoths emerging as the dominant power and converting, by the early 7th century, the peninsula to Christianity; and in the early 8th century Moorish Arabs arrived from North Africa to set up an Umayyad dynasty distinguished by wealth and learning.

However, by the end of the 13th century the Moors had been driven back from most of the peninsula by the Christian kingdoms of Castile and Aragon. These were formally joined in 1479 as a consequence of the earlier marriage of Isabella of Castile and Ferdinand II of Aragon, and in 1492 Granada, the last Moorish stronghold, was reconquered.

Imperial riches

Spain then flexed its imperial muscles. The Atlantic crossing by Colombus in 1492 gave his Spanish patrons colonies in the Americas (the colonial reach soon embraced the globe, from North Africa to the Philippines); gold and silver came back from the New World by the galleon-load.

Meanwhile, the dynasties changed. The Habsburgs (whose origins were Germanic) ruled from 1516 to 1700, to be followed until 1870 by the Bourbons. But the change of dynasty sparked the War of the Spanish Succession (1701–14), in which Spain lost Belgium, Luxembourg, Milan, Naples and Sardinia. There was also an interruption to Bourbon rule when Napoleon Bonaparte in 1808 installed his brother Joseph as king (the Bourbons were restored to power in 1814 by joint British and Spanish action). However, the military action encouraged revolution within Spain's American colonies, and by 1898, with its defeat by the United States, Spain had lost all its overseas possessions.

Civil war: uncivil scars

The monarchy ended in 1931 with the election of a Republican-Socialist popular front and the abdication and exile of King Alfonso XIII. Five turbulent years later a rebel nationalist, General Francisco Franco, led a revolt against the Second Republic (the First had been a brief affair in 1873–74). The civil war was a bloody struggle not just of armies but of ideologies: the Republicans, supported by the Soviet Union, represented the progressive left; Franco's forces, supported by Hitler and Mussolini, represented fascism.

The Franco era

The outcome was victorious fascism and four decades of dictatorship under Franco. Only one party, the Falange (later called the Movement), was permitted; unions were government-organised; there was no universal suffrage; and the Cortes, or parliament, had only very limited powers.

For a time Spain was ostracised. After the second world war (in which the country was officially neutral), the United Nations approved an economic boycott and Spain was excluded from aid given to Europe in the Marshall Plan. But then the Cold War came to Spain's rescue. In 1953 President Eisenhower offered huge loans in return for the establishment of American bases in Spain; America signed a Treaty of Friendship and the UN boycott was lifted. There followed a period of rapid economic development into the 1970s. But while Franco lived there could, it seemed, be relatively little loosening of political controls.

Welcome democracy

The question was what to do after Franco's death in November 1975. The dictator had in 1969 chosen Alfonso XIII's grandson, Prince Juan Carlos of Bourbon, to be his successor, and on Franco's death he duly took his oath as king. But the restoration of the monarchy still left Spain's political future open to definition. Finally, in November 1976 the government of Adolfo Suarez brought in the Law of Political Reform, creating a bicameral parliament elected by universal suffrage. The following February was marked by the Law of Political Association, allowing political parties to be formed, and in April the Communist Party was legalised. In the same year free trade unions were authorised and in June 1977 Spain enjoyed its first free elections for 40 years.

The new Cortes embarked on a programme of political

and economic reform, with a referendum in 1978 approving a new constitution that repealed Franco's laws, guaranteed free enterprise and human rights, gave limited regional autonomy and ended the official status of the Roman Catholic Church. Democracy had arrived, not without challenge – witness the terrorism of the Basque separatists and an attempted military coup in 1981 – but surely to stay.

Politics: making the new republic

Spain has a system of proportional representation but as a check on the formation of coalitions for purely electoral purposes, no party may take seats in the Cortes unless it fought the election on an independent basis. As a check on the centralisation of power, considerable autonomy has been devolved to the country's 17 regions; the Basques and Catalans, for example, chose to elect their own parliaments in 1980, and the Galicians in 1981.

In the immediate aftermath of the Franco era, Spanish politics was dominated by the Union of the Democratic Centre (UCD), which in 1979 won 168 out of the lower house's 350 seats. But the UCD was crushed in the 1982 elections by the Socialists (PSOE), who during the Franco era had had to operate in secret. The Socialists, who discarded Marxism in the late 1970s, dominated Spain after the 1982 victory, with Felipe Gonzales proving a charismatic prime minister able to take tough economic decisions. However, the PSOE's popularity waned in the early 1990s; after the 1993 elections, when the conservative Popular Party came second, Mr Gonzales found himself leading a minority government.

Meanwhile, whatever the fortunes of the parties, King Juan Carlos has remained extraordinarily popular. One reason for this was his reaction to the 1981 coup attempt. While the lower house of parliament and the cabinet were being held hostage for 18 hours, the king bravely persuaded the rebels to surrender.

Foreign policy: part of democratic Europe

Although Spain's defence relationship with America survived the transition from fascism to democracy, in 1988 the United States was compelled to close down its air base at Torrejon and to rely instead on the Rota base near Cadiz. Spain's NATO membership dates from 1982, and was confirmed by a 52.2% referendum vote in 1986 which specifically maintained Spain's exclusion (decided by the Socialists in October 1982) from NATO's military structure.

Even so, Spain acts as an important member of the Western alliance: it joined the Western European Union in 1988 and sent troops in 1991 to counter the Iraqi invasion of Kuwait. Accession to the European Union had already been won in 1986. This membership came despite Spain's gentlemanly quarrel with Britain over the future of Gibraltar and arguments over fishing. Spain's fishing fleet is the largest in the EU and is seen by some countries as a threat to their own fish stocks.

Society: regional pride

The Spanish have always had regional identities, suppressed under Franco but now officially allowed to flourish. Although Castilians, Valencians, Andalusians and Asturians normally rejoice in a Spanish identity, the Catalans – some 16% of the population – have a fierce pride in their ethnic separateness. So too do the Basques, around 2% of the population, and at times the Galicians (8%). Indeed, ETA, a Basque separatist movement, has for decades waged a war of terror against the state. Although nine of out ten Spaniards are at least nominally Roman Catholic, the fertility rate has fallen to around 1.3 children per woman of childbearing age – one of the lowest rates in the world.

The economy: the drive to compete

Spain is one of the European Union's least developed countries, with a tenth of its workforce still in the agricultural sector (compared with two-fifths in 1960). As such it has benefited immensely from EU regional aid and the Common Agricultural Policy.

All this is accelerating a process of economic change that was already under way. During the 1960s and early 1970s the economy grew by around 9% a year, spurred both by industrialisation and a surge in foreign tourism. But the OPEC price rises of 1973–74 led to a decade of stagnation before membership of the European Union sparked a second period of fast growth.

But growth has not been without its pains. Throughout the late 1980s and early 1990s Spain has had to liberalise its industry and services to match foreign competition. The Gonzales government, keen to become a "first class" member of the EU, pursued a tight monetary policy to suppress inflation and stop public spending running out of control. But the policy proved too ambitious, and recession in 1992 provoked three devaluations of the peseta. These helped to restore competitiveness, but unemployment has soared.

Total area	504,782 sq km	% agricultural area	60.6
Capital	Madrid	Highest point metres	Mulhacen
Other cities	Barcelona,Valencia,		3,478
	Seville	Main rivers	Tagus (Tajo), Ebro,
		Duero, Guadiana, Guadalquivir	

The economy

GDP $bn	548	GDP per head $	14,022
% av. ann. growth in		GDP per head in purchasing	
real GDP 1985–92	3.5	power parity (USA=100)	57.3

Origins of GDP	% of total	Components of GDP	% of total
Agriculture	5	Private consumption	63
Industry	38	Public consumption	16
of which:		Investment	23
manufacturing	...	Exports	18
Services	57	Imports	-21

Structure of manufacturing
			% of total
Agric. & food processing	18	Other	48
Textiles & clothing	8	Av. ann. increase in industrial	
Machinery & transport	25	output 1985–92	1.6

Inflation and exchange rates
Consumer price 1993	4.6%	Pta per $ av. 1993	127.3
Av. ann. rate 1988–93	5.8%	Pta per ecu av. 1993	142.6

Balance of payments, reserves and aid
			$bn
Visible exports fob	63.9	Capital balance	6.4
Visible imports fob	-95.0	Overall balance	-17.5
Trade balance	-31.0	Change in reserves	-20.3
Invisible inflows	45.7	Level of reserves	
Invisible outflows	-39.0	end Dec.	49.7
Net transfers	5.8	Aid given	1.5
Current account balance	-18.5	as % of GDP	0.3
as % of GDP	-3.4		

Principal exports	$bn fob	Principal imports	$bn cif
Raw materials & intermediate		Raw materials & intermediate	
products (excl. fuels)	27.0	products (excl. fuels)	44.2
Non-food consumer goods	18.6	Non-food consumer goods	20.2
Capital goods	9.0	Capital goods	17.8
Food & drink, etc	8.2	Energy products	9.9
Total incl. others	63.9	Total incl. others	99.7

Main export destinations	% of total	Main origins of imports	% of total
France	19.0	France	16.8
Germany	15.0	Germany	15.6
Italy	9.3	Italy	9.0
UK	8.4	UK	7.6
USA	4.7	USA	6.8

Government

System The monarch is head of state. The head of government, appointed by the monarch but responsible to parliament, is the president of the government (prime minister). The two-chamber parliament, the Cortes, comprises the 254-member Senate (208 directly elected and 45 appointed as regional representatives) and the 350-member Congress of Deputies, elected by a form of proportional representation, both for four years. There are 17 autonomous communities (regions) with their own parliaments.

Main political parties Spanish Socialist Workers' Party (PSOE), Popular Party (PP), United Left (IU), including Comunist Party (PCE), Democratic and Social Centre (CDS); regional: Convergence and Unity (CIU, Catalan), Basque National Party (PNV, Basque), Herri Batasuna (HB, Basque)

People

Population m	39.1	% under 15	17.1
Pop. per sq km	78	% over 65	14.7
% urban	79	No. men per 100 women	97
% av. ann. growth 1985–92	0.2	Human Development Index	92

Life expectancy	yrs		per 1,000 pop.
Men	75	Crude birth rate	11
Women	81	Crude death rate	9

Ethnic groups*	% of total	Workforce	% of total
Spanish	72.3	Services	48.0
Catalan	16.3	Industry	32.2
Galician	8.1	Agriculture	10.1
Basque	2.3	Construction	9.7
		% unemployed	18.4

Society

No. households m	14.6	**Consumer goods ownership**	
Av. no. per household	2.5		% of households
Marriages per 1,000 pop.	5.6	TV	98
Divorces per 1,000 pop.	0.2	Video recorder	40
		Microwave oven	9

Household spending	% of total	Education	
Food/drink	24.0	Spending as % of GDP	5.0
Clothing/footwear	7.0	Years of compulsory education	8
Housing/energy	16.0	Enrolment ratios:	
Household goods	6.0	primary school	109
Health	7.0	secondary school	107
Transport/communications	14.0	tertiary education	34
Leisure/other	21.0		

Tourism		Health	
Tourist arrivals m	34.3	Pop. per doctor	280
Tourist receipts $bn	18.6	Pop. per hospital bed	208

a Classified by ethno-linguistic composition.

SWEDEN

Total area	449,964 sq km	Population	8.7m
GDP	$233bn	GDP per head	$26,784
Capital	Stockholm	Other cities	Gothenburg, Malmo, Uppsala

The Swedes enjoy one of the highest standards of living in the world and the highest in Scandinavia. Long experienced in democracy and neutral through the two world wars, they have enjoyed peace with political stability. A sophisticated welfare system has gone hand in hand with high economic growth, but in recent years Swedes have realised that the two may no longer be compatible.

History: a once great power

After more than a century under Danish rule, Sweden became independent again in the 16th century under Gustavus Vasa who established Lutheranism as the state religion in 1527. The Vasa line ruled until 1818 when the French Marshal Bernadotte, the first of the present line, ascended the throne. During the 16th and 17th centuries Sweden made extensive territorial gains which gave it control of the Baltic and made it one of the great powers in Europe. But overambition led to defeat and the collapse of its Baltic empire in the early part of the 18th century. Sweden later lost Finland to Russia in 1809, but the Congress of Vienna a few years later confirmed the transfer of Norway from Denmark to Sweden, a union that lasted until 1905.

Politics: Social Democrats have dominated

Between 1932 and 1976 the Social Democrats headed every government, ruling in coalition for only nine of those years. In 1982, after six years of disenchanting non-socialist rule, they were returned to power which, with the help of the Communists and later the Greens, they managed to hold on to until the 1991 elections when, despite remaining the largest party, a centre-right coalition took over. But many expected that this aberration from the Social Democratic norm would not last long.

Foreign policy: tradition of neutrality

Unlike other Scandinavian countries, Sweden maintained its neutrality during the second world war. It has remained neutral ever since and is therefore not a member of NATO. It was a founder member of EFTA and in 1991 applied to join the European Union. Negotiations on the terms of accession were concluded in 1994 with agreement that Sweden would become a member of the EU at the beginning of 1995. Accession was to be subject to a referendum.

The economy: slow progress

Sweden has a broad industrial base, which evolved from its natural resources of forests, iron ore and water power. Pulp and paper products, metallurgy, motor vehicles, engineering and high technology are all important. Other key minerals include copper, zinc and uranium. But Sweden is heavily dependent on imported oil. Some 85% of business is in the private sector; the government has stopped bailing out the unviable and state industries are being given management autonomy. In 1991 Sweden entered its most severe post-war recession: in 1991 GDP fell by 1.1%; in 1992 it fell by 1.3%. The result of poor economic growth has been a virtual stagnation of living standards.

Whittling down the costs of welfare

The main political debate in recent years has been about the size and cost of the public sector. In 1960 the public sector was about the average for the OECD, accounting for 31% of GDP. But in the 1970s public-sector spending as a proportion of GDP grew much faster than elsewhere and by 1982 was 66% of GDP. Swedish public-sector spending has since remained the largest in the OECD and was 70% in 1993, although half of that was made up of transfers back to the private sector.

Emphasising the market

Among the tasks the centre-right coalition set itself on assuming government in 1991 were the encouragement of the private sector and the development of a more market-driven economy. It succeeded in reducing labour costs which helped employers. Nonetheless, by the beginning of 1994 its reforms had barely dented the welfare state and the budget deficit, at 13% of GDP, was one of the highest in the OECD. But the economy was expected to pick up, which in conjunction with lower interest rates and a relaunch of the privatisation programme will help reduce the budget deficit. It was also accepted that public-sector reforms would continue, even if slowly. Swedes may continue to demand sophisticated social services as before, but the way those services are provided will change.

Total area	449,964 sq km	% agricultural area	7.9
Capital	Stockholm	Highest point metres	
Other cities	Gothenburg, Malmö,		Kebnekaise 2,111
	Uppsala	Main rivers	Ume, Torne, Ångerman

The economy

GDP $bn	233	GDP per head $	26,784
% av. ann. growth in		GDP per head in purchasing	
real GDP 1985–92	1.2	power parity (USA=100)	79.0

Origins of GDP	% of total	Components of GDP	% of total
Agriculture	3	Private consumption	54
Industry	28	Public consumption	28
of which:		Investment	17
manufacturing	23	Exports	28
Services	69	Imports	-26

Structure of manufacturing

			% of total
Agric. & food processing	10	Other	56
Textiles & clothing	2	Av. ann. increase in industrial	
Machinery & transport	32	output 1985–92	-1.0

Inflation and exchange rates

Consumer price 1993	4.7%	SKr per $ av. 1993	7.78
Av. ann. rate 1988–93	6.5%	SKr per ecu av. 1993	9.11

Balance of payments, reserves and aid

			$bn
Visible exports fob	55.4	Capital balance	7.4
Visible imports fob	-48.5	Overall balance	7.1
Trade balance	6.9	Change in reserves	4.3
Invisible inflows	25.3	Level of reserves	
Invisible outflows	-34.7	end Dec.	22.9
Net transfers	-2.5	Aid given	2.5
Current account balance	-4.9	as % of GDP	1.0
as % of GDP	-2.1		

Principal exports	$bn fob	Principal imports	$bn cif
Machinery incl. electric	15.6	Machinery incl. electric	13.0
Wood products, pulp & paper	9.7	Chemicals	5.3
Transport equipment	8.4	Transport equipment	5.0
Chemicals	5.1	Mineral fuels	4.3
Iron & steel	3.2	Food & agric. products	3.6
Total incl. others	57.2	Total incl. others	51.8

Main export destinations*	% of total	Main origins of imports*	% of total
Germany	15.0	Germany	18.5
UK	9.7	USA	8.8
Norway	8.4	UK	8.6
USA	8.3	Denmark	7.8
Denmark	7.2	Norway	6.9

Government

System The monarch is the ceremonial head of state, without any executive role. Executive power is exercised by a cabinet headed by a prime minister who is responsible to the legislature. The one-chamber Riksdag (parliament) has 349 members elected by a form of proportional representation for three years (310 by constituency and the remainder apportioned to contending parties on the basis of votes received nationally).

Main political parties Social Democratic Labour Party, Conservative Party, Liberal Party, Centre Party, Moderate Unity Party, New Democrats, Ecology Party, Christian Democrats

People

Population m	8.7	% under 15	18.8
Pop. per sq km	19	% over 65	17.4
% urban	84	No. men per 100 women	98
% av. ann. growth 1985–92	0.6	Human Development Index	98

Life expectancy	yrs		per 1,000 pop.
Men	75	Crude birth rate	14
Women	81	Crude death rate	12

Ethnic groups	% of total	Workforce	% of total
Swedish	95.3	Services	70.2
Finnish	1.7	Industry	20.2
Other Scandinavian	0.6	Agriculture	3.2
Yugoslav	0.5	Construction	6.4
		% unemployed	4.8

Society

No. households m	3.8	**Consumer goods ownership**	
Av. no. per household	2.2		% of households
Marriages per 1,000 pop.	4.7	TV	97
Divorces per 1,000 pop.	2.2	Video recorder	48
		Microwave oven	37

Household spending	% of total	Education	
Food/drink	13.0	Spending as % of GDP	5.7
Clothing/footwear	5.0	Years of compulsory education	9
Housing/energy	19.0	Enrolment ratios:	
Household goods	7.0	primary school	107
Health	11.0	secondary school	91
Transport/communications	11.0	tertiary education	33
Leisure/other	21.0		

Tourism		Health	
Tourist arrivals m	0.8	Pop. per doctor	370
Touris receipts $bn	2.9	Pop. per hospital bed	161

SWITZERLAND

Total area	41,293 sq km	Population	6.7m
GDP	$249bn	GDP per head	$36,231
Capital	Berne	Other cities	Zurich, Basel, Geneva

Although geographically at the heart of Western Europe, the Swiss – who enjoy the highest income per head in the world – prefer to remain somewhat separate from other countries in the region. Their neutrality in both world wars benefited the Swiss economy enormously and has helped strengthen these isolationist tendencies.

History: canton confederation

In 1991 Switzerland celebrated the 700th anniversary of the pact between the people of the three valley communities from which the present Swiss Confederation (Confederatio Helvetica) evolved. The region became part of the Holy Roman Empire in the 11th century and achieved virtual independence within the empire in the late 15th century. The Reformation of the early 16th century brought religious wars as some parts of Switzerland embraced Calvinism, while the more rural districts remained faithful to Roman Catholicism. Complete independence from Habsburg control was finally recognised by the Treaty of Westphalia in 1648. (None of the Swiss cantons had joined in the Thirty Years' War that treaty ended.) Having been allied to royalist France since 1777, Switzerland was invaded by French revolutionary forces in 1798 and a centralised republic was created. But this was later modified by Napoleon in 1803 when the cantons were given back their powers. Following a brief and almost bloodless civil war, a new constitution was introduced in 1848. It gave considerable power to central government and the parliament but also guaranteed the cantons' rights in important areas. Revisions to the constitution in 1874 increased federal powers but also introduced the principle of the referendum. The country industrialised rapidly in the 19th century and by 1850 was considered the second most industrialised nation in Europe after Britain.

Politics: changing reluctantly

A remarkable degree of consensus has given Swiss politics considerable stability despite the existence of four distinct language communities: German, French, Italian and Romanisch. The country is organised along federal, cantonal and communal lines.

The federal government is responsible for foreign policy,

defence, pensions, post, telecommunications, railways and the currency. Anything not in the hands of the federal government is in principle the responsibility of the cantons. Each canton comprises numerous communes, varying greatly in size, which also have certain political responsibilities. The 3,000 or more communes lie at the heart of the Swiss federation. They generally carry out cantonal directions but also levy their own income taxes and provide amenities such as water. The holding of referendums has ensured that the people have a strong influence on government. The use of referendums has increased in recent years while the turnout of those voting in them has, with a few exceptions, fallen to below 30%.

The political system gives all major parties a share in government. The resulting coalitions have a tendency to favour a conservative line. A brief shift to the left, brought about by the oil price crisis in 1973, was reversed at the beginning of the 1980s.

Foreign policy: no end to neutrality?

Switzerland's policy of neutrality has made it a popular place for the headquarters of international agencies such as the Red Cross and the Bank for International Settlements. It has only observer status at the UN and in a 1986 referendum voted by three to one against joining. UN membership has been declared to be a priority for the 1990s, though opinion polls continue to show hostility to the idea. A new flexibility in foreign policy was indicated by the decision to support UN sanctions against Iraq in 1990 and against Libya and Serbia in 1992, the year it became a member of the IMF and the World Bank. In 1991 it signed up for the EEA, but membership was rejected in a 1992 referendum. Nonetheless, the government reaffirmed its desire to join the European Union.

The economy: secrecy and skills

Lacking raw materials, Switzerland's economic prosperity has been based on labour skills (though it depends heavily on foreign workers to supplement its workforce) and technological expertise in manufacturing as well as earnings from services. Strengths include pharmaceuticals, watches and precision instruments, engineering, food, financial services (helped by laws that allow banking secrecy) and tourism. Exports account for roughly one-third of GDP. The early 1990s saw the Swiss economy in the doldrums and unemployment rising. An upturn was expected in 1994.

Total area	41,293 sq km	% agricultural area	48.9
Capital	Berne	Highest point metres Dufourspitze	
Other cities	Zürich, Basle, Geneva		4,634
		Main rivers	Rhine (Rhein), Aare, Rhône, Inn, Ticino

The economy

GDP $bn	249	GDP per head $	36,231
% av. ann. growth in		GDP per head in purchasing	
real GDP 1985–92	2.3	power parity (USA=100)	98.4

Origins of GDP	% of total	Components of GDP	% of total
Agriculture	4	Private consumption	61
Industry	35	Public consumption	15
of which:		Investment	28
manufacturing	25	Exports	43
Services	62	Imports	-45

Structure of manufacturing   % of total

Agric. & food processing	...	Other	...
Textiles & clothing	...	Av. ann. increase in industrial	
Machinery & transport	...	output 1985–92	2.6

Inflation and exchange rates

Consumer price 1993	3.3%	SFr per $ av. 1993	1.48
Av. ann. rate 1988–93	3.9%	SFr per ecu av. 1993	1.65

Balance of payments, reserves and aid $bn

Visible exports fob	78.6	Capital balance	-8.7
Visible imports fob	-78.9	Overall balance	4.4
Trade balance	-0.3	Change in reserves	4.3
Invisible inflows	46.9	Level of reserves	
Invisible outflows	-30.2	end Dec.	41.4
Net transfers	-2.9	Aid given	1.1
Current account balance	13.4	as % of GDP	0.5
as % of GDP	5.4		

Principal exports	$bn fob	Principal imports	$bn cif
Machinery	18.1	Machinery	13.0
Chemicals	15.2	Chemicals	8.2
Precision instruments,		Precision instruments,	
watches & jewellery	13.6	watches & jewellery	7.4
Metals & metal manufactures	5.5	Automobiles	7.1
Total incl. others	65.8	Total incl. others	66.0

Main export destinations	% of total	Main origins of imports	% of total
Germany	23.4	Germany	33.4
France	9.5	France	10.8
Italy	8.8	Italy	10.0
USA	8.5	USA	6.4
UK	6.6	UK	5.8

Government
System The president of the Federal Council is head of state, elected for one year by the parliament from members of the Federal Council (cabinet). This seven-member council, elected for four years by parliament, exercises executive power. The two-chamber Federal Assembly comprises the 200-member National Chamber directly elected by proportional representation for four years, and the 46-member National Council representing the cantons. Each of the cantons has its own parliament and government.
Main political parties Radical Democratic Party (RDP), Social Democratic Party (SDP), Christian Democratic Party (CDP), Swiss People's Party (PP), Liberal Party, Green Party, Independent Alliance

People
Population m	6.7	% under 15	17.1
Pop. per sq km	188	% over 65	15.1
% urban	60	No. men per 100 women	96
% av. ann. growth 1985–92	0.9	Human Development Index	98

Life expectancy	yrs		per 1,000 pop.
Men	76	Crude birth rate	13
Women	81	Crude death rate	10

Ethnic groups[a]	% of total	**Workforce**	% of total
German	65	Services	60.5
French	18	Industry	24.7
Italian	10	Agriculture	5.6
Other	7	Construction	9.2
		% unemployed	1.1

Society
No. households m	2.8	**Consumer goods ownership**	
Av. no. per household	2.3		% of households
Marriages per 1,000 pop.	6.9	TV	93
Divorces per 1,000 pop.	1.9	Video recorder	41
		Microwave oven	15

Household spending	% of total	**Education**	
Food/drink	17.0	Spending as % of GDP	5.1
Clothing/footwear	4.0	Years of compulsory education	9
Housing/energy	17.0	School enrolment ratios:	
Household goods	…	primary	…
Health	15.0	secondary	…
Transport/communications	9.0	tertiary	26
Leisure/other	38.0		

Tourism		**Health**	
Tourist arrivals m	13.2	Pop. per doctor	630
Tourist receipts $bn	6.8	Pop. per hospital bed	91

a Classified by ethno-linguistic composition.

TURKEY

Total area	779,452 sq km	Population	58.5m
GDP	$114bn	GDP per head	$1,954
Capital	Ankara	Other cities	Istanbul, Izmir, Adana, Bursa

Modern Turkey remains strategically important, straddling the borders of Western Europe, the former Soviet Union and the Middle East, and it is a member of the OECD, the rich nation's club. But for all that it is a poor country with considerable problems.

History: rise and fall of Ottoman empire

The Seljuk Turks, who adopted Islam in the 7th century, settled in Anatolia in the 11th century. The Ottoman Turks began their rise under Osman I in the late 13th century. After overrunning Asia Minor they moved into Europe. By the late 15th century they had control of the Balkans. By the mid-16th century their empire had expanded to include Egypt, Syria, Arabia, Mesopotamia, Tripoli and most of Hungary. Cyprus and Crete were added later but towards the end of the 17th century the Turks were defeated at Vienna and lost Hungary. The decline of the empire had begun. By 1913 most of it had gone. By the end of the first world war, in which Turkey fought on the side of Germany, the territories in the Middle East had been lost too. Under the Treaty of Sevres (1920) Greece was given Izmir. But the treaty was repudiated by the provisional government set up under Mustapha Kemal (who later took the surname Ataturk). His forces expelled the Greeks in 1922, the year that the last sultan was deposed and the sultanate abolished. The Treaty of Lausanne, signed in 1923, restored eastern Thrace and Izmir to Turkey. The country was declared a republic with Ataturk as president and Ankara the capital. In theory it was a parliamentary democracy. In practice it was run by Ataturk's Republican People's Party (RPP). Ataturk died in 1938; the party ruled on. Turkey's first multi-party elections did not take place until after the second world war.

Politics: interrupted democracy

The Democrat Party (DP) under Adnan Menderes crushed the RPP in the 1950 elections. Menderes cultivated the rural communities but antagonised the urban groups. Additionally the economy was running out of control, with inflation and debt levels booming. In an attempt to control the opposition, Menderes imposed martial law. However, some parts of the army were not prepared to support him and he was overthrown in 1960. In 1961 the army withdrew from government and under the system of proportional representation that was introduced Turkey experienced 18 governments in 19 years. By 1980 the instability was such that political violence was claiming some 20 lives a day and there was another coup. In 1982 a new constitution was agreed and elections took place the following year. Turgut Ozal's centre-right Motherland Party won both the 1983 and 1987 elections but in 1991 it was beaten into second place by another centre-right party, the True Path Party, which formed a coalition with the Social Democrat Populist Party. In 1993 Tansu Ciller replaced prime minister Demirel. Although personally popular, by 1994 dissatisfaction with Turkey's first female premier's inability to bring inflation down or solve the Kurdish problem was growing.

Foreign policy: leaning West

Although neutral from 1924 to 1944, Turkey has allied itself with the West since 1947 and in 1952 joined NATO. It has an association agreement with the EU but its application in 1987 for full membership met with a lukewarm reception. One obstacle to membership is Turkey's age-old rivalry with Greece and in particular the issue of northern Cyprus. Another is its treatment of the Kurdish minority in the south-east. The break-up of the Soviet Union removed the major threat to Turkey's security but the unsettled state of the newly independent republics on its borders has brought new problems.

The economy: in need of restructuring

Since 1960 there has been a marked shift from agriculture to industry. After high growth of respectively 8.1% and 7.5% in 1986 and 1987, GDP grew by only 3.6% in 1988 and 1.6% in 1989. In 1990 there was a marked recovery but in 1991, with uncertainties in the Gulf after Iraq's invasion of Kuwait, growth was minimal. Since then the economy has been growing at a reasonable rate, though 1994 saw a slow-down. Structural problems remain which contribute to such problems as controlling the budget deficit (15% of GDP in 1994) and inflation (70% by the end of 1993). The government is now going for the highest possible growth: a risky policy, but one that worked in the mid-1980s.

Total area	779,452 sq km	% agricultural area	46.6
Capital	Ankara	Highest point metres	
Other cities	Istanbul, Izmir, Adana		Mt Ararat 5,165
		Main rivers	Euphrates (Firat),
			Tigris (Dicle), Kizilirmak

The economy

GDP $bn	114	GDP per head $	1,954
% av. ann. growth in		GDP per head in purchasing	
real GDP 1985–92	5.0	power parity (USA=100)	21.9

Origins of GDP	% of total	Components of GDP	% of total
Agriculture	18	Private consumption	60
Industry	34	Public consumption	19
of which:		Investment	24
manufacturing	24	Exports	20
Services	49	Imports	-23

Structure of manufacturing
% of total

Agric. & food processing	16	Other	54
Textiles & clothing	14	Av. ann. increase in industrial	
Machinery & transport	17	output 1985–92	...

Inflation and exchange rates

Consumer price 1993	66.0%	Lira per $ av. 1993	10,985
Av. ann. rate 1988–93	66.5%	Lira per ecu av. 1993	12,303

Balance of payments and debt
$bn

Visible exports fob	14.9	Capital balance	3.6
Visible imports cif	-23.1	Overall balance	1.5
Trade balance	-8.2	Change in reserves	1.0
Invisible inflows	10.5	Level in reserves end Dec.	7.7
Invisible outflows	-7.3	Foreign debt	54.8
Net transfers	4.1	as % of GDP	50.6
Current account balance	-0.9	Debt service	9.1
as % of GDP	-0.8	Debt service ratio	31.9

Principal exports	$bn fob	Principal imports	$bn cif
Textiles	4.6	Machinery & apparatus	5.9
Iron & steel	1.5	Crude oil	2.6
Hides & leather	0.5	Metals	2.1
Food	0.4	Chemicals	0.9
Total incl. others	14.9	Total incl. others	23.1

Main export destinations	% of total	Main origins of imports	% of total
Germany	24.9	Germany	16.4
Italy	6.4	USA	11.4
USA	5.9	Italy	8.4
France	5.5	Saudia Arabia	7.3
UK	5.4	Japan	5.2

Government

System The president, as head of state, is elected by parliament for seven years. The cabinet, headed by the prime minister, is appointed by the president. The one-chamber Meclis (Grand National Assembly) has 450 members directly elected for five years.

Main political parties Motherland Party (Anap), Social Democrat Populist Party (SHP), True Path Party (DYP), Democratic Left Party (DLP), Welfare Party (Islamic), National Endeavour Party (neo-fascist)

People

Population m	58.5	% under 15	33.7
Pop. per sq km	80	% over 65	4.8
% urban	63	No. men per 100 women	106
% av. ann. growth 1985-92	2.2	Human Development Index	72

Life expectancy	yrs		per 1,000 pop.
Men	65	Crude birth rate	28
Women	70	Crude death rate	7

Ethnic groups	% of total	Workforce	% of total
Turkish	80	Services	32.0
Kurd	17	Industry	17.6
Other	3	Agriculture	45.0
		Construction	5.4
		% unemployed	7.8

Society

No. households m	9.6	**Consumer goods ownership**	
Av. no. per household	5.6		% of households
Marriages per 1,000 pop.	7.9	TV	...
Divorces per 1,000 pop.	0.4	Video recorder	...
		Microwave oven	...

Household spending	% of total	Education	
Food/drink	40.0	Spending as % of GDP[a]	1.8
Clothing/footwear	15.0	Years of compulsory education	5
Housing/energy	13.0	Enrolment ratios:	
Household goods	...	primary school	110
Health	4.0	secondary school	54
Transport/communications	5.0	tertiary education	14
Leisure/other	23.0		

Tourism		Health	
Tourist arrivals m	4.8	Pop. per doctor	1,260
Tourist receipts $bn	3.3	Pop. per hospital bed	476

a Expenditure on tertiary education excluded.

UKRAINE

The roots of Ukrainian statehood go back to the principality of Kievan Rus, which in the 9th century became the first Russian state. After the subjugation of Russian principalities by the Mongols in the 13th and 14th centuries, Ukrainians pursued a separate path, being influenced mainly by their conquerors, Poland and Lithuania. In the 17th century most of Ukraine was annexed by Russia, with more territory being ceded a century later. Ukraine was part of the core of the Soviet Union, and when it moved towards independence in mid-1991 the Union's days were numbered. But Ukraine has failed to build a credible independent state and has edged back into the Russian embrace.

Politics: the travails of independence

In 1991 the push for independence was spearheaded by the former communist boss, Leonid Kravchuk, who was elected the country's president in December that year. But Ukraine's experiment with independence has not been a success. Former communist officialdom refused to implement the radical reforms needed to revitalise the stagnant economy, and the 1994 elections failed to clear the way for such reforms. Part of the reason for the intransigence was a fear of a split in the country between the nationalist west and the mainly Russian-inhabited, heavily industrialised, eastern provinces, which would be vulnerable to market reforms. Another problem has been the secessionist movements in the mainly Russian-inhabited Crimean peninsula, given to Ukraine by Khrushchev in 1954. Ukraine has also clashed with Russia over the ownership of the former Soviet Black Sea Fleet. Ukraine is one of four former Soviet republics with nuclear missiles, although it has committed itself to transfer them to Russia for dismantling.

The economy: deep trouble

The failure to get to grips with economic reform has led the economy into deeper and deeper trouble. National income fell by 12% in 1992. By mid-1993 the budget deficit had reached 40% of GDP, inflation had soared to well over 50% a month, and the currency, the karbovanets, was in virtual freefall. In 1994, because Ukraine could not pay for the oil and gas it depends on, Russia threatened to cut supplies and demanded the transfer of assets in payment.

Total area	603,700 sq km	Capital	Kiev

Government

System Ukraine has yet to adopt its post-Soviet constitution, though the Soviet-style parliament, the Supreme Soviet, has been renamed the Supreme Council. The president, elected by direct vote, is executive head of government, with the right to appoint the prime minister.

Main political parties Socialist Party of Ukraine (SPU), Communist Party of Ukraine (CPU), Rukh (nationalist party), Congress of National Democratic Forces, Ukrainian Social Democratic Party, Green Party of Ukraine

The economy

GDP $bn	87.0	GDP per head $	1,670
% av. ann. growth		GDP per head in purchasing	
in real GDP 1985–92	...	power parity (USA=100)	23.4

Debt

Foreign debt $m	415.3	Debt service $m	5
as % of GDP	...	Debt service ratio	...

People and society

Population m	52.1	% under 15	21.2
Pop. per sq km	86	% over 65	13.2
% urban	67	No. men per 100 women	106
% av. ann. growth 1985–92	0.3	Human Development Index	84

Life expectancy	yrs		per 1,000 pop.
Men	65	Crude birth rate	14
Women	75	Crude death rate	12

Ethnic groups	% of total	Health	
Ukrainian	73	Pop. per doctor	230
Russian	22	Pop. per hospital bed	74
Other	5		

UNITED KINGDOM

Total area	244,046 sq km	Population	57.7m
GDP	$1,025bn	GDP per head	$17,760
Capital	London	Other cities	Manchester, Birmingham, Leeds

Geography has had a great effect on Britain's history and character. An island people, the British have been both the most inward looking and the most international of the world's great nations. After winning two world wars but losing an empire, Britain is still struggling to find its place in the international pecking order.

History: from conquered to conqueror

Julius Caesar's expeditionary forces landed in Britain in 55BC, though the Romans did not invade and conquer until 43AD in the reign of Claudius. The Romans finally left in 426 after raids by the Angles and Saxons, two Germanic tribes which drove the indigenous Celts out of England and into the mountains of Wales and Scotland. This clash can still be traced in the British identity today, which is dominated by Anglo-Saxon pragmatism but leavened by Celtic imagination and eloquence.

For the next 1,000 years British history was turbulent. Divided into warring kingdoms and invaded repeatedly by Vikings, Britain achieved a fleeting unity after William the Conqueror's successful invasion in 1066 – the last in British history – established the Norman monarchy. And yet Britain remained restive under the Normans, who were more concerned with their holdings in France. Dynastic struggles reached their apogee in the Wars of the Roses in the 15th century, from which Henry Tudor emerged with the crown. His son, Henry VIII, ruled with an iron fist, breaking with the Roman Catholic Church, despoiling the monasteries and establishing Protestantism in England. His daughter, Elizabeth I, gave her name to an age in which literature and the arts flourished, and the beginnings of a vast empire were established

The Puritan revolution

Elizabeth's successor, James VI of Scotland, became James I of England, uniting the two countries and so creating, for the first time, the United Kingdom as it still survives today (Wales had been incorporated in the 13th century). But it took another 85 years to lay the foundations of the modern British state. In 1649 James's son, Charles I, lost his crown and his head to Puritan revolutionaries after a bitter civil war and Oliver Cromwell set up a republic. After Cromwell's death, Charles II returned from France to re-establish the monarchy, but it was only after the peaceful "Glorious Revolution" of 1688, with the deposition of the Catholic James II and the invitation to William of Orange, a Dutch Protestant, to take the crown, that the rights (and so eventually the sovereignty) of Parliament were firmly established.

World power house

In the 18th century Britain pioneered two developments which were to help transform the world in the 19th century: it founded a global empire based on trade and conquest and it began the industrial revolution. It also engaged in a long rivalry with France, which culminated in Wellington's victory over Napoleon at Waterloo in 1815. After that, Britain's rapid industrialisation made it the world's most powerful economy. Under Queen Victoria's long reign (1837–1901), Britain became a society of haves and have-nots, but avoided the revolutions and political turmoil of continental countries with a combination of gradual political reforms, which extended the voting franchise, and the acceptance of trade unions, which gave the working class both a voice and a stake in the existing order.

Winning the wars, losing the peace

Though Britain was on the winning side in the first world war, the horrendous number of young men killed shattered the nation's self-confidence, a blow from which it has never really recovered. That war also made clear that Britain had lost its pre-eminent economic position. The 1920s and 1930s were decades of drift and stagnation. The shared sacrifices of the second world war restored Britain's spirits, but signalled the unmistakable demise of its empire. At the war's end in 1945, the Labour Party won a surprise victory over Winston Churchill's Conservatives. The first Labour government established Britain's modern welfare state, most notably the country's cherished National Health Service. The Tories returned to power in 1951, but retained, and even expanded, Labour's welfare measures, as have all subsequent governments of both parties.

Politics: two-party dominance

One of Europe's first true democracies, Britain is also one of its few surviving monarchies. But it is unusual in not having a written constitution. Politicians, civil servants, judges and the monarch are all supposed to know, and abide by, the rules of precedent, which in many instances are open to widely differing interpretations.

The post-war dominance of Britain's two major political parties – Conservative and Labour – has been challenged, but has not yet been broken. In 1981 some right-wing Labour MPs departed to form the Social Democrats, which then formed an alliance with the Liberals, who had not held office since 1924. The Alliance went on to win 25.4% of the vote, but only 23 seats in the House of Commons. The parties merged to form the Liberal Democrats in 1987, but the Lib Dems have never matched the Alliance's 1983 showing. One reason may be that the centre ground is now crowded by all three parties. The ideological left–right battles of earlier years have petered out and there is now no huge gulf between any of the major parties.

Foreign policy: not so influential now

Britain is still reluctantly coming to terms with the fact that it is no longer a superpower, a view best summed up by the boast that the British can still "punch above our weight". The Commonwealth, the successor to the British empire, has faded into insignificance. Mrs Thatcher tried, with some success, to stress the "special relationship" between the America and Britain. At the same time she often acted obstreperously with her partners in Europe, demanding "her" money back from the EU budget when she felt Britain was paying too much. This attitude embittered Britain's European partners and attracted opposition to British polices even when they were right.

The "special relationship" with America, which never meant that much to America, has not survived Mrs Thatcher's departure and the arrival of Bill Clinton, who prefers to deal with the European Union as a whole, or its most powerful members, Germany and France. But British ambivalence about Europe has survived. In 1991 John Major won "opt outs" from the Maastricht Treaty, but still only got the treaty through Parliament by narrowly winning a vote of confidence which nearly brought the government down. Britain's future undoubtedly lies in Europe, but what role Britain will play there remains unclear.

Society: multicultural

The spread of English as the language of international commerce, diplomacy and even entertainment has helped maintain Britain's cultural self-confidence. And as a combination of four distinct nationalities – English, Welsh, Scottish and Irish – Britain represents one of the more successful combinations of multiculturalism in the old world. But there is the glaring exception of the strife in Northern Ireland, where history has left the age-old conflict between Ireland and Britain, now largely resolved, concentrated in a small province. Like other European countries, Britain has also been less than skilful at absorbing the many Asian, West Indian and African immigrants, most of whom have come, as British citizens, from former territories.

The economy: now following, not leading

Since the second world war Britain has recorded slower economic growth than most Western, industrialised countries and in terms of total output it now ranks ninth in the world. The British themselves seemed resigned to the relative decline of their economy until Margaret Thatcher's election victory in 1979. The Thatcherites abandoned European-style corporatism and tried to reintroduce free-market disciplines. Many Thatcherite reforms were successful, though painful. Privatisation of state industries cut government losses and, even in the case of many which remained quasi-monopolies, boosted efficiency. The curtailment of union power was confirmed by the defeat of the miners after a year-long strike in 1984. Deregulation of the City of London in the "Big Bang" of 1986 ensured that London remained one of the world's most important financial centres. A huge shakeout of inefficient and overmanned companies in manufacturing left the surviving firms more competitive. But the price was high unemployment and increased social discontent. These changes also accelerated a shift away from manufacturing towards services as well as making Britain the most successful country in Europe in attracting foreign investment, much of it Japanese and American.

What the Thatcherites failed to do was to re-introduce into Britain much entrepreneurial spirit, at least compared with that of America. Many of the high-flying entrepreneurial stars of the Thatcher era have since gone bust, to the delight of many. The Thatcherites also failed to cut back the size of the government, as they pledged to do. Government spending still accounts for some 45% of GDP, though that is not that much less than in most other European countries. And their errors on macroeconomic policy first caused, and then prolonged, the country's most recent recession, from which it is only now slowly emerging.

Total area	244,046 sq km	% agricultural area	75.7
Capital	London	Highest point metres	Ben Nevis
Other cities	Manchester,		1,343
	Birmingham, Leeds	Main rivers	Severn, Thames,
			Trent, Ouse, Wye, Tay

The economy

GDP $bn	1,025	GDP per head $	17,760
% av. ann. growth in		GDP per head in purchasing	
real GDP 1985–92	2.2	power parity (USA=100)	73.8

Origins of GDP	% of total	Components of GDP	% of total
Agriculture	2	Private consumption	65
Industry	32	Public consumption	22
of which:		Investment	15
manufacturing	20	Exports	23
Services	67	Imports	-25

Structure of manufacturing

			% of total
Agric. & food processing	13	Other	49
Textiles & clothing	5	Av. ann. increase in industrial	
Machinery & transport	32	output 1985–92	1.2

Inflation and exchange rates

Consumer price 1993	1.6%	£ per $ av. 1993	0.68
Av. ann. rate 1988–93	5.5%	£ per ecu av. 1993	0.78

Balance of payments, reserves and aid

			$bn
Visible exports fob	187.4	Capital balance	17.3
Visible imports fob	-212.1	Overall balance	-2.1
Trade balance	-24.6	Change in reserves	5.3
Invisible inflows	175.7	Level of reserves	
Invisible outflows	-162.8	end Dec.	41.3
Net transfers	-9.0	Aid given	3.2
Current account balance	-20.7	as % of GDP	0.3
as % of GDP	-2.0		

Principal exports	$bn fob	Principal imports	$bn cif
Finished manufactures	100.7	Finished manufactures	116.9
Semi-manufactures	52.7	Semi-manufactures	56.8
Food, beverages & tobacco	15.1	Food, beverages & tobacco	23.6
Fuels	12.0	Fuels	12.3
Basic materials	3.3	Basic materials	8.2
Total incl. others	187.4	Total incl. others	222.4

Main export destinations	% of total	Main origins of imports	% of total
Germany	13.9	Germany	15.1
USA	11.3	USA	10.9
France	10.6	France	9.7
Netherlands	7.8	Netherlands	7.9
Italy	5.7	Japan	5.9

Government

System The monarch is head of state. Executive power lies with the prime minister, nominally appointed by the monarch, and usually leader of the majority party in the Commons. The two-chamber parliament comprises the 651-member House of Commons, directly elected on a first-past-the-post-basis (except in Northern Ireland) for five years and the 1,176-member non-elected House of Lords (consisting of hereditary members, life peers, Anglican bishops and senior judges).

Main political parties Conservative Party, Labour Party, Liberal Democrat Party, Green Party; regional: Scottish National Party, Plaid Cymru (Welsh National Party); Northern Ireland: Social Democratic and Labour Party, Official Ulster Unionist Party, Democratic Unionist Party, Sinn Fein, Alliance Party

People

Population m	57.7	% under 15	19.7
Pop. per sq km	238	% over 65	15.6
% urban	89	No. men per 100 women	96
% av. ann. growth 1985–92	0.3	Human Development Index	96

Life expectancy	yrs		per 1,000 pop.
Men	74	Crude birth rate	14
Women	79	Crude death rate	12

Ethnic groups	% of total	Workforce	% of total
English	81.5	Services	71.6
Scottish	9.6	Industry	26.2
Irish	2.4	Agriculture	2.2
Welsh	1.9	Construction	…
Other	4.6	% unemployed	8.1

Society

No. households m	21.2	**Consumer goods ownership**	
Av. no. per household	2.6		% of households
Marriages per 1,000 pop.	6.8	TV	98
Divorces per 1,000 pop.	2.9	Video recorder	58
		Microwave oven	48

Household spending	% of total	Education	
Food/drink	12.0	Spending as % of GDP	4.7
Clothing/footwear	6.0	Years of compulsory education	11
Housing/energy	17.0	Enrolment ratios:	
Household goods	7.0	primary school	107
Health	8.0	secondary school	84
Transport/communications	14.0	tertiary education	25
Leisure/other	31.0		

Tourism		Health	
Tourist arrivals m	18.0	Pop. per doctor	611
Tourist receipts $bn	15.0	Pop. per hospital bed	146

VATICAN

Total area	0.44 sq km	Population '000	1

This tiny city state in the heart of Rome is the Holy See of the Roman Catholic church. The pope's temporal auhority was first recognized by the king of the Franks in the 8th century. A palace was built on the Vatican hill in the late 14th century and by the mid-16th century the papacy controlled much of central Italy. Between 1859 and 1870, when troops entered Rome, the Papal States were gradually subsumed into Italy. Succesive popes refused to leave the Vatican and in 1929 Pope Pius X1 and Mussolini signed the Lateran Treaty by which the pope's sovereignty over the Vatican was recognised.

The treaty was reaffirmed by the Italian constitution of 1947. In 1978 a Pole, Karol Wojtyla, became Pope John Paul II. He was the first non-Italian pontiff since the 16th century.

Politics: less influential now

The pope is elected bishop of Rome and head of the Roman Catholic Church for life by the Sacred College of Cardinals. A papal commission for the Vatican City, appointed by the pope, exercises the papal power of government. Historically, the pope has wielded considerable political clout in international affaris but today his power to sway governments around the world is limited. Pope John Paul II has sought to increase the papacy's influence in international affairs by, among other things, restoring diplomatic links with Eastern Europe.

The economy: financially fallible

The Vatican city state has its own bank, post office and stamps as well as coinage. Its main sources of revenue are income from investments and voluntary contributions, known as Peter's pence. Budget figures show an increasing deficit. During the last decade the Vatican found itself involved in a financial scandal arising out of its alleged involvement in the collapse of the Banco Ambrosiano, whose chairman, Robert Calvi, had been found hanged under Blackfriar's Bridge in London.

=Part III=
ORGANISATIONS

THE EUROPEAN UNION

The four main EU institutions are the Council of Ministers, the European Commission, the European Parliament and the Court of Justice. The European Parliament (initially called the Assembly) and the European Court were founded as the common institutions of the ECSC, the EEC and Euratom (see below). The Council of Ministers and the Commission were founded in 1967 with the merger treaty. The EC was incorporated into the European Union (EU) in November 1993. The EC institutions continue their function under the Treaty on European Union (the Maastricht treaty). In addition, powers have been acquired by the EU that are not subject to the institutions of the EC, but are dealt with on an inter-governmental basis. These include a common foreign and security policy and co-operation over judicial, police and immigration issues.

1951 Treaty of Paris establishes European Coal & Steel Community (ECSC); members were Belgium, France, West Germany, Italy, Luxembourg, Netherlands.
1955 Six ECSC members form committee to investigate the feasibility of a common market.
1957 Treaty of Rome forms European Economic Community (EEC). European Atomic Energy Community (Euratom) set up.
1961 UK, Ireland, Denmark, Norway apply for membership.
1962 Common market in agriculture established.
1963 France vetoes UK membership of EEC; Ireland, Norway and Denmark withdraw applications.
1966 UK again applies for membership; France again vetoes.
1967 EEC, ECSC, Euratom become European Community (EC).
1972 Renewed applications for membership from UK, Ireland, Denmark and Norway; Norway rejects membership in referendum, other three become members on January 1st 1973.
1979 European Monetary System established. First direct elections to European Parliament.
1981 Greece becomes a member of the EC.
1985 Greenland (no longer under full Danish rule) withdraws.
1986 Spain and Portugal join. Single European Act signed.
1987 Turkey and Morocco apply to join. Morocco's application rejected, further negotiations on Turkey's membership may begin in 1993.
1988 Committee established to discuss monetary union.
1990 East Germany joins EC with German unification.
1991 Agreement to set up European Economic Area (EEA). Treaty on European Union agreed at Maastricht summit.
1993 Treaty on European Union comes into force.
1994 EEA comes into force. Accession negotiations completed with Austria, Finland, Norway and Sweden.

The institutions

Council of Ministers

Base: Brussels; April, June, October, Luxembourg

Composition
The council, the centre of political control, consists of representatives of the governments of the 12 member states. Its membership constantly changes, depending on the topics discussed, since relevant ministers are called upon to discuss their areas of responsibility.

The General Affairs Council
The foreign ministers' meeting, which is held at least once a month except in August, is known as the General Affairs Council. The ministers discuss foreign policy and exercise general co-ordination over the work of the other ministerial councils, tackling particularly complicated and urgent matters. They also prepare the summit meetings of EU leaders, known as the European Council.

The presidency
The council has a rotating presidency, with member states taking turns for a six-month period. The foreign minister of the country holding the presidency assumes the title of president of the Council of Ministers, and his country's foreign ministry undertakes, with the help of the council secretariat, the organisation of the council's business during the six months.

The role of the presidency Part of the presidency's unofficial duty is to strive to get agreement on as many issues as possible by producing compromise proposals whenever there is a deadlock and cajoling its own national representatives as well as those of other member states.

Tasks
Legislative powers The Council of Ministers performs the legislative role in the Union. Legislation, known as directives or regulations, is initiated by the European Commission and is adopted by the Council after consultation with the European Parliament and the Economic and Social Committee.

Other responsibilities The council has a wide range of activities including joint responsibility with the European Parliament (whose role, however, is a subordinate one) to adopt the budget. It has the power of appointment to the other institutions, such as the Economic and Social Committee and the Court of Auditors.

Meetings

In its various forms the council meets around 80–90 times a year, usually for a day, but sometimes for longer. Two or three different meetings may take place simultaneously.

The meetings, which are also attended by at least one commissioner and by officials of its own secretariat.

Informal gatherings Most of the specialist councils also hold informal meetings to exchange views on long-term issues. These gatherings are known in Euro-circles as Gymnich-type meetings, after Schloss Gymnich, in former West Germany, where the first of them was held.

COREPER

The Council of Ministers is assisted by the very important Committee of Permanent Representatives, known by its French language initials as COREPER, and based in Brussels. It consists of the permanent representatives (ambassadors) of the member states of the EU.

Working methods The representatives meet at least once a week to work through all the issues which are awaiting ministerial decision. If they are in agreement on a draft Commission proposal, it is placed on the council agenda as an "A" point, and is adopted without discussion.

If viewpoints are fairly wide apart, the proposals are referred to expert groups at a lower level. Only when no more than one or two governments are in disagreement with the rest is an issue passed on to the council.

COREPER II and SCA

Since the permanent representatives cannot maintain a uniform level of expertise on the highly detailed topics on the agenda, many subjects are entrusted to their deputies who have weekly meetings, known as COREPER II. Agricultural issues, for example, are dealt with by the Special Committee for Agriculture (SCA), consisting of senior officials of national ministries or of the agricultural councillors at the representations.

Voting procedure

When a proposal actually reaches a Council of Ministers meeting, except as an "A" point, it is by no means assured of being adopted. The Treaty of Rome lays down precise rules on decision making within the council, but these have not been applied in the manner originally intended. Under Article 148 of the treaty, decisions may be taken by: a simple majority, qualified majority and unanimously.

Simple majority Member states have one vote each.

These decisions are restricted to minor matters, often of a purely procedural nature.

Qualified majority Votes are allocated very roughly in proportion to the size of the member state. Germany, France, Italy and the UK have ten votes each, Spain eight votes, Belgium, Greece, the Netherlands and Portugal five votes each, Denmark and Ireland three votes each, and Luxembourg two votes. As 54 votes (out of 76) are needed for a proposal to be adopted, it follows that a "blocking minority" must muster 23 votes. Thus, three large states acting together, or two large states plus one small one (except for Luxembourg) can block a proposal, but it would require at least five of the smaller states (with five votes each or less) to do so.

The arithmetic will change in January 1995 if four new members join the EU. Austria and Sweden will have four votes each and Finland and Norway three, increasing the total number of votes to 90. It will then be necessary to win 64 votes for a decision to be taken, raising the blocking majority to 27. Following objections from the UK and Spain, the Council of Ministers agreed that if between 23 and 26 votes were cast against a proposal a decision should be delayed "for a reasonable period of time" while a compromise was sought.

Unanimity Under the Rome treaty, it was envisaged that the unanimity rule would apply for a limited number of issues of major importance, with most decisions reached by a qualified majority. However, the 1966 disagreement between the French government and the other five original members of the EEC on some important issues led to the "Luxembourg compromise", which extended the unanimity rule to a vast range of decisions which were regarded as affecting the "very important interest" of member states. As a result, some proposals were held up for years because one or two member states objected to them. The result was that many decisions were reached on a "log-rolling" basis, governments giving way on points on which they were not convinced in exchange for concessions on often quite unrelated issues.

Changes under the Single European Act Although the Luxembourg compromise, which has no legal force, still stands, the Single European Act has much reduced the number of issues on which unanimity is required.

European Commission

Base: Brussels

The European Commission is the executive organ of the Community. It is often seen as the embodiment of the European idea as its members, while appointed by national governments, are under no obligation to them, and their total loyalty is pledged to the interests of the EU as a whole.

The Commission's tasks

The tasks of the Commission have been summarised as being those of initiative, supervision and implementation.

Initiative As initiator of policy, the Commission has the specific right to put proposals before the Council of Ministers, which in most circumstances is unable to make decisions in the absence of such a proposal.

Implementation The Commission:

• is entrusted with the implementation of the decisions taken by the Council of Ministers;

• has a wide range of decision-making powers in respect of the coal and steel industries, inherited from the former High Authority of the ECSC, which it may exercise without reference to the Council of Ministers;

• has substantial autonomous powers relating to competition policy and the running of the common agricultural policy;

• administers the various funds established by the Community (Agricultural Guidance and Guarantee Fund, Social Fund, Regional Fund, etc);

• prepares a draft budget which must be approved by the Council of Ministers and the European Parliament;

• negotiates international agreements on behalf of the EU, though these can only be concluded by the council.

Supervision The Commission:

• has a general responsibility to ensure that treaty provisions are carried out;

• supervises the implementation of Community law by the member states;

• is required to deliver an "opinion" whenever it concludes that a member state has infringed its treaty obligations, and may afterwards bring an action in the European Court of Justice against the state concerned.

The commissioners

The Commission is composed of 17 members, two each from the UK, France, Germany, Italy and Spain, and one each from Belgium, Denmark, Greece, Ireland, Luxembourg, Netherlands and Portugal. Under the enlargement treaties negotiated with Austria, Finland, Norway and Sweden, each country will have a member of the Commission, whose size will increase to 21 in January 1995 if all four countries ratify their treaties.

Commissioners are appointed by the Council of Ministers, nominated by their own national governments, for a four-year term, which is renewable. At the end of each four-year period typically about half of the commissioners are reappointed, and the remainder are replaced by new nominees.

Most of the commissioners are politicians, but a minority have been senior administrators, trade union leaders or businessmen.

The president and vice-presidents

One of the commissioners is appointed president, also by agreement among the member governments, for a two-year term, though in practice this is now normally extended to four years. Each four-year Commission term is referred to colloquially under the name of its president, for example the Jenkins Commission, the Thorn Commission, the Delors Commission.

Six of the other commissioners are appointed as vice-presidents, a distinction which has little practical significance, except that they draw somewhat larger salaries than their colleagues.

The influence of the president The president is often misleadingly compared to a prime minister of a member state in relation to his cabinet. In fact, he neither selects nor dismisses his colleagues, and does not himself determine what portfolios they should hold. His influence is considerable, as he proposes the distribution of responsibilities at the outset of each four-year term, but the actual decision is taken by the commissioners themselves, if necessary by majority vote.

Administrative apparatus

Each commissioner has an area of responsibility, and parts of the administrative machine report directly to him.

He has the assistance of a small cabinet of half a dozen personal appointees who not only act as his advisers but also customarily intervene on his behalf at all levels of the Commission's bureaucracy.

Organisation The Commission's staff is organised in 23 directorates-general (from External Relations to Financial

Control) and 14 special services (Secretariat-General, Legal Services, Statistical Office, etc). The directorates-general (DGS) are grouped together under the responsibility of individual commissioners.

Numbers The staff, some of whom are based in Luxembourg, consists of about 15,000 employees, one-third of whom are concerned with interpreting or translating. A further 1,350 men and women are employed in scientific research work at Ispra in Italy, Culham in the UK, Geel in Belgium and various other centres.

Working practices
The Commission meets every Wednesday. Additional meetings are frequently scheduled, occasionally in more relaxed surroundings, to discuss particular topics or long-term perspectives.

Decisions within the Commission are adopted on the basis of a simple majority vote; subsequently the principle of collective responsibility applies.

All official documents are translated, and meetings involving national officials are simultaneously interpreted into all official languages. Most day-to-day business within the Commission is conducted in French or English.

European Parliament

Base: Strasbourg

The European Parliament is intended to bring a measure of democratic control and accountability to the other institutions. The advocates of closer political union envisage a very influential role for the parliament, but at present its powers are severely restricted.

Election

Since 1979 the European Parliament has been directly elected. The term of office is five years, and there is no provision for early dissolution. The Rome treaty stipulated that there should be a common electoral system, and parliament itself proposed a uniform system in 1982. But the Council of Ministers was unable to agree to this, largely because of the British government's reluctance to change its first-past-the-post system to proportional representation (PR). So for the first four direct elections — in June 1979, June 1984, June 1989 and June 1994 – each member state used its own systems, which (except for the UK) were variations of PR.

Country	Seats	Voting method
Belgium	25	PR, regional lists
Denmark	16	PR, national lists
France	87	PR, national lists
Germany	99	PR, regional lists
Greece	25	PR, national lists
Ireland	15	PR, single transferable vote
Italy	87	PR, regional lists
Luxembourg	6	PR, national lists
Netherlands	31	PR, national lists
Portugal	25	PR, national lists
Spain	64	PR, regional lists
UK	87	plurality
of which		
N. Ireland	3	PR, single transferable vote

Powers

The powers of the European Parliament can be defined under three headings.

Supervisory Parliament has the right to dismiss the Commission by a vote of censure, requiring a two-thirds majority of votes cast and representing a majority of Euro-MPs. (This power has never been used.) It can discuss the Commission's annual general report and can put questions to the Commission and Council of Ministers. In 1990 some 2,732 written and 835 oral questions were put to the Commission, and a further 343 written and 520 oral questions to the council. These were answered by ministers from the country holding the presidency, who attend each plenary session of the parliament for this purpose.

Legislative   Parliament has an advisory role in the legislative process, since the Council of Ministers cannot enact certain legislation without consulting parliament. In practice, parliament is normally invited to submit an opinion on any draft directive or regulation tabled by the Commission. The powers were significantly strengthened under the Single European Act and by the Maastricht treaty. This strengthens the parliament's ability to amend legislation and gives it the right to veto certain legislation.

Budgetary   Under a 1975 amendment to the Rome treaty, parliament can amend non-obligatory spending and adopt or reject the draft budget. On three occasions parliament did refuse to adopt the draft budget, which resulted in the Community entering a new calendar year without a budget being approved.

Operation and voting

The European Parliament meets in plenary session for one week each month except August, with additional part-sessions in March and October to consider its opinions on agricultural prices and the annual budget. Much of its work takes place in committees or subcommittees, of which there are currently 45, and which usually meet during two other weeks each month, leaving at least one week free for party or constituency activities.

The member states have not yet fulfilled their obligation to establish a single seat for the parliament. Plenary sessions are normally held in Strasbourg, most committees meet in Brussels and the bulk of the secretariat is based in Luxembourg. This geographical fragmentation, together with the fact that it conducts its business in nine different languages, with simultaneous interpretation, and the requirement that all documents shall be translated into all nine languages, greatly increases the cost of running the institution, which in 1991 amounted to some 508m ecus. Most Euro-MPs would undoubtedly prefer the parliament's activities to be concentrated in Brussels, but the Luxembourg and French governments are vehemently opposed to this and they have prevented a decision on a permanent seat from being taken – and under the treaties this would need to be unanimous.

Euro-MPs are paid the same salary as MPs in their own countries, which means that there is a wide variation, with Portuguese Euro-MPs being paid the least, and French and Germans the most. In addition, there are generous travel, attendance, research and secretarial allowances which are paid on the same basis to all members.

Voting in the European Parliament is less disciplined than in most national parliaments and ad hoc coalitions are often formed on individual issues which cross normal ideological and national barriers. There is, accordingly, often some uncertainty about how the parliament may vote. Euro-MPs sit in cross-national political groups. At the end of the 1989–94 parliament the membership of the groups was as follows.

Party of European Socialists	198
European People's Party (Christian Democrats)	162
Liberal, Democratic and Reformist Group	44
Greens	28
European Democratic Alliance	20
Rainbow Group	16
Technical Group of the European Right	14
Left Unity Group	13
Non-affiliated	23

The party of European Socialists comprised Labour, Socialist or Social Democratic parties in all 12 member states, including the former Italian Communist Party, renamed the Party of Democratic Socialism. The Left Unity Group consisted mostly of French Communists. British Conservatives, who had previously belonged to the European Democratic Group along with Danish Conservatives, became members of the European People's Party in 1992, although the Conservative Party itself declined to affiliate to the European Federation of Christian Democratic parties. The European Democratic Alliance was made up of French Gaullists and Irish Fianna Fail members, while the Rainbow Group consisted mostly of regionalist and nationalist parties. There was a small left-wing majority in the parliament, but the centre-left predominated as the Socialists and the Christian Democrats, who together made up more than two-thirds of the membership, reached an agreement to co-operate on a wide range of issues.

After the 1994 elections the seats won by party groups were as follows:

Belgium 6 Party of European Socialists; 7 European People's Party; 6 Liberal, Democratic and Reformist Group; 2

Greens; 3 Technical Group of the European Right; 1 Rainbow Group

Denmark   3 Party of European Socialists; 3 European People's Party; 5 Liberal, Democratic and Reformist Group; 1 Greens; 4 Rainbow Group

France   16 Party of European Socialists; 7 European People's Party; 8 Liberal, Democratic and Reformist Group; 14 Group of the European Democratic Alliance; 10 Technical Group of the European Right; 6 Left Unity; 26 others

Germany   40 Party of European Socialists; 47 European People's Party; 12 Greens

Greece   10 Party of European Socialists; 9 European People's Party; 3 Left Unity; 1 non-attached; 2 others

Ireland   1 Party of European Socialists; 4 European People's Party; 1 Liberal, Democratic and Reformist Group; 2 Greens; 7 Group of the European Democratic Alliance

Italy   19 Party of European Socialists; 9 European People's Party; 1 Liberal, Democratic and Reformist Group; 3 Greens; 24 non-attached; 31 others

Luxembourg   2 Party of European Socialists; 2 European People's Party; 1 Liberal, Democratic and Reformist Group; 1 Greens

Netherlands   8 Party of European Socialists; 10 European People's Party; 10 Liberal, Democratic and Reformist Group; 1 Greens; 2 non-attached

Portugal   10 Party of European Socialists; 1 European People's Party; 8 Liberal, Democratic and Reformist Group; 3 Group of the European Democratic Alliance; 3 Left Unity

Spain   22 Party of European Socialists; 30 European People's Party; 2 Liberal, Democratic and Reformist Group; 1 Rainbow Group; 9 non-attached

UK   63 Party of European Socialists; 19 European People's Party; 2 Liberal, Democratic and Reformist Group; 2 Rainbow Group; 1 non-attached

Total   200 Party of European Socialists; 148 European People's Party; 44 Liberal, Democratic and Reformist Group; 22 Greens; 24 Group of the European Democratic Alliance; 13 Technical Group of the European Right; 12 Left Unity; 8 Rainbow Group; 37 non-attached; 59 others

Court of Justice

Base: Luxembourg

The task of ensuring that the law is applied throughout the Community in accordance with the provisions of the treaties falls to the Court of Justice.

The judges and advocates-general

The court consists of a judge from each member state, one other from one of the larger member states and six advocates-general.

The judges are chosen by the Council of Ministers, on the nomination of member states. They are appointed for a renewable term of six years, half the court being renewed every three years. The advocates-general are appointed on the same basis.

The judges select one of their number to be president of the court for a renewable term of three years.

Plenary sessions and chambers

Cases brought by a member state or a Community institution, and other important cases, are heard in full court. Other cases are assigned to chambers set up within the court. At any stage, a chamber may refer a case to the full court if it considers that it raises points of law requiring definitive rulings.

The various forms of action

In general, six types of cases come before the court or its chambers.

- Disputes between member states.
- Disputes between the Community and member states.
- Disputes between the institutions.
- Disputes between individuals, or corporate bodies, and the Community (including staff cases).
- Opinions on international agreements.
- Preliminary rulings on cases referred by national courts.

Relations with lower courts

The court is the EU's supreme court; there is no appeal against its rulings. Because it has no hierarchical relationship with the lower national courts, a system of preliminary rulings was introduced to ensure that Community law is uniformly applied.

In national cases involving Community law, which takes

precedence over national laws, where there is any question as to the effect of the Community law, the national court should, and in some cases must, ask the court for a preliminary ruling, which it must then apply.

In the application and interpretation of purely national laws, which of course make up the great bulk of cases in other courts, the Court of Justice has no jurisdiction whatever.

Court procedure

Proceedings before the court may be initiated by a member state, a Community institution (most often, the Commission) or by a corporate body or individual (providing he has a direct personal interest in the subject of the case). The court procedure involves two separate stages, one written and one oral.

Written procedure On receipt of a written application from a plaintiff, the court first establishes that it falls within its jurisdiction and that it has been lodged within the time limitations determined by the treaties. The application is then served on the opposing party, which normally has one month in which to lodge a statement of defence. The applicant has a further month to table a reply to this, and the defendant one more month for a rejoinder.

Each case is supervised by a judge-rapporteur, who is appointed by the president. On receipt of all the documents, he presents a preliminary report to the court, which decides whether a preparatory enquiry (involving the appearance of the parties, requests for further documents, oral testimony, etc) is necessary, and decides whether the case should be heard by the full court or one of the chambers.

Oral procedure The two sides appear before the judges, present their arguments and call evidence if they so wish. Questions are asked by the judges and the advocate-general (whose role is somewhat similar to that of the public prosecutor in French courts). Some weeks later the advocate-general gives his opinion, at a further hearing, analysing the facts and the legal aspects in detail and proposing his solution to the dispute.

Judgments The advocate-general's opinion often gives a clear indication of which way the judgment will go, but this is not invariably the case. The judges consider their ruling in private, on the basis of a draft prepared by the judge-rapporteur. If, during their deliberations, they require additional information they may reopen the procedure and ask the parties for further explanation, oral or written, or order further enquiries.

The judgments of the court are reached by majority vote; where the court is equally divided the vote of the most junior judge being disregarded, though in most cases it is arranged that an uneven number of judges will be sitting. The judgment is given at a public hearing, which, on average, occurs some 18 months after the receipt of an application.

The Court of First Instance

The Single European Act provided for the establishment of a court of first instance, which would hear certain classes of cases brought by individuals, including actions brought by officials of the Community, which used to clog up the main court. This court began work in September 1989.

Direct action cases

Proceedings against member states These are often initiated by the Commission, normally alleging failure to carry out their obligations under the treaties. Occasionally, one member state is brought to court by another. Italy has figured very frequently, both as a complainant and as a defendant. The Italian parliament is notoriously slow in passing laws, and a large number of these actions have been for failure to apply directives adopted by the Council of Ministers within the appointed time.

The Commission easily heads the lists both of complainants and defendants. It is its responsibility to take action, against individuals and companies, as well as member states, to ensure that the treaties are being applied, for example in competition cases. The Commission is also the defendant in virtually all actions alleging loss or damage caused by the carrying out of Community policies.

Proceedings against institutions Occasionally one institution lodges a complaint against another. The EC Council of Ministers has more than once initiated action against the European Parliament for allegedly exceeding its budgetary powers, while the parliament took the council to the Court of Justice for failure to implement a common transport policy within the period foreseen by the Rome treaty.

European Council

The Treaty of Rome made no provision for meetings of the heads of government of the member states. It was the Single European Act that gave the European Council legal status, without defining its powers.

Beginnings and development

In the first ten years of the EEC the heads of government met on only three occasions. Yet it gradually became clear that a more regular exchange of views was necessary to give a sense of strategic direction to the Community and to resolve problems to which the Council of Ministers and the Commission had not been able to find solutions through the normal processes. In December 1974 at a summit meeting in Paris, the heads of government formally decided to meet three times each year under the name "European Council".

Since 1974   Starting in Dublin in March 1975, the European Council duly met on this basis until December 1985, when it was agreed that only two meetings a year would henceforward be held. The Single European Act stipulated that the council would meet at least twice a year, and that extraordinary meetings could also be held; in 1990 two "emergency" summits were held in addition to the regular meetings, and in 1991 one extra "emergency" summit was held. It seems probable that in future three or four meetings of the European Council will be held each year.

Composition and meetings

The heads of government meet accompanied only by their foreign ministers. The president of the Commission also attends, and is supported by only one of his vice-presidents.

   Meetings take place in the member state currently holding the presidency of the Council of Ministers, and its prime minister (or, in the case of France, its president) takes the chair and is responsible for the organisation of the meetings.

Informal exchange of views   Deliberations are informal. The more sensitive discussions normally take place in the intervals between the actual sessions (which spread over two days), particularly during and after dinner on the evening of the first day, when most if not all of the heads of government speak in English and simultaneous interpretation is dispensed with.

Political influence

The European Council has had the same status as an ordinary meeting of the Council of Ministers, though it has usually avoided giving formal effect to the decisions it has taken, leaving it to a subsequent meeting of foreign ministers to adopt them on a "rubber stamp" basis.

Increasing importance It has, however, to a large extent, replaced the Commission as the motor of the Community, and has given the green light for recent new initiatives, such as the launching of the 1992 programme, the acceptance of a united Germany within the EC, the convening of inter-governmental conferences (IGCs) on economic and monetary union and on political union, and the offer of economic aid to the former Soviet Union.

Court of Auditors

Base: Luxembourg

The least known of the Community's institutions, established in 1977, when it replaced an Audit Board which had less sweeping authority.

Its operation and influence

The Court of Auditors examines all accounts of revenue and expenditure of Community institutions and other bodies.

The court produces an annual report, as well as periodic specific reports for instance on wasteful expenditure (especially on support to agriculture) or on financial misconduct. These reports have led to a considerable tightening up of procedures. Its role is highly influential.

The auditors

The Court of Auditors consists of an auditor from each member state. They are appointed by the Council of Ministers for a renewable six-year term, and appoint their own chairman from among their number for a renewable term of three years.

European Investment Bank (EIB)

Base: Luxembourg

Set up to finance capital investment projects promoting the balanced development of the Community.

Financial resources
The bank's capital stands at 57.6 billion ecus (of which 4.32 billion ecus is paid up). Most of its financial resources come from borrowing on capital markets. On a non-profit making basis, it on-lends the proceeds for capital investment projects with priority objectives. Up to end-1992 the bank had raised 126 billion ecus in loans. During 1992 it borrowed 13 billion ecus and loaned 17 billion ecus.

Activities
Within the EU In 1990 EIB loans went to each of the member states, mostly to less prosperous regions.

The main headings of EIB loans within the Community during 1990 were regional development, energy, industry, advanced technology, the modernisation and conversion of enterprises, transport, telecommunications and other infrastructure development, and environmental protection.

Outside the EU The EIB contributes towards implementating EU development aid programmes. It finances projects in countries under EU co-operation or association agreements and in 69 African, Caribbean and Pacific (ACP) countries under Lomé IV.

Since 1990 the bank has lent money to Eastern European countries to help their transition to market economies. It has a 3% share in the $10 billion capital of the European Bank for Reconstruction and Development (EBRD), which was set up in 1990 for this purpose.

Structure
The EIB's board of governors consists of the finance ministers of the member states, who meet once a year. It also has a part-time board of directors and a full-time management committee comprising the bank's president and six vice-presidents, appointed by the board of governors, on the nomination of the board of directors, for a renewable six-year term.

Economic and Social Committee (ESC)

Base: Brussels

The Treaty of Rome specifies a number of areas where the Commission and the Council of Ministers must consult the ESC before directives and regulations may be approved. In practice, the Commission and the council customarily consult with the committee over many other issues. There is in practice little hindrance to the ESC offering opinions on any subject on which its members may wish to pronounce.

Composition

The members are divided into three groups – Group I representing employers, Group II workers, and Group III various interests, which includes consumers, farmers, the self employed, academics, and so on. Members are appointed by the Council of Ministers, and nominated by governments, which consult the interest groups most concerned (particularly the trade unions and employers' organisations) before choosing their nominees.

Members are appointed for a renewable term of four years. They elect a chairman, who serves for two years, and it is customary to rotate the chairmanship between the three groups. Members are part-timers, who are allowed time off from their normal jobs.

Plenary sittings and specialist sections

The committee meets every month. Its detailed work is undertaken in nine specialist sections, which draft opinions for approval by the committee meeting in plenary session. rather than the employers' side. On most questions, however, divisions occur within groups rather than between them. The real influence of the ESC, which by now has given over 2,000 opinions, is on more technical issues, where the expertise of its members is valuable.

A similar body, known as the Committee of the Regions, was appointed under the Maastricht treaty provisions, and met for the first time in March 1994. This committee is asked to give its opinion on proposed legislation likely to have a particular impact on the various regions of the member states.

OTHER ORGANISATIONS

Bank for International Settlements – BIS

Base: Basle, Switzerland

Foundation and aims
The BIS was founded following The Hague Agreements of 1930. Its main aim is to promote co-operation between national central banks and to provide additional facilities for international financial operations.

Structure
General Meeting Held annually. The central banks (or financial institutions acting in their stead) of the following countries are represented and their voting rights exercised in proportion to the number of shares subscribed in each country.

Australia	Greece	Portugal
Austria	Hungary	Romania
Belgium	Iceland	Slovakia
Bulgaria	Ireland	South Africa
Canada	Italy	Spain
Czech Republic	Latvia	Sweden
Denmark	Lithuania	Switzerland
Estonia	Japan	Turkey
Finland	Netherlands	UK
France	Norway	USA
Germany	Poland	

Board of directors Comprises the governors of the central banks of Belgium, France, Germany, Italy and the UK, each of whom appoints another member of the same nationality. The USA does not occupy the two seats to which it is entitled. Nine governors of other member central banks may be elected to the board; those of the Netherlands, Sweden and Switzerland are also members. The BIS has a staff of about 360.

Activities
The BIS is the central banks' central bank. It is an international organisation governed by international law, possessing special privileges and immunities. There are some private shareholders, but they cannot participate in the General Meeting; 85% of the total share capital is held by central banks. The bank's authorised capital is 1,500m gold francs,

divided into 600,000 shares of 2,500 gold francs each.

The BIS helps central banks manage and invest their monetary reserves. In 1989 it managed more than 10% of world foreign exchange reserves and held deposits from about 80 central banks. The funds are used partly for lending to central banks but the bank also participates in traditional types of investment. Since central banks' monetary reserves must be available at short notice, funds are placed with the BIS for short-term fixed periods and the bank must maintain a high degree of liquidity.

The central bank governors have regular meetings to discuss and co-ordinate international monetary policy, and the close relationship with the IMF allows the bank to act as a contact between East and West.

The Euro-currency Standing Committee advises central bank governors of the G-10 on policy aspects of Euro-currency markets.

The Monetary and Economic Department carries out research and publishes data and statistics.

The BIS acts as an agent for the European Monetary Co-operation Fund, undertaking operations in connection with the European Monetary System (EMS). It is also an agent in a private international clearing and settlement system for ecu-denominated bank deposits.

Commonwealth of Independent States (CIS)

The CIS is a voluntary association of 12 (originally 11) states, established by the Minsk Agreement at the time of the collapse of the Soviet Union in December 1991. The members are:

Armenia	Kazakhstan	Tajikistan
Azerbaijan	Kirgizstan	Turkmenistan
Belorussia	Moldova	Ukraine
Georgia	Russia	Uzbekistan

Under the agreement the states pledge to develop relations on the "basis of mutual recognition and respect for state sovereignty, the inalienable right to self-determination, the principles of equality and non-interference in internal affairs".

Conference on Security and Co-operation in Europe – CSCE

The headquarters of the CSCE opened in Prague, Czechoslovakia, in May 1992.

Foundation and aims

The first CSCE meeting, known as the Helsinki Conference, was held in Helsinki from 1973 to 1975. It was the first conference in the history of Europe in which all European countries with the exception of Albania took part. The main aim of the CSCE is to develop friendly relations and co-operation between participants in order to lessen the likelihood of military confrontation and promote disarmament.

Structure

Participating countries are represented at the main CSCE meetings by their head of state or government. Other meetings are attended by government representatives. Non-participating countries may be invited.

Participants

Albania	Germany	Portugal
Armenia	Greece	Romania
Austria	Hungary	Russia
Azerbaijan	Iceland	San Marino
Belgium	Ireland	Slovakia
Belorussia	Italy	Slovenia
Bosnia-	Kazakhstan	Spain
Hercegovina	Kirgizstan	Sweden
Bulgaria	Latvia	Switzerland
Canada	Liechtenstein	Tajikistan
Croatia	Lithuania	Turkey
Cyprus	Luxembourg	Turkmenistan
Czech Republic	Malta	Ukraine
Denmark	Moldova	UK
Estonia	Monaco	USA
Finland	Netherlands	Uzbekistan
France	Norway	Vatican
Georgia	Poland	

Activities

The Final Act of 1975 contained a declaration on ten principles to guide relations between participating states. It included clauses on respect for sovereignty, restraint from the use of force, the inviolability of frontiers, peaceful settlement of disputes, respect for human rights and fundamental freedoms, security building and disarmament. The participants also agreed to co-operate in economics, science, technology, the environment, humanitarian and other fields. Follow-up meetings were to be held on a regular basis.

The Final Act also committed the participants to encourage the practices of openness and access to the host country, and agreed open sessions of the CSCE for the media, non-governmental organisations, religious groups, private individuals, and so on.

Council of Europe

Base: Strasbourg, France

Foundation and aims
Founded in May 1949, the Council of Europe aims to achieve greater unity between its members, to encourage their economic and social progress and to uphold the principles of parliamentary democracy.

Members

Austria	Hungary	Portugal
Belgium	Iceland	Romania
Bulgaria	Ireland	San Marino
Cyprus	Italy	Slovakia
Czech Republic	Liechtenstein	Slovenia
Denmark	Lithuania	Spain
Estonia	Luxembourg	Sweden
Finland	Malta	Switzerland
France	Netherlands	Turkey
Germany	Norway	UK
Greece	Poland	

Israel has permanent observer status and the Holy See is an observer, while Albania, Belorussia, Bosnia-Hercegovina, Croatia, Latvia, Former Yugoslav Republic of Macedonia, Moldova, Russia and Ukraine have "guest status".

Structure
Committee of Ministers Comprising the foreign ministers of all member states, the committee takes decisions on questions of internal organisation, makes recommendations to governments, draws up agreements and conventions and discusses political matters. Meetings normally take place in April/May and November each year.

19 conferences of specialised ministers meet regularly for inter-governmental co-operation in various fields.

Most of the routine work is dealt with at monthly meetings of senior diplomats accredited to the Council as permanent representatives of their governments. Their decisions have equal force with those of ministers.

Parliamentary Assembly Headed by a president. Members are elected or appointed by their national parliaments from among their members. Political parties in each delegation follow the proportion of their strength in the national parliament. The members speak for public opinion and do not represent their governments.

The Assembly meets once a year in ordinary session for not more than one month. The session is normally divided into three parts held in January/February, April/May and September/October.

A Standing Committee consisting of the president, vice-presidents, chairmen of ordinary committees and some ordinary members represents the Assembly when it is not in session. It meets at least three times a year. There are a number of Ordinary Committees and a Secretariat.

Activities

The Council has issued a number of conventions and agreements on aspects of European co-operation in an attempt to co-ordinate national laws, put the citizens of member countries on an equal footing and create a pool of resources.

A major task of the Council of Europe is the promotion and development of human rights. All member countries are parties to the 1950 European Convention for the Protection of Human Rights and Fundamental Freedoms.

European Commission of Human Rights   The Commission can examine complaints made by a contracting party, or in some cases by individuals, non-government organisations or groups of individuals, that the European Convention has been violated by one or more of the contracting parties. If a friendly settlement cannot be reached the case is referred to the Committee of Ministers or the Court of Human Rights.

European Court of Human Rights   The Court can deal with a case only after the Commission has acknowledged that a friendly settlement has not been reached. The judgment of the Court is final.

Committees and conventions   There are a number of expert bodies covering: Mass Media, Social Welfare, Health, Population, Migrant Workers and Refugees, Social Development Fund, Legal Matters, Crime, Education and Culture, Youth, Sport, Environment and Regional Planning, Local and Regional Government, Monuments and Sites, External Relations, Finance.

Economic Commission for Europe – ECE

Base: Geneva, Switzerland

Foundation and aims

Established in 1947, the ECE includes representatives from all European countries and the USA and Canada who study the economic, environmental and technological problems of the region and recommend courses of action.

Members

Albania	Greece	Poland
Andorra	Hungary	Portugal
Armenia	Iceland	Romania
Austria	Ireland	Russia
Belgium	Italy	San Marino
Belorussia	Kirgizstan	Slovakia
Bosnia-	Latvia	Slovenia
Hercegovina	Liechtenstein	Spain
Bulgaria	Lithuania	Sweden
Canada	Luxembourg	Switzerland
Cyprus	Macedonia	Turkey
Czech Republic	(Former Yugoslav	Turkmenistan
Denmark	Republic of)	Ukraine
Estonia	Malta	UK
Finland	Moldova	USA
France	Monaco	Uzbekistan
Georgia	Netherlands	
Germany	Norway	

Structure

The ECE holds an annual plenary session which is headed by a president. Meetings of subsidiary bodies are convened throughout the year.

A secretariat services the ECE's meetings and publishes statistics, surveys and reviews. Close contact is maintained with the UN and its commissions and agencies. It is headed by an executive secretary.

Activities

The ECE's work programme consists of environmental protection, scientific and technical co-operation; energy; transport policies; trade and industrial co-operation between Eastern and Western Europe; and economic projections. It is carried out by 15 committees.

European Bank for Reconstruction and Development – EBRD

Base: London, UK

Foundation and aims

The EBRD was established in May 1990 and inaugurated in April 1991. It aims to foster the transition towards open market oriented economies and to promote private and entrepreneurial activities in the countries of central and eastern Europe. The bank will try to help these countries integrate into the international economy, with particular concern for strengthening democratic institutions, respect for human rights and for environmentally sound policies.

The bank intends to become a centre for the accumulation and exchange of knowledge on the region's problems, including, in particular, transition to a market economy. It also intends to play a significant role in co-ordinating projects.

Members

The bank has 41 members (39 countries and two institutions – the EU and the EIB), spanning Europe, the USA, Japan, and other countries. Membership is open to all European countries and non-European countries which are members of the IMF.

The board of directors has recommended that Albania be admitted as the 40th member. Estonia, Latvia and Lithuania have applied for membership.

Structure

The powers of the bank are vested in a board of governors. Each member appoints one governor and one alternate to the board. The board of governors has delegated powers to a board of directors whose 23 members hold office for three years.

The president is elected by the board of governors for a four-year term. Vice-presidents are appointed by the board of directors on the recommendation of the president. The board of directors is responsible for the general direction of the bank, including approval of its budget and general operations.

The EBRD has the following departments: merchant banking, development banking, finance, personnel and administration, project evaluation, secretary-general, chief economist, general counsel, political unit, communications.

Activities

The initial subscribed capital is 10 billion ecus, of which 30% was paid in five equal annual instalments commencing in 1991. The bank will also borrow in various currencies on world capital markets. The terms of the bank's funding are designed to enable it to co-operate with both international and public and private financial institutions through co-financing arrangements.

The EBRD performs a variety of functions in order to assist Central and East European countries to implement structural and sectoral reforms.

It merges the principles and practices of merchant and development banking. Funding of private or privatisable enterprises in the competitive sector is carried out through merchant banking, while funding of physical and financial infrastructure projects is carried out through development banking.

The EBRD offers loans, guarantees, underwriting and equity investment. Advisory services and technical assistance are a major feature of its activities.

European Economic Area – EEA

Europe's newest club. After the single market programme was initiated, negotiations started in December 1989 between the seven members of EFTA and the twelve members of the EC to form a closer association. The EFTA states would take on some of the obligations of EC membership, including rules about the movement of capital, persons and services, in exchange for some of the benefits of the single market. The EEA treaty was signed in October 1991 and should have come into effect on January 1st 1993, but Switzerland rejected it in a referendum in December 1992. It finally came into force on January 1st 1994 with Switzerland left out and Liechtenstein's membership deferred to a later date. It looks as if joining the organisation is merely a staging post to full EU membership. Austria, Finland, Norway and Sweden are expected to become full members in January 1995, while a Swiss application remains in abeyance.

European Free Trade Association – EFTA

Base: Geneva, Switzerland

Foundation and aims

EFTA was established in 1960 with the object of promoting free trade in industrial goods and expanding trade in agricultural goods between its members, and encouraging the liberalisation of world trade.

Members

Austria	Liechtenstein	Sweden
Finland	Norway	Switzerland
Iceland		

The applications of Austria, Finland, Norway and Sweden to join the EU were accepted in 1994. Provided the results of national referendums are in favour the four countries will become full EU members in January 1995.

Structure

There is a Council consisting of delegations led by ministers, which is normally held twice a year. Meetings led by heads of national delegations take place every two weeks. Each country holds the chair for six months. There is a secretariat headed by a secretary-general and a deputy.

There are ten Standing Committees: Trade Experts, Origin and Customs Experts, Technical Barriers to Trade, Legal Experts, Economic, Consultative, Members of Parliament of EFTA Countries, Budget, Economic Development, Agriculture and Fisheries.

Activities

EFTA combines the markets of its members in a single free trade area and its principal task is to ensure that this works efficiently. Since each member is also linked by free trade agreements with the EU, EFTA acts as consultant and co-ordinator on matters connected with these agreements and promotes closer collaboration in areas such as research and development.

Nordic Council

Base: Stockholm, Sweden

Foundation and aims
Founded in 1952, the Nordic Council promotes co-operation between the Nordic parliaments and governments.

Members
Denmark (with the autonomous territories of the Faeroe
    Islands and Greenland)
Finland (with the autonomous territory of the Aland Islands)
Iceland
Norway
Sweden

Structure
Council This is convened annually in a plenary session
lasting about one week. There are 87 members elected
annually by the parliaments of each country from among
their members. Political parties follow the proportion of
their strength in the national parliaments.

    Each delegation has a secretariat at its national parlia-
ment.

Allocation of members

Denmark	16	Aland	2
Faeroes	2	Iceland	7
Greenland	2	Norway	20
Finland	18	Sweden	20

Standing Committees There are six: Economic, Legal,
Communications, Cultural, Social and Environmental, Budget and Control.

Presidium The five countries each have two parliamentary representatives. As the supreme executive body, it
administers the day-to-day work of the council between
sessions.

Activities
The Nordic Council is not a supranational parliament and
its members take decisions guiding Nordic co-operation.
The Nordic Council of Ministers, representing the governments of Nordic countries, undertakes the implementation
of council decisions.

    The Council issues recommendations and statements of
position in order to initiate and follow up collaborative
efforts among its members. These usually result in measures being taken by the national governments.

Nordic Council of Ministers

Base: Copenhagen, Denmark

Foundation and aims

Co-operation between the governments of the member countries through the Nordic Council of Ministers is regulated by treaties signed in 1962 and 1971. The prime ministers and ministers of defence and foreign affairs do not meet within the Council, although the prime ministers do meet annually on an informal basis with the ministers of Nordic co-operation.

Members

Denmark	Iceland	Sweden
Finland	Norway	

Structure

Council of Ministers This is attended by ministers with responsibility for whatever subject is under discussion. In addition, each member country appoints a minister for Nordic co-operation in its own cabinet.

Decisions must be unanimous, apart from those on procedural matters which may be decided by a simple majority, and are binding.

An annual report is made to the Nordic Council.

Secretariat Headed by a secretary-general, there are seven main divisions: budget and administration; cultural and educational co-operation; research, higher education, computer technology, environmental protection, energy; labour, occupational environment, social policy, health care, equality; finance and monetary policy, industry, housing, trade, development aid; regional policy, transport, communications, tourism, farming, forestry, fishing, consumers' affairs; information.

Committees The Committee of Ministers' Deputies prepares material for ministers' meetings. Other committees cover the subjects listed above.

Activities

Foremost is economic co-operation, which is particularly important in view of the single European market. Nordic institutions include the following: Nordic Investment Bank, Nordic Industrial Fund, Nordic Economic Research Council, NORDTEST, Nordic Project Fund.

There are other agreements and conventions on co-operation.

North Atlantic Treaty Organisation – NATO

Base: Brussels, Belgium

Foundation and aims

Founded in 1949, NATO's objective was to create a defence organisation linking a group of European states with the USA and Canada. It was agreed that an attack on any one member would be regarded as an attack against all.

Members

Belgium	Iceland	Spain
Canada	Italy	Turkey
Denmark	Luxembourg	UK
France*	Netherlands	USA
Germany	Norway	
Greece	Portugal	

* France withdrew from the military structure in 1966 but remains a member of the Atlantic Alliance.

Structure

North Atlantic Council The highest authority, comprising representatives of the member countries. Ministerial meetings are held twice a year; permanent representatives meet once a week.

NATO's secretary-general chairs the Council and the foreign minister of a member country is nominated honorary president annually.

The Council provides a forum for consultation between its members on wide-ranging issues. Decisions are taken by common consent.

Defence Planning Committee Deals with defence and has the same functions and authority as the council. Regular meetings are held at ambassadorial level and ministers of defence meet twice a year. All member countries except France are represented.

Nuclear Planning Group Follows a similar pattern to the Defence Planning Committee and the Council. All member countries except France participate; Iceland participates as an observer.

Other committees Cover a wide range of general and specialised subjects.

International secretariat Headed by a secretary-general and a deputy.

There is an assistant secretary-general for: political affairs, defence planning and policy, defence support, infrastructure, logistics and civil engineering planning, scientific and environmental affairs.

Military structure
Military Committee   The highest military body in NATO, composed of allied chiefs of staff or their representatives of all member countries except France. (France maintains a Military Mission to the committee for regular consultation.) Meetings of chiefs of staff are held twice a year but permanent military representatives remain in permanent session. Makes recommendations to the council and Defence Planning Committee and gives guidance to supreme allied commanders.

European Command at Casteau, Belgium (Supreme Headquarters Allied Powers in Europe – SHAPE).

Atlantic Ocean Command at Norfolk, Virginia, USA.

Channel Command at Northwood, UK.

Activities
NATO aims to prevent war by maintaining its forces at a sufficient level and state of readiness to present a credible deterrent to an aggressor. It draws up joint defence plans, organises the relevant infrastructure and arranges joint training and exercises. There are three types of NATO forces: conventional; intermediate and short-range nuclear; and strategic nuclear (the UK and the USA).

A defence review is held annually to assess the contribution of member countries. Ministers of defence review allied defence policy from time to time.

The North Atlantic Council provides a forum for discussion of East-West relations and arms reduction.

There are a number of NATO agencies. One group comprises civilian and logistics organisations responsible to the North Atlantic Council. Another group is responsible to the Military Committee.

Western European Union – WEU

Base: London, UK

Foundation and aims
The WEU was set up in 1955 and was based on the Brussels Treaty of 1948. The members aim to co-ordinate their views on security and defence matters.

Members

Belgium	Italy	Portugal
France	Luxembourg	Spain
Germany	Netherlands	UK
Greece		

Structure
Council   Responsible for formulating policy and issuing directives to the secretary-general and agencies. Comprises the foreign and defence ministers of the member countries or their ambassadors resident in London and an under-secretary of the British Foreign and Commonwealth Office. Meetings are held twice a year at ministerial level and usually twice a month at permanent representative level. The presidency is held for one year by each country.

Assembly   Comprises the delegates of the member countries to the Parliamentary Assembly of the Council of Europe. Meetings are held twice a year in Paris. Defence policy in Western Europe (as well as other matters) is discussed and recommendations are passed on.

Committees   There are permanent committees on: defence and armaments, general affairs, scientific matters, budgetary affairs and administration, rules of procedure and privileges, parliamentary and public relations.

Secretariat   Headed by a secretary-general and a deputy.

Agencies for security questions   Three; in Paris.

Activities
The organisation was restructured in 1984 when it was agreed to hold more frequent ministerial meetings in order to co-ordinate members' views on questions of defence, arms control and disarmament, East-West relations, Europe's contribution to NATO and European armaments co-operation.

In 1987 the Council resolved to develop more cohesion in European defence. Decisions taken at the Maastricht summit in December 1991 envisage a heightened role for the WEU in achieving a common European defence policy.

Notes on data

For a list of the main sources used in preparing this book see page 216. For further details of publications of The Economist Intelligence Unit, EIU, contact

The Marketing Department,
The Economist Intelligence Unit,
15 Regent Street, London SW1Y 4LR
Telephone: 071 830 1000 Fax: 071 491 2107

Coverage

The extent and quality of the statistics available vary from country to country. Every care has been taken to specify the broad definitions on which the data are based and to indicate cases where data quality or technical difficulties are such that interpretation of the figures is likely to be seriously affected. Nevertheless, figures from individual countries will often differ from standard international statistical definitions. Data for Cyprus normally refer to Greek Cyprus only.

Statistical basis

The research for this section was carried out in 1994 using the latest published sources. The data, therefore, unless otherwise indicated, refer to the year ending December 31st 1992. Exceptions are: population under 15 and over 65, number of men per 100 women and urban population which refer to estimates for 1991; crude birth and death rates and life expectancy are based on 1985–90 averages; GDP per head in PPP and tourism refer to 1991; structure of manufacturing and household, consumer goods and expenditure data refer to 1991; ethnic groups, marriage and divorce, education and health data refer to the latest year with available figures.

Figures may not add exactly to totals, or percentages to 100, because of rounding. Sums of money have generally been converted to US dollars at the official exchange rate ruling at the time to which the figures refer.

UN data have been used for projections, based on medium-growth assumptions.

Definitions

Agricultural area   The area of arable land, land under permanent crops and pasture land expressed as a percentage of a country's total area.

Balance of payments   The record of a country's transactions with the rest of the world. The **current account** of the balance of payments consists of: exports of visible trade (goods) less imports of visible trade; "invisible" trade: receipts and payments for services such as banking, tourism and shipping plus dividend and interest payments and profit remittances, private transfer payments, such as remittances from those working abroad; official transfers, including payments to international organisations and some current expenditure aid flows (such as famine relief). Visible imports and exports are normally compiled on rather different definitions to those used in the trade statistics (shown in principal imports and exports) and therefore the statistics do not match. The **capital account** consists of long- and short-term transactions relating to a country's assets and liabilities (for example loans and borrowings). Adding the current to the capital account gives the overall balance. This is compensated by net monetary movements and changes in reserves. In practice methods of statistical recording are neither complete nor accurate and an errors and omissions item, sometimes quite large, will appear. In the country facts pages of this book this item is included in the overall balance. Changes in reserves are shown without the practice of reversing the sign often followed in balance of payments presentations. They exclude monetary movements and therefore do not equal the overall balance.

Cif/fob When goods pass through customs and are recorded in trade statistics they are normally registered at their value at the point of passage through customs. Imports, which are valued at the point of entry to a country, will include the cost of "carriage, insurance and freight" (cif) from the exporting country to the importing one. The value of exports does not include these elements and is recorded "free on board" (fob). The value of imports will therefore automatically be greater than the equivalent amount of exports – in many cases by a factor of 10–12%. In most (but not all) countries the crude trade statistics record imports cif and exports fob; balance of payments statistics are generally adjusted so that imports are shown fob.

Crude birth rate The number of live births in a year per 1,000 population. The crude rate will automatically be relatively high if a large proportion of the population is of childbearing age and low if this is not the case.

Crude death rate The number of deaths in one year per 1,000 population. Like the crude birth rate this is affected by the population's age structure. It will be relatively high if there is a high proportion of old people in the population.

Debt, foreign Financial obligations owed by a country to the rest of the world and repayable in foreign currency. **Debt service** consists of interest payments on outstanding debt plus any principal repayments due. **The debt service ratio** is debt service expressed as a percentage of the country's earnings from exports of goods and services.

Enrolment ratio (gross) The number enrolled at a specific level of education, whether or not they belong to the age group relevant to that level, as a percentage of the total population in the relevant age group. The ratio can therefore be over 100% if children start an education stage early or stay in it late; conversely, a ratio below 100% can be consistent with full education if children of the appropriate age group have passed on early to the following stage.

GDP Gross Domestic Product. It is the sum of all output produced by economic activity within that country. Economic activity normally refers to goods and services that are exchanged for money or traded in a market system (activities such as housework, childcare by parents and household repairs or improvements carried out by occupiers are excluded). Subsistence farming and other activities that could potentially be exchanged for money are theoretically also included but national statistics vary in the extent to which they cover them.

GDP can be measured in three ways: by summing the output of all production (origins of GDP); by measuring all expenditure on a country's production and adding stockbuilding (components of GDP); or by measuring the income of businesses and individuals generated by the production of goods and services. The exports and imports figures shown in national accounts statistics are defined differently from visible and invisible exports and imports used in the balance of payments, notably by excluding interest, profits and dividends payments.

GDP can be measured either at "market prices", the prices at which goods and services are bought by consumers, or at "factor cost", the cost of producing an item excluding taxes and subsidies. In general the expenditure breakdown is shown at market prices and the production breakdown at factor cost. Data on total GDP generally refer to market prices. National income is obtained by deducting an estimate of depreciation of capital goods (capital consumption) from GDP.

The average annual increase in real GDP shows the growth in GDP excluding any increase due solely to the rise in prices.

Human Development Index This new index is an attempt by the United Nations Development Programme to assess relative levels of human development in various countries. It combines three measures: life expectancy, literacy and whether the average income, based on purchasing power parity (PPP) estimates (see below), is sufficient to meet basic needs. For each component a country's score is scaled according to where it falls between the minimum and maximum country scores; for income adequacy the maximum is taken as the official "poverty line" incomes in nine industrial countries. The scaled scores on the three measures are averaged to give the Human Development Index, shown here scaled from 0 to 100. Countries scoring less than 50 are classified as low human development, those from 50 to 80 as medium and those above 80 as high.

As with any statistical exercise of this sort the results are subject to caveats and the small number of indicators used places some limitations on its usefulness. The index should not be taken as a quality of life indicator since in particular it excludes any direct notion of freedom.

Inflation The rate at which prices are increasing. The most common measure and the one shown here (but not the only one) is to take the increase in the consumer price index.

Life expectancy rates refer to the average length of time a baby born today can expect to live.

NMP Net Material Product. The equivalent measure to GDP used in Marxist national accounting; a system used in eastern Europe and certain other planned economies. It differs from GDP in excluding certain services and in deducting capital consumption. **Gross Material Product** is equal to NMP plus consumption. In general, NMP is 80–90% of GDP.

PPP Purchasing Power Parity. Comparing GDP per head is an unsatisfactory way of comparing relative living standards since it does not take account of differences in prices of goods and services (the cost of living). PPP statistics adjust for cost of living differences by replacing normal exchange rates with rates designed to equalize the prices of a standard "basket" of goods and services. These are used to obtain PPP estimates of GDP per head. PPP estimates are normally shown on a scale of 1–100, taking the USA, where the average standard of living is highest, as 100. The World Bank is the source for the PPP estimates given in this book.

Real terms Figures adjusted to allow for inflation.

Unemployment ratio The number of unemployed people expressed as a percentage of a country's total workforce.

Abbreviations

bn	billion (one thousand million)	GNP	Gross National Product
CIS	Commonwealth of Independent States	kg	kilogram
		km	kilometre
CMEA	The former eastern bloc economic grouping known as Comecon, which was abolished in 1991	m	million
		NMP	Net Material Product
		PPP	Purchasing Power Parity
		–	zero
GDP	Gross Domestic Product	...	not available

Sources

The Economist Books/Hamish Hamilton, *The Economist Guide to the European Union,* Dick Leonard

The Economist Intelligence Unit, *Country Reports.*
The Economist Intelligence Unit, *Country Risk Service.*

Euromonitor, *European Marketing Data and Statistics.*

Europa Publications, *Europa World Year Book*

FAO, *Production Yearbook.*

ILO, *Year Book of Labour Statistics.*

IMF, *International Financial Statistics.*

OECD, *Development Co-operation Report.*
OECD, *Monthly Economic Indicators.*

UN, *Monthly Bulletin of Statistics.*
UN, *World Population Prospects.*
UN, *Demographics Yearbook.*
UN Development Programme, *Human Development Report.*
UN Economic Commission for Europe, *Economic Survey of Europe.*
UNESCO, *Statistical Yearbook.*

US Central Intelligence Agency, *The World Factbook*

WHO, *World Health Statistics.*

World Bank, *World Debt Tables.*
World Bank, *World Development Report.*

World Tourist Organisation, *Yearbook of Tourism Statistics.*